Blue Line 2

Ausgabe für Bayern (Mittelschulen) Klasse 6

Herausgeber: Wolfgang Hamm

Ernst Klett Verlag
Stuttgart • Leipzig

Inhalt

L = Listening M = Mediation R = Reading S = Speaking V = Viewing W = Writing

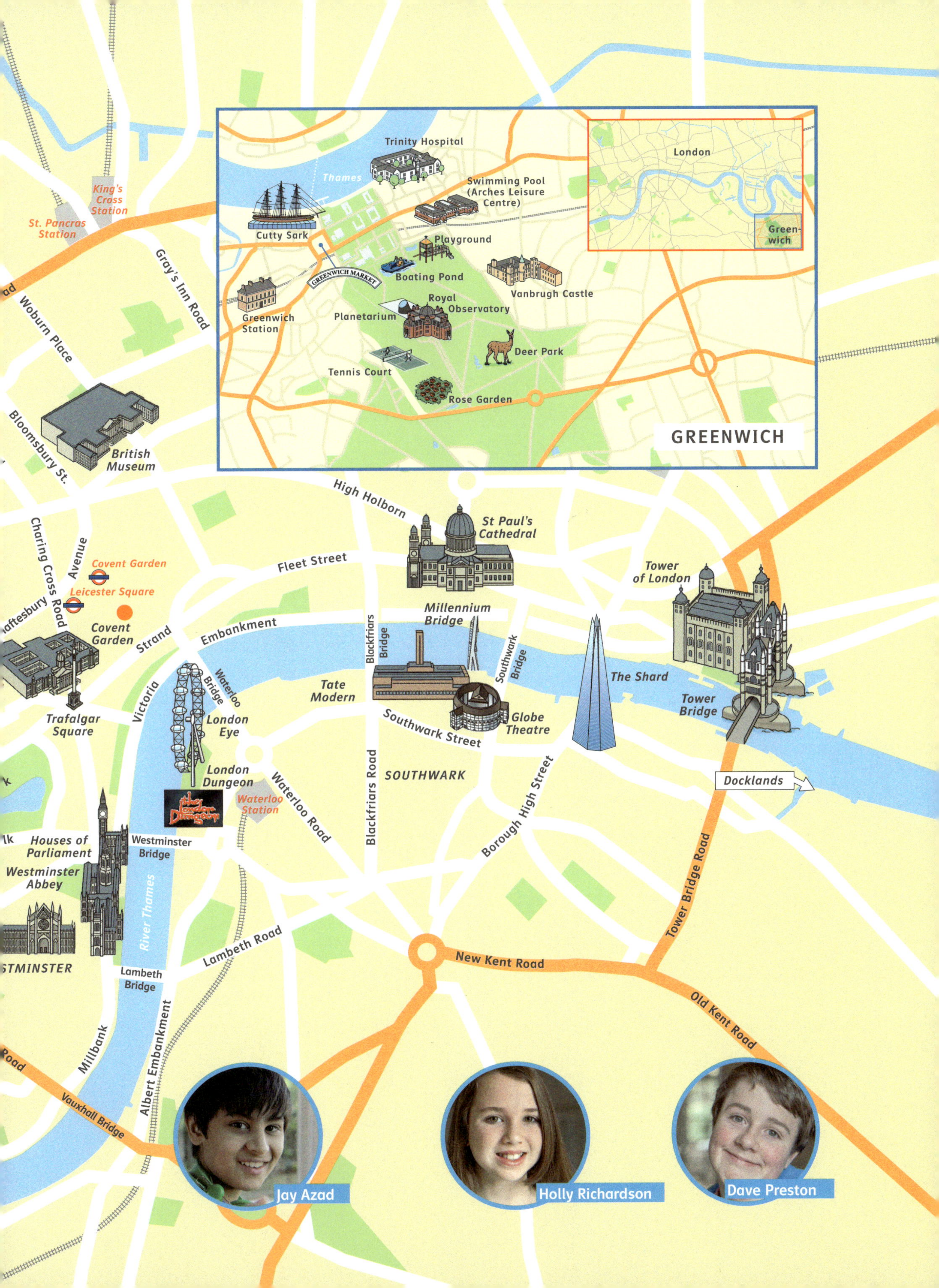
GREENWICH
Trinity Hospital
Thames
Swimming Pool (Arches Leisure Centre)
Cutty Sark
Playground
GREENWICH MARKET
Boating Pond
Vanbrugh Castle
Greenwich Station
Royal Observatory
Planetarium
Deer Park
Tennis Court
Rose Garden
London
Green-wich
King's Cross Station
St. Pancras Station
Gray's Inn Road
Woburn Place
Bloomsbury St.
British Museum
High Holborn
St Paul's Cathedral
Fleet Street
Charing Cross Road
Avenue
Covent Garden
Leicester Square
Covent Garden
aftesbury
Strand
Embankment
Millennium Bridge
Blackfriars Bridge
Tower of London
Southwark Bridge
The Shard
Tower Bridge
Trafalgar Square
Victoria
Waterloo Bridge
London Eye
Tate Modern
Southwark Street
Globe Theatre
London Dungeon
Waterloo Station
Waterloo Road
Blackfriars Road
SOUTHWARK
Borough High Street
Docklands
Houses of Parliament
Westminster Bridge
Westminster Abbey
River Thames
Lambeth Road
New Kent Road
Tower Bridge Road
STMINSTER
Lambeth Bridge
Old Kent Road
Millbank
Albert Embankment
Vauxhall Bridge
Road
Jay Azad
Holly Richardson
Dave Preston

Blue Line **2**

Ausgabe für Bayern (Mittelschulen) Klasse 6

Die Mediencodes (Beispiel: Find more online: 8x6p93) enthalten zusätzliche Unterrichtsmaterialien, die der Verlag in eigener Verantwortung zur Verfügung stellt.

Im Lernmittel wird in Form von Symbolen auf eine CD verwiesen. Diese enthält – bis auf die Hörverstehensübungen – ausschließlich optionale Unterrichtsmaterialien. Die CD unterliegt nicht dem staatlichen Zulassungsverfahren.

Zusatzmaterial für Schülerinnen und Schüler u.a.:
Blue Line 2 Bayern Workbook mit Audio-CD (ISBN 978-3-12-548352-1)

1. Auflage 1 10 9 8 7 6 | 29 28 27 26 25

Alle Drucke dieser Auflage sind unverändert und können im Unterricht nebeneinander verwendet werden.
Die letzte Zahl bezeichnet das Jahr des Druckes.

Herausgeber: Wolfgang Hamm, Marktredwitz
Autorinnen und Autoren: Daniel Shatwell, Hanau sowie
Jo Cummins, London; Elizabeth Daymond, Kronshagen; Timo Dorsch, Hamburg; Leanne Garrity, London; Patrick Hoke, Hamburg; Melanie Ku, Köln; Dave Lambert, Cambridge; Howard Rayner, London; Karen Seekings, London; Clare Treleaven, Castellón
Beratung: Michaela Cavallucci, München; Gaby Fruhmann, Parsberg; Michael Meisenzahl, Karlstadt; Felicitas Müller, Weidenberg; Lisa Schubert, Altdorf; Anna Weber, Taufkirchen

Für besondere Unterstützung danken wir herzlich Susan Bolton und Ken Jones von der Thomas Tallis School, London.

Redaktion: Claudia Schwarz-Brownbill; Daniel Shatwell, Hanau; Regina Kleinhenz, Stuttgart; Judith Ley, Mainz
Herstellung: Sabine Kienzle; Kathrin Schindler

Umschlaggestaltung und Gestaltungskonzept: know idea, Freiburg; Koma Amok, Stuttgart
Umschlagfoto: February Films (Andrew Kemp), London; Alamy Stock Photo (Andriy Kravchenko), Abingdon, Oxon;
Fotografen: February Films (Elke Bock), London; February Films (Andrew Kemp), London; Thomas Weccard, Ludwigsburg
Illustrationen: Kirill Chudinskiy, Köln; Katja Rau, Berglen; Marcus Wilder, Hamburg; Steffen Wolff, Brohl-Lützing; Dorothee Wolters, Köln sowie Friederike Ablang, Berlin; Dorothea Ackroyd, Bielefeld; Verena Ballhaus, München; Matthias Balonier, Lützelbach; Uta Bettzieche, Leipzig; Susanne Bochem, Mainz; Audrey Bongiorno, La nouvière; Martina Burghart-Vollhardt, Kamenz; Francois Davot, Troyes; Christian Dekelver, Weinstadt; Andreas Florian, Lübeck; Mascha Greune, München; Josef Hammen, Trierweiler; Christian Hansen, Berlin; Rob Harvey, Cirencester Glos; Susann Hesselbarth, Leipzig; Carmen Hochmann, Bielefeld; Steffen Jähde, Sundhagen; Peer Kramer, Düsseldorf; Hendrik Kranenberg, Drolshagen; Cornelia Kurtz, Boppard; Jeongsook Lee, Köln; Katja Leuschner, Halle/S.; Jörg Mair Computergraphik, München; Helga Merkle, Albershausen; Axel Nicolai, Brauweiler; David Norman, Liliane Oser, Hamburg; Meerbusch; Simone Pahl, Berlin; Sven Palmowski, Barcelona, El Prat de Llobrega; Rosanna Pradella, Ludwigsburg; Myrtia Rockstroh, Berlin; Carolin Ina Schröter, Berlin; Friederike Schumann, Berlin; Birgit Tanck, Hamburg; TEBITRON GmbH, Edward Eckstein, Gerlingen; Ursula Wedde, Göppingen; Sylvia Wolf, Wiesbaden; Katrin Wolff, Wiesbaden
Satz: graphitecture book & edition
Reproduktion: Schwabenrepro GmbH, Stuttgart
Druck: Firmengruppe APPL, aprinta druck, Wemding

Printed in Germany
ISBN 978-3-12-548342-2

9 783125 483422

L = Listening M = Mediation R = Reading S = Speaking V = Viewing W = Writing

Inhalt

L = Listening M = Mediation R = Reading S = Speaking V = Viewing W = Writing

So lernst du mit Blue Line

So lernst du mit deinem Buch.
Das Buch hat sechs Units (Kapitel).
Jede Unit ist gleich aufgebaut.

Intro

Hier steigst du in das neue Thema ein.
Dazu gibt es auch einen kurzen Film.

Im gelben Kasten siehst du, was du in der *Unit* lernen wirst.

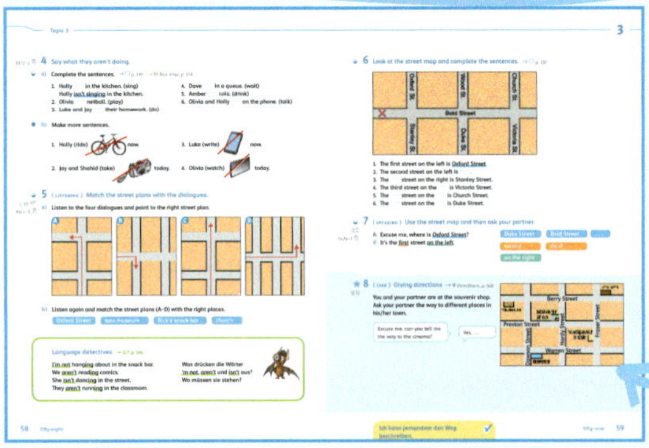

Topics

In jeder *Unit* gibt es 2–3 *Topics*, in denen du viele neue Dinge lernst.
Hier kannst du erkennen, wie schwer eine Übung ist:
● schwer ◒ mittel ○ leicht

In der *Task* kannst du zeigen, dass du alles verstanden hast, und deine eigenen Ideen einbringen.

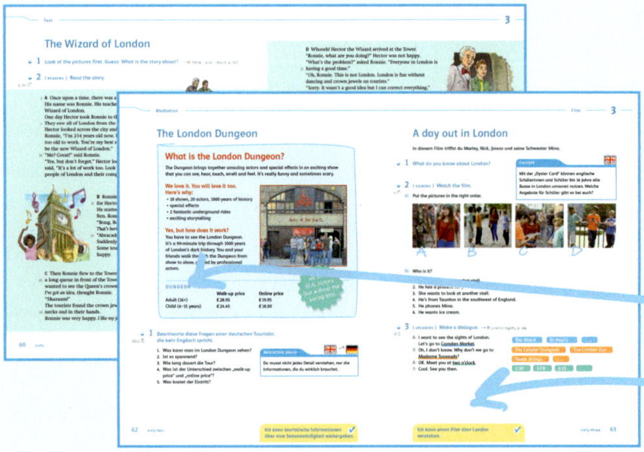

Text

Auf den *Text*-Seiten findest du spannende Geschichten und andere Texte.

Mediation/Film

Auf der linken Seite geht es darum, englische Informationen auf Deutsch weiterzugeben.
Das nennt man *Mediation*.

Auf der *Film*-Seite geht es um einen englischen Film.

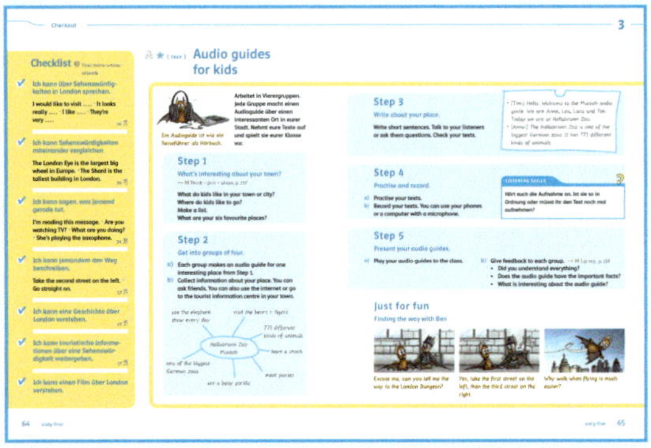

Checkout

Auf dieser Doppelseite kannst du zeigen, ob du in der *Unit* alles verstanden hast.
In der *Checklist* sind alle Lernziele noch einmal aufgelistet.

Die Abschluss-Aufgabe (*Unit task*) sollt ihr zu zweit oder in der Gruppe lösen.

Look at Great Britain / Look at the USA

Hier kannst du Großbritannien und die USA entdecken. Schau genau hin. Vieles kannst du verstehen oder erraten.

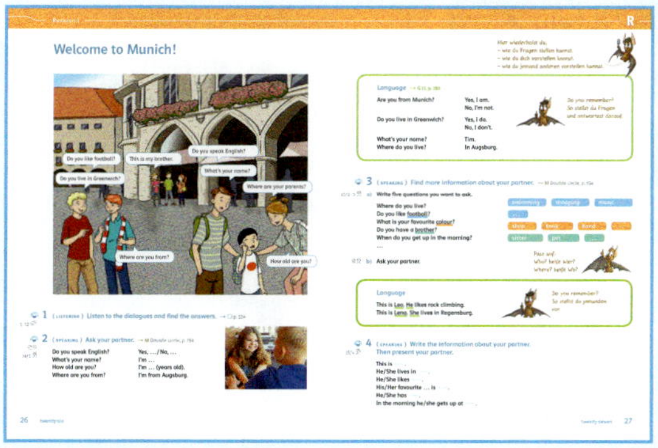

Revision

Hier kannst du das Wichtigste aus Klasse 5 wiederholen.

Im Anschluss an die sechs *Units* gibt es noch weitere nützliche Seiten:

Grammar: Hier findest du alle Regeln und Erklärungen zur Grammatik, Übungen und eine Liste der unregelmäßigen Verben.

Methods: Manche Übungen könnt ihr auf eine bestimmte Art und Weise bearbeiten. Das erkennst du an diesem Symbol: → M.
Wie es genau funktioniert, kannst du hier nachlesen.

Vocabulary: Im *Vocabulary* findest du alle neuen Wörter in der Reihenfolge, in der sie in der *Unit* auftauchen. Im *Dictionary* sind die Wörter noch einmal alphabetisch aufgelistet: zuerst Englisch-Deutsch und dann Deutsch-Englisch.

Symbol	Erklärung
○ ◒ ●	leicht/mittel/schwer (Niveaudifferenzierung)
remember ◒	(Re)Aktivierung von Wissen aus Klasse 5
✿	individualisierende Aufgabe (natürliche Differenzierung)
→ ○ p. 131	Verweis auf leichtere Parallelübung auf der *Diff corner*-Seite
OR	Aufgabe zur Auswahl (Wahldifferenzierung)
P	Hier entsteht ein Produkt für das Portfolio.
4/1	Verweis auf eine Übung im *Workbook*
→ G6, p. 145	Verweis auf den Grammatikanhang (*Grammar*)
→ M	Verweis auf die Methodenseite (*Methods*)
→ V	Verweis zum Wortfeld im Vokabular (*Vocabulary*)
	Partnerarbeit
	Gruppenarbeit
	Verweis auf die Lehrer-CD (Audio)
	Verweis auf die Lehrer-DVD (Film)
Find more online: w8e4f8	Code auf www.klett.de eingeben und Zusatzinformationen erhalten

It's great to be back

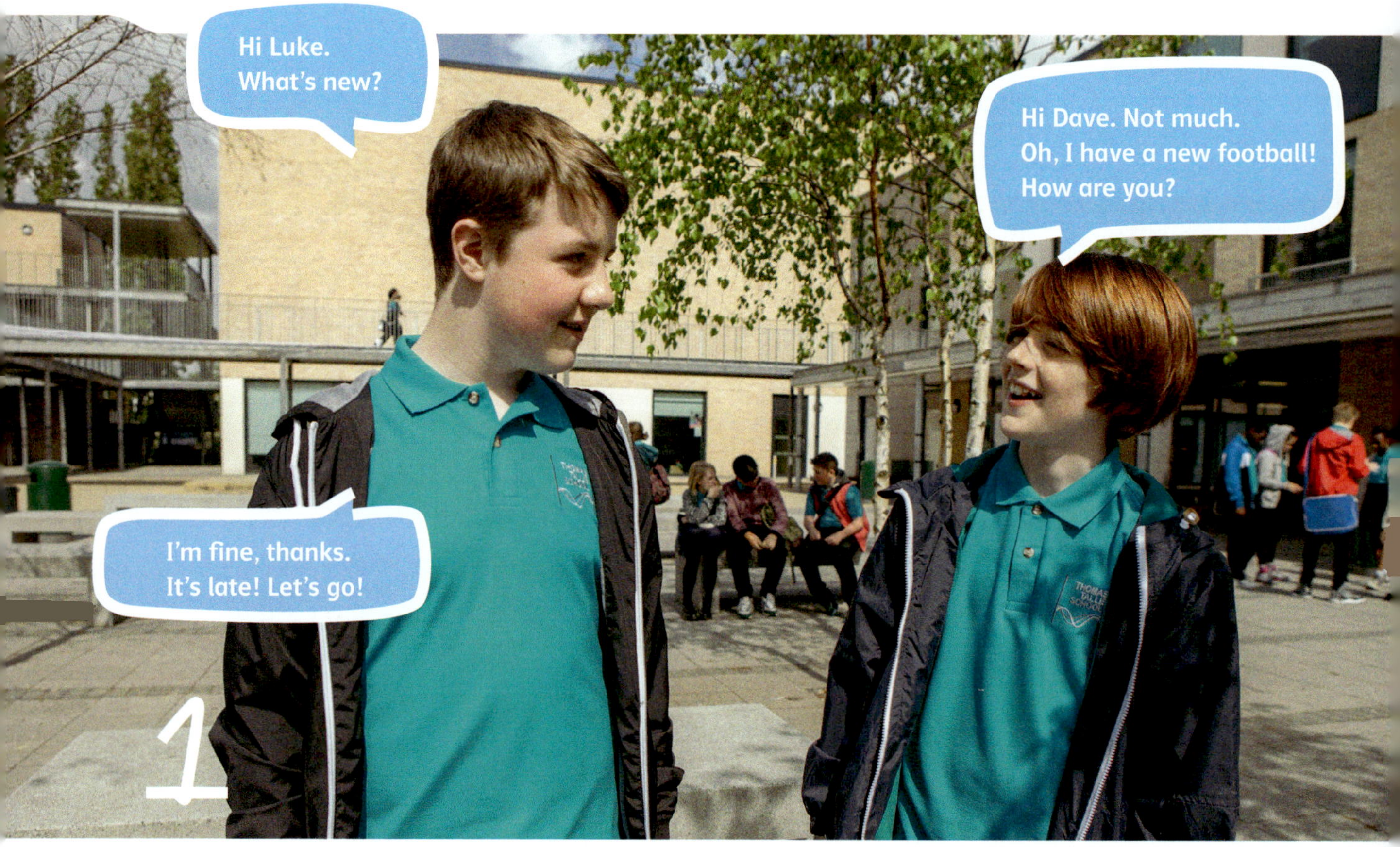

1 Who is it?

2/1

1. … has a new football.
   Luke has a new football.
2. … doesn't want to be late.
3. … was in Jamaica.
4. … has a new scarf.
5. … visited his grandparents.
6. … asks Holly about her holidays.

2 (LISTENING) Right or wrong?

1, 2

a)
1. A girl and a boy talk about their weekend.
2. The girl wants to be on the beach again.
3. The boy got up at eight o'clock.

1, 3

b)
1. The boy visited his uncle.
2. He went to Margate.
3. They had homework.

Am Ende dieser Unit kann ich …
- meine Freunde nach den Ferien begrüßen.
- über meine Sommerferien sprechen.
- Missverständnisse klären.

1

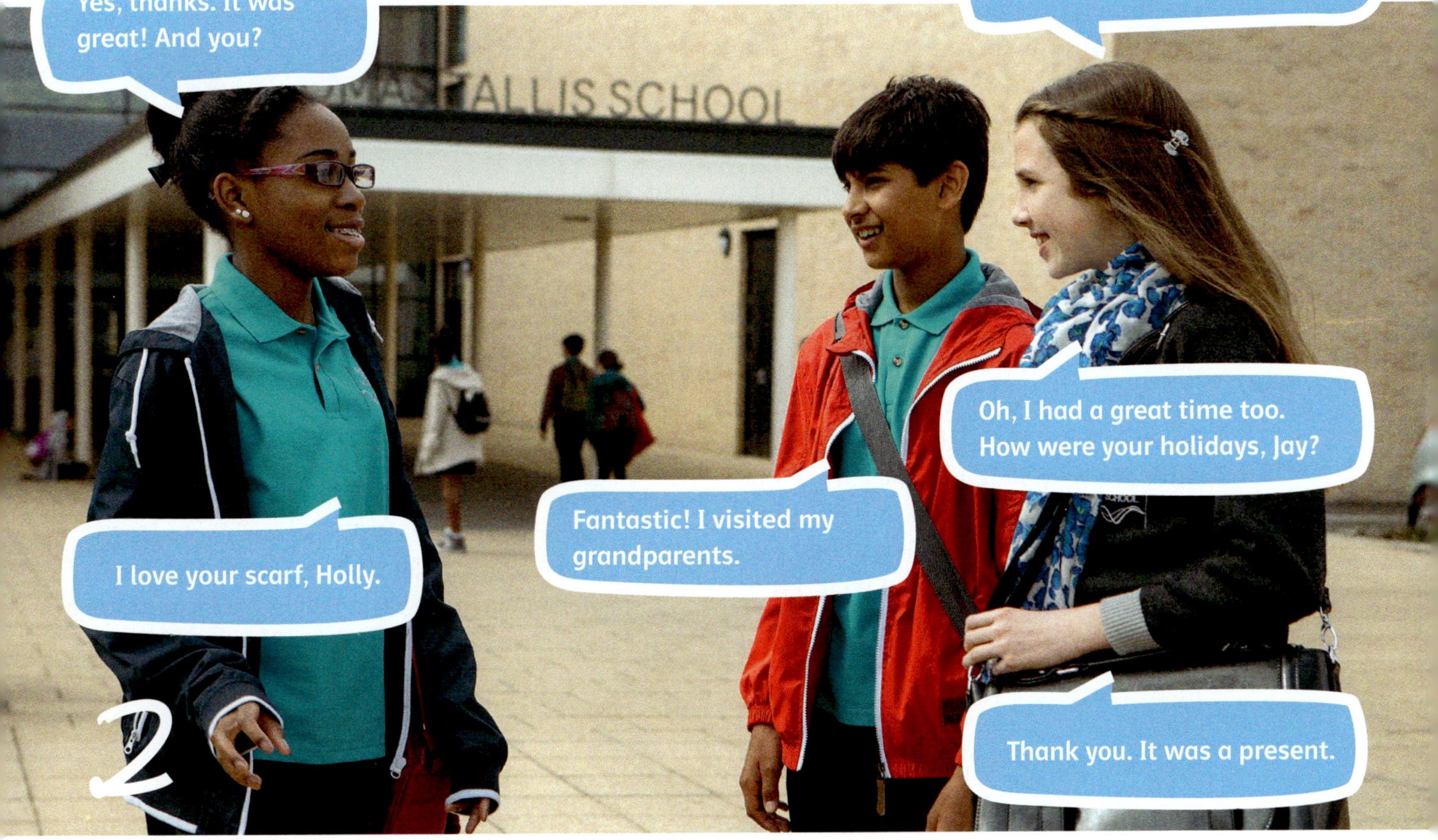

3 (TASK) Hi! → V Everyday English, p. 161 → M Double circle, p. 154

2/2

Talk to your partner. Choose 1 or 2.

1. A: Hi!
   B: Hi! How were your holidays?
   A: Great. What's new?
   B: Not much.

OR

2. A: How are you?
   B: Fine, thanks. And you?
   A: OK. I like your bag. Is it new?
   B: Yes, thank you.

CULTURE

In Großbritannien beginnt man Gespräche oft mit der Frage „How are you?". Die Antwort ist meist „Fine, thanks." Oft fragt man auch zurück: „And you?"

OK. | Fine, thanks. | Good. | Fantastic!

I have a new bike. | I have a new bag. | …

bag | bike | … | I bought it in Jamaica / in …

It's a present from my mum / my sister / my …

Ich kann meine Freunde nach den Ferien begrüßen. ✓

Hier lerne ich, über meine Sommerferien zu sprechen.

My summer holidays

1 (READING) Read the dialogue.

1, 4
3/1

The students talk about the school holidays.

Jay: In August I went to Manchester for a week with my parents. We visited my grandparents and stayed at their house. Manchester is a cool city with a lot of music shops. I took a lot of photos and I met my two cousins. They like music too and we sang every day. We started a band!

Gwen: When can we hear your songs?

Jay: I need more practice. Then I can sing them here.

Olivia: Why do you have a cricket ball, Jay?

Jay: I played cricket with my grandfather.

Teacher: Give the ball to Gwen. You know she can't see very well, but she can feel it.

Jay: Here you are, Gwen.

Teacher: Thanks, Jay. What about you, Gwen?

Gwen: I had a great time. I went tandem bike riding with my cousin. She was in front and told me about things on the road. One day we made a trip to a small town and ate lots of ice cream.

Teacher: Thank you, Gwen. Now it's Holly's turn.

Holly: I was at home in the holidays but I had a lot of fun …

CULTURE

Manchester liegt im Nordwesten Englands. Es ist eine sehr große Stadt mit berühmten Fußballmannschaften und Bands. Welche deutschen Städte mit bekannten Fußballmannschaften kennst du?

2 What did they do?

a) Which pictures are wrong?

1

2

3

4

b) Make a sentence for each right picture.

3 Make mind maps. → M Think – pair – share, p. 157

3/2

You stay at home in your holidays. What can you do?

1 visit – friends

2 play – football every day

3 go – to the sports centre – to the swimming pool

4 have – a picnic

5 …

4 Holiday activities

What can you do here? Match the activities with the places.

1 

2 

3 

4 

At the supermarket I can …
In the park I can …

have a burger | watch a film | buy fruit | take the dog for a walk | buy bread | have a sandwich | play frisbee

5 (LISTENING) Listen to Holly's report.

1, 5
3/3

Choose the right answer.

1. Holly went swimming with her mum / her dad.
2. Holly had lunch in a snack bar / at the market.
3. Holly went to the shops with Amber / her mum.
4. Holly went to the cinema with Olivia / her dad.

Do you remember the simple past?

Language detectives → G1, p. 140

Jay: I visited my grandparents.
Jay: I played cricket.

Erinnerst du dich? Die meisten Verben enden in der Vergangenheitsform auf …

Gwen: I went tandem bike riding.
Gwen: I ate lots of ice cream.

Einige Verben haben eine unregelmäßige Vergangenheitsform. Went und ate sind die Vergangenheitsformen von … und … . Welche anderen unregelmäßigen Vergangenheitsformen kennst du noch?

6 Match the pictures from Amber's holidays with the sentences.

1. We played frisbee on the beach.
2. We went swimming in the sea.
3. Then I ate a lot of fish and chips.
4. We met some cool boys and girls.
5. Later I saw a nice scarf at a market.
6. I bought the scarf for Holly.

7 What did Olivia do in her holidays? → M Bus stop, p. 154

4/4–5

a) Put in the verbs in the right form. → ○ p. 120

1. It was Olivia's mother's birthday, so Olivia helped (help) her with the party.
2. She (ask) her friends for ideas.
3. At the party she (play) with her sister.
4. Later she (talk) to her friends.
5. They all (dance).

b) Put the words in the right order and use the right form of the verb. → M Walking sentences, p. 158

1. at her aunt's house • (stay) • In Jamaica • Olivia
2. cricket • She • (play)
3. (watch) • a cool film • She
4. Lucy • with her postcards • She • (help)

8 (GAME) Last weekend

a) What did you do last weekend? Write the past form of these verbs on a card. One card for one verb.

organize | play | start | watch | help | dance

b) Put the cards on the table. Take a card (e. g. organized). Say what you did last weekend and ask your partner. Your partner takes a card and answers. → ○ p. 120

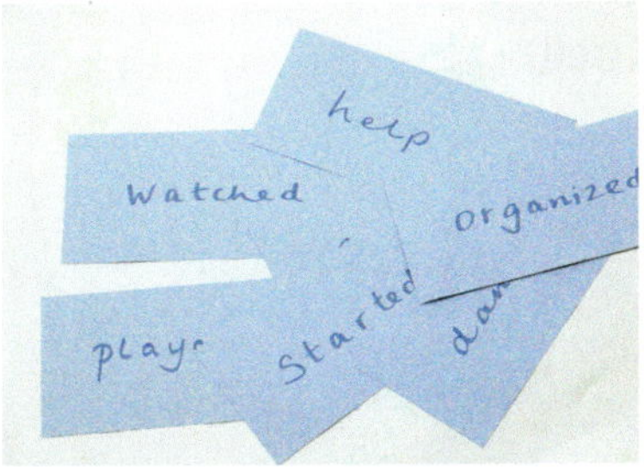

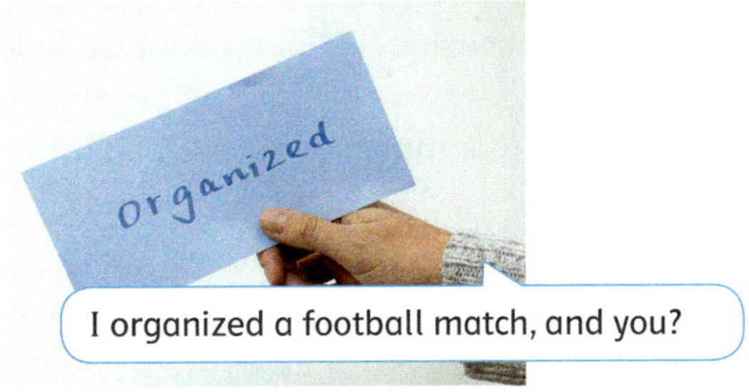

The game is over when there are no more cards on the table.

9 (SONG) Last summer

1, 6

Sing the song in groups.

Last summer we walked on the beach,
We had a great time together.
We went swimming every day,
The summer days were beautiful.

Last summer we all slept in a tent,
At the campfire we counted stars.
We sang songs and played some games,
The summer nights were beautiful.

(Chorus:) Sunshine, friends and good vibes,
picnics in the sun,
We always sang and danced, we had a lot of fun.
Holidays, holidays, eating ice cream on the sand,
I can't wait, I can't wait, to see my friends again.

Next summer I want to go to the beach again
Because I really liked it there.
Next summer I want to lie in the sun,
When will summer come again?
(Chorus)

10 Put in was or were.

4/6

1. Yesterday Dave was at Luke's house.
2. Luke: My holidays —— good.
3. Dave: Where —— you?
4. Luke: I —— in London with Dad and Jamie.
5. Dave: We —— at the beach in Margate.
6. It —— great!

11 (SPEAKING) Ask your partner. → M Milling around, p. 156

5/7

two | three | ... | with friends | in town | at school | ...

A: Where were you yesterday at five o'clock?
B: I was at home.

12 (WRITING) Write about Jay's holidays.

a) Complete the sentences. → ○ p. 121

5/8

1. Jay had a great time in Manchester! (have)
2. He —— a cool DVD at a music shop. (buy)
3. Jay and his brother —— to a concert. (go)
4. They —— some famous bands. (see)
5. Jay —— breakfast for his grandparents. (make)
6. His cousins —— him about cool places in Manchester. (tell)

b) Make four more sentences. Use these ideas.

Jay had a picnic. He ...

sing ... | eat ... | meet ... | take photo of ...

13 (TASK) My holidays → V Holidays, p. 162

a) Write about your holidays.

My holidays were great.
I went to Salzburg with my brother.
We went swimming and played football.
That was exciting.
I took a lot of photos for my friends.

cool | OK | awful
boring | good | ...
went to ... | was at home | ...
family | friends | parents
grandparents | ...
visited | saw | ate
liked | played table tennis
bought | went rock climbing

b) Tell your class about your holidays.

Ich kann über meine Sommerferien sprechen. ✔

Hier lerne ich, Missverständnisse zu klären.

An argument about a scarf

1 Look at the photo. Is Holly happy?

2 (READING) Read the three dialogues.

1, 7

Holly: Hi Olivia, can I have my new scarf, please?
Olivia: The blue scarf?
Holly: Yes, you borrowed it last week. Did you bring it to school?
Olivia: Yes, I did. You weren't here so I put the scarf in your black bag.
Holly: It wasn't there. Did you lose it?
Olivia: No, I didn't lose it.
Holly: I have to go. Can you find it, please?

Gwen: Hi Olivia. Here's your scarf.
Olivia: Oh thank you! It's Holly's scarf. I put it in her bag. How did you find it?
Gwen: I looked in my bag and was surprised. There it was!
Olivia: Oh! Your bag looks like Holly's. That's what happened. I put the scarf in the wrong bag. I was really worried! Let's give it back to her. She was very unhappy.

Olivia: Holly! Gwen found your scarf. Here it is.
Holly: Where was it?
Olivia: It was in Gwen's bag. She has the same bag as you. I'm really sorry I lost your scarf, Holly!
Holly: I'm sorry I was angry.
Olivia: Never mind.

3 Find the right order.

a) Put the pictures in the right order. → ○ p. 121

1 

2 

3 

b) Find a sentence from the text for each picture.

4 (WRITING) What are the words? → M Bus stop, p. 154

6/1

a) Find the words. → ○ p. 122

hap | an | py | gry | wor | sur | un | hap | ried | prised | py

b) Match the feelings from a) with the pictures.

1. He is worried.

5 (SOUNDS) Listen, read and say.

1, 8
6/1

1. I'm sorry I was angry. (sorry)
2. Did you lose it? (angry)
3. It's not there. (worried)
4. What's this? It isn't my scarf! (surprised)

SPEAKING SKILLS

Denke an eine Situation, in der du dich schon einmal so gefühlt hast.
Sag den Satz dann mit diesem Gefühl.

6 (LISTENING) How do they feel?

1, 9
6/1

1. Holly is angry.
2. Gwen is ....

sorry | angry ✓ | worried | surprised | unhappy | happy

7 Say how you feel.

a) Match the sentences with the words from exercise 6. → ○ p. 122

1. Your friend is not happy because you ate his/her last sandwich.
   I am sorry.
2. Your cat doesn't come home. Where can he be?
3. You had an argument and your friend doesn't want to talk to you.
4. You find some money.
5. Your little sister lost your phone.
6. You find your friend's book in your bag.

b) Think about two more situations and make sentences for the class.

8 (SPEAKING) Act it!

6/2

Act a dialogue with your partner.

A: Oh, sorry!
B: Why, what happened?
A: I took your pencil.
B: Never mind.

what's the problem? | ...

borrowed your pen | took your bag | ...

Don't worry. | It was old. | It's OK. | ...

Language detectives → G 2, p. 141

Holly: Did you lose my scarf?
Olivia: No, I didn't lose it!

Welches Wort brauchst du, um eine Frage in der Vergangenheit zu stellen?

Do you remember?

Olivia: I'm sorry I lost it.

Schau dir die beiden Antworten von Olivia an. Welche Form des Verbs verwendest du mit didn't?

9 What didn't you do in your last holidays?

7/3

a) Make sentences about yourself with didn't. → ○ p. 123

1 I didn't play cricket.

2 visit

3 sing

4 watch

5 do

6 take

b) Make more sentences.

10 (SPEAKING) Ask your partner. → M Milling around, p. 156

7/4

A: Did you + watch TV / play a computer game / visit the stadium / play netball/football + yesterday? / on Saturday? / last week? / at the weekend?

B: Yes, I did. It was cool! / I had a fantastic time! / …
No, I didn't. I was busy/tired/…

11 (LISTENING) What happened?

1, 10
8/5

Listen to the three dialogues and answer these questions: → ○ p. 123

Dialogue A
1. What happened?
2. Where did Luke lose it?

Dialogue B
1. What happened?
2. Where did Olivia lose it?

Dialogue C
1. How was Jay's weekend?
2. What happened?
3. Where did Jay and his cousins sing?
4. Did people like it?

12 (SPEAKING) Act the dialogues.

Spielt den Dialog mit Ausdruck!

1.
A: How was your weekend?
B: Not very good. — Bad. / Awful. / …
A: What happened?
B: I lost my bag. — my new phone / my new pencil / my new torch / …
A: Where did you lose it?
B: At school. — At the sports centre. / At the swimming pool. / …

OR

2.
A: How was your trip?
B: Great. — OK. / Exciting. / …
A: What did you do?
B: I went canoeing. — I went bike riding. / I played …
A: Great.

13 Match the questions with the answers.

8/6

1. Where did you go for your holidays, Jay? ✓
2. When did you go?
3. Did you like Manchester?
4. How did you go there?
5. What did you do in Manchester?
6. Where did you stay?

a. I met my cousins and we started a band.
b. I stayed with my grandparents.
c. I went to Manchester. ✓
d. I went in August.
e. Yes, it's a really cool city.
f. We went by car.

14 What did Olivia's mum ask?

→ M Walking sentences, p. 158

a) Put the words in the right order. → ○ p. 124

8/6

1. did • What • borrow? • you
   What did you borrow?
2. you • it? • borrow • When did
3. did • you • Where • put the scarf?
4. didn't you • the scarf to Holly? • give • Why
5. get her scarf back? • Holly • How • did

b) Match Olivia's answers with the questions from a).

Because Holly wasn't there. | Gwen and I gave it to her. | Holly's scarf. | I put it in Gwen's bag. | On Monday.

15 (TASK) I'm sorry! → V Everyday English, p. 161

Act a dialogue with your partner.

A: Can I have my pen, please?
B: I put it in your bag.
A: It's not there. I looked. Did you lose it?
B: No, I didn't. Look! It was under your books.
A: Oh I'm sorry. I didn't see it.
B: It's OK.

new scarf | football | ruler | rubber | ...

on your chair | on your table | ...

exercise book | bag | ...

Never mind. | No problem. | ...

Ich kann Missverständnisse klären. ✓

A lucky day for Luke

1 Look at the photos.

1. Where are Luke and Gwen in photo 1?
2. Where are they in photo 3?
3. What happened? Guess.

READING SKILLS

Bilder helfen dir, eine Geschichte zu verstehen. Deshalb sieh dir immer zuerst die Bilder an. Dann lies den Text. Dabei brauchst du nicht gleich jedes Wort zu verstehen.

2 (READING) Read the story.

1, 11

1

It was after school. Luke and Gwen were on the bus.

"Dad said we can get a pet," said Gwen. "Isn't that great?"

Luke didn't answer.

"Did you hear me?" asked Gwen.

"Sorry. This game on my phone is great," said Luke. "Look!"

"I can't see that," said Gwen.

"Sorry. I forgot you have a problem with your eyes."

"You forgot Dave's birthday. You forgot your homework. You forget everything," said Gwen.

"No, I don't," said Luke. "Oh no! This is my stop. I forgot where we are! Bye Gwen."

2

Luke got off the bus. He wanted to finish his game so he put his hand in his bag. His phone wasn't there! "Oh no, I forgot it on the bus!"

Luke went home and phoned the bus company. They wanted to help but first they needed a special number from his phone – and he didn't know the number!

3

Later the doorbell rang.

Luke went to the door. Gwen and her dad were there.

"I heard your phone fall on the bus," said Gwen.

Gwen gave Luke his phone.

"Wow! Your hearing is really good," said Luke. "It's my lucky day! Thanks Gwen."

3 Right or wrong?

9/1

a)
1. Luke and Holly were on the bus.
   That's wrong.
2. Gwen was angry with Luke.
3. Luke doesn't forget things.
4. Gwen gave Luke his phone.
5. It was Luke's lucky day.

b) Why did Luke forget his phone on the bus?

STUDY SKILLS

So kannst du vorgehen, wenn du die Bedeutung eines Wortes nicht kennst:

- Fällt dir ein deutsches Wort ein, das ähnlich klingt? Z. B. bei forget, fall oder lucky.
- Oder kannst du das Wort von einem anderen englischen Wort ableiten? Z. B. everything → every

4 Choose one of the tasks.

a) Make a poster about friends.
Find words in the story for the poster.
Put pictures on the poster.

OR

b) Act scene 1 or scenes 2 and 3.

Ich kann eine Geschichte über Freunde verstehen. ✔

Postcards from Bavaria

Hi Andy,
Greetings from Munich!
Yesterday we walked through the city centre and visited the Town Hall.
There were a lot of people … and the Bayern Munich team on the balcony! Great!
See you soon, Henry

Deutschland

Mr Andy Dawson
28 Bristol S
Birmingha
West Mid
UK

Hello Rosie,
Landshut is great. We were in a huge park and swam in a river. The river has a funny name: Isar. People are very nice but I can't understand what they say … After 3 years of German!
Lots of love, Amy

Deutschland

Ms Rosie Williams
10 Hartshill Rd.
Stoke-on-Trent
Staffordshire, ST47RB
ENGLAND

Dear Mum,
We go rock climbing, swimming and walking every day. It's great … Today we wanted to have a picnic but the weather is terrible. It's too wet and too cold – brrr. On the postcard you can see the Alps and our village with the campsite.
Everything is fine.
Robin

Mrs Belinda Simp
14 Albion St.
Exeter
Devon, EX41AZ
UK

1 (MEDIATION) **Fasse die Informationen auf Deutsch zusammen.**

9/2

1. Wo waren die Kinder im Urlaub?
2. Was haben sie gemacht?
3. Gab es Probleme? Wenn ja, welche?

2 (WRITING) **Write a holiday postcard to one of your classmates.**

Ich kann Informationen aus einer Postkarte weitergeben. ✓

The new boy

In diesem Film triffst du Marley, Jinsoo und ihren neuen Mitschüler Nick.

1 (VIEWING) Watch the film.

2 a) Put the pictures in the right order.

b) Match the words from the film to the correct pictures.

penny | lemon | battery | wire | nail

1 

2 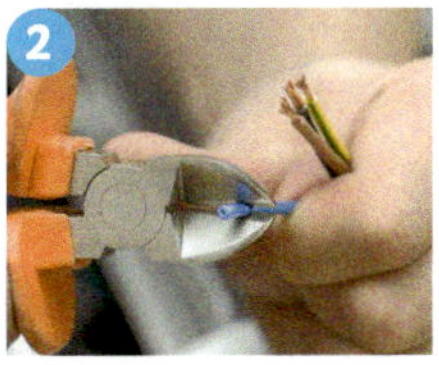

3 

4 

5 

2 (MEDIATION) Explain the experiment in German.

3 Choose the best film title.

a. Where is the penny?
b. The experiment
c. An argument about a lemon
d. A new friend

Ich kann einen Film über ein Experiment verstehen.

Checklist

Find more online: 6ag9ry

✔ **Ich kann meine Freunde nach den Ferien begrüßen.**

How were your holidays? • Fine, thanks. • I like .... Is it new? • Yes, thank you.

10

✔ **Ich kann über meine Sommerferien sprechen.**

I had a great time. • I went to ... with .... • We .... • I had a lot of fun.

10

✔ **Ich kann Missverständnisse klären.**

Did you ...? • I'm sorry. • I didn't .... • Never mind. • That's OK.

10

✔ **Ich kann eine Geschichte über Freunde verstehen.**

11

✔ **Ich kann Informationen aus einer Postkarte weitergeben.**

11

✔ **Ich kann einen Film über ein Experiment verstehen.**

(UNIT TASK)

A role play

In dieser Aufgabe geht es darum, eine Streitszene zu schreiben und sie dann vorzuspielen. Lies zuerst alles durch. Dann suche zwei Mitschüler, mit denen du zusammenarbeiten kannst.

Step 1

Collect ideas about arguments.

Student A is angry with student B and they have an argument. Student C tries to help.
What can you have an argument about?
Make a list. Here are some ideas:

- A saw B with another boy/girl yesterday.
- A or B is always late / forgets ....
- A or B always wants to do the same things/....

Step 2

Plan the role play.

Choose one of the ideas from Step 1 and talk about it.

- How can student C help?
- How can the argument end?
- Choose roles. Who is student A, who is student B and who is student C?

WRITING SKILLS

Euer Dialog sollte aus folgenden vier Teilen bestehen:

1. Begrüßung ("Hi!")
2. Problem ("You didn't talk to me.")
3. Streit ("You're not my friend.")
4. Lösung ("I'm sorry.")

Step 3

Write the role play.

a) Write a draft of your role play.

Students A and B can use these phrases:

- You always ....
- That isn't fair!
- Why can't you ...?
- Don't say that!
- Why don't you ...?
- That's not true.

Student C can use these phrases:

- Stop it!
- What happened?
- Let's talk about the problem.
- He/She didn't want to ....

b) Show the draft to a teacher and your classmates and listen to their ideas.

Step 4

Practise the role play. → M Read and look up, p. 157

- Learn each line of your dialogue.
- Practise the dialogue.

SPEAKING SKILLS

Wenn du deinen Dialog vorspielst, vergiss nicht, laut und deutlich zu sprechen. Schau deine Partnerin oder deinen Partner an. Du kannst auch Gesten einsetzen.

Step 5

Do your role play for your class. Then ask the class for feedback.

That was great!

I didn't hear all of the sentences.

I think your dialogue was fantastic / very interesting / funny / OK.

Well done!

Just for fun

Ben's holidays

That's the last time I go with Batbus Tours.

Ow!

Ouch!

Now I really need a holiday!

Welcome to Munich!

1, 12

1 (LISTENING) **Listen to the dialogues and find the answers.** → ○ p. 124

14/1

2 (SPEAKING) **Ask your partner.** → M Double circle, p. 154

Do you speak English?	Yes, … / No, …
What's your name?	I'm …
How old are you?	I'm … (years old).
Where are you from?	I'm from Augsburg.

Hier wiederholst du,
- wie du Fragen stellen kannst.
- wie du dich vorstellen kannst.
- wie du jemand anderen vorstellen kannst.

Language → G 11, p. 150

Are you from Munich?	Yes, I am. No, I'm not.
Do you live in Greenwich?	Yes, I do. No, I don't.
What's your name? Where do you live?	Tim. In Augsburg.

Do you remember?
So stellst du Fragen und antwortest darauf.

3 (SPEAKING) Find more information about your partner. → M Double circle, p. 154

15/2–3 a) Write five questions you want to ask.

Where do you live?
Do you like football?
What is your favourite colour?
Do you have a brother?
When do you get up in the morning?
…

swimming | shopping | music | …

shop | book | band | …

sister | pet | …

b) Ask your partner.

Pass auf:
Who? heißt Wer?
Where? heißt Wo?

Language

This is Leo. He likes rock climbing.
This is Lena. She lives in Regensburg.

Do you remember?
So stellst du jemanden vor.

4 (SPEAKING) Write the information about your partner. Then present your partner.

15/4

This is ___ .
He/She lives in ___ .
He/She likes ___ .
His/Her favourite … is ___ .
He/She has ___ .
In the morning he/she gets up at ___ .

3 1,, 13

Unit 2 Intro

Where I live

1 Where is it?

16/1

1. Luke and Holly live in this road.
   It's Brook Lane.
2. Luke likes to play computer games there.
3. Luke often goes there with his friends and Sherlock.
4. Holly often does her homework there.
5. Holly often goes there on Saturdays.

1, 14

2 (LISTENING) Listen to Dave.

a) Which places does Dave talk about?

Brook Lane | snack bar | shopping centre | cinema | Kidbrooke Gardens

b) What is his favourite place in Greenwich? Say why.

Am Ende dieser Unit kann ich …
- sagen, wo ich wohne.
- über Aufgaben im Haushalt sprechen.
- mich über mein Zimmer unterhalten.
- Kleidung aussuchen und kaufen.

2

3 (TASK) Where I live

16/2

Tell a partner about where you live. What's your favourite place?

I live in Bamberg.
Our flat is in Schillerstraße.
There's a park and a supermarket.
My favourite place is the shopping centre.

house | swimming pool | snack bar | cinema | playground

Ich kann sagen, wo ich wohne. ✔

Hier lerne ich, über Aufgaben im Haushalt zu sprechen.

At home with Holly

1 (READING) Read about Holly and her family's jobs at home.

1, 15 17/1

Holly lives with her mother and her sister Amber in a flat in Brook Lane. Sometimes her mother is busy and Holly has to help at home.

Holly:

I get up at 7 o'clock every morning. I usually feed my guinea pigs, Fluff and Honey. After school I often empty the dishwasher. On Saturdays I have to tidy my bedroom and clean the guinea pigs' cage.

Amber:

I make my bed every morning. I also have to take out the rubbish before school. I often load the dishwasher. I sometimes help Mum with the cooking. Holly never hoovers the living room. I usually do it.

Mrs Richardson:

I sometimes have to work at the market or clean old people's houses. I clean our kitchen and bathroom every week. I cook for the family every evening.

2 Who does what? Complete the sentences.

17/2

1. —— often loads the dishwasher.
2. —— has to cook for the family.
3. —— feeds the guinea pigs in the morning.
4. —— sometimes helps her mother with the cooking.
5. —— has to tidy her bedroom on Saturdays.
6. —— cleans the kitchen every week.

Holly

Mrs Richardson

Amber

1, 16

3 (LISTENING) Look at the pictures. → ○ p. 124

Listen to the sounds in Holly's flat and put the pictures in the right order. Write the names of the rooms.

1 
2 
3 
4 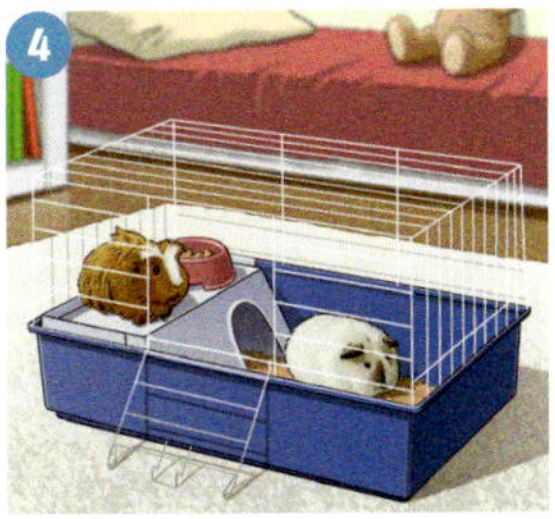

17/3

4 Write about Dave's day. → M Bus stop, p. 154

Complete the sentences.

empties the dishwasher | makes breakfast | takes out the rubbish | makes lunch | feeds Sid | tidies the living room

It's his mum's birthday today and Dave wants to help her. He gets up at 8 o'clock. First he  . Then he  for his mum. At 9 o'clock he  . At 9:30 he  . At 10 o'clock he 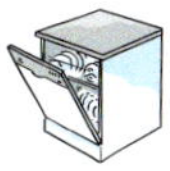 in the kitchen. At 12 o'clock he  .

Mrs Preston is very happy. "You're fantastic, Dave!" she says.

1, 17

5 (SOUNDS) Listen, read and say.

fish, dishwasher, give, his, rubbish [ɪ]

tidy, sometimes, arrive, behind, like [aɪ]

6 Make questions.

18/4

a) Write the questions.

Do you have to	+	eat clean be go	+	to bed before 10:00 in the evening? in school before 8:00 in the morning? lunch in the school cafeteria? the classroom? to school by bus?

b) Ask your partner questions about his or her day. → M Double circle, p. 154

You: Do you have to go to school by bus?
Partner: Yes, I do. / No, I don't.

Language detectives → G 3, p. 142

Amber always makes her bed in the morning.
Holly never hoovers the living room.
Mrs Richardson sometimes works at the market.
Amber usually hoovers the living room.
Holly often empties the dishwasher.

Was bedeuten die grün unterstrichenen Wörter auf Deutsch? Wo stehen sie, vor oder nach dem Verb?

18/5

7 (WRITING) How often do they do it?

a) Put the words in the sentences. → ○ p. 124

1. Amber loads the dishwasher. (++)
2. Dave takes out the rubbish. (+)
3. Olivia makes her bed in the morning. (++++)
4. Luke tidies the living room. (–)
5. Holly feeds her guinea pigs chocolate. (–)
6. Dave hoovers the living room on Saturday. (++++)

– = never
\+ = sometimes
++ = often
+++ = usually
++++ = always

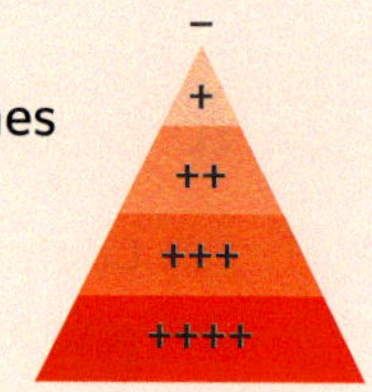

b) Write about Holly, Amber and Mrs Richardson. Look at page 30 if you need help.

1. Holly (hoover) –
2. Mrs Richardson (clean) +
3. Amber (help) +
4. Holly (feed) +++

8 (SPEAKING) What about you? → M Double circle, p. 154

Say what you do at home: I often …

9 (TASK) Jobs at home → V Jobs at home, p. 163

a) Ask a partner about his or her jobs at home. Find out three things and write them.

hoover the living room • tidy the bedroom • take out the rubbish • load/empty the dishwasher • feed the pets • do your homework • help with the cooking • make your bed

Do you have to make your bed?

Yes, I do.

No, I don't.

Yes, often.

No, never.

b) Tell your class about your partner.

"Leonie often has to make her bed. She sometimes has to …. She never has to …."

Ich kann über Aufgaben im Haushalt sprechen. ✔

Hier lerne ich, mich über mein Zimmer zu unterhalten.

Luke's new room

1 (READING) Read the text.

1, 18

In the summer holidays, Luke changed things in his bedroom. Now it looks very different. Jay visits Luke.

Luke: Close your eyes and come with me, Jay! Welcome to my new room!

Jay: Wow! It's really different!

Luke: Yes, now the wardrobe is next to the window and there's a new shelf above the bed.

Jay: What's that on the wall above your desk?

Luke: Oh, that's my new Arsenal lamp. And look, there are my new Arsenal posters.

Jay: No, thanks. I think Arsenal posters look best behind a wardrobe.

Luke: Ha, ha. That's only because you're a Manchester United fan.

Jay: Are your comics in the wardrobe now?

Luke: No, they're in the black boxes on the shelf, next to the books.

Jay: Is the carpet new too?

Luke: Yes, the old carpet was blue. I like this red carpet.

Jay: It's OK. The blue carpet was better. Errr – Can we go to the shopping centre now?

Luke: Great idea! Let's go to the new sports shop.

2 Complete the sentences.

19/1

1. Luke's  is next to the .
2. His new  is above his 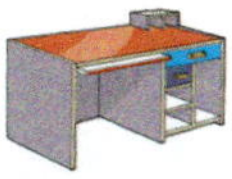.
3. There's a new  on the wall above his 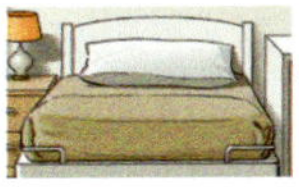.
4. My  are new.
5. Luke's comics are in the 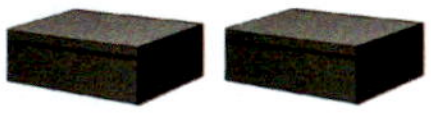 on the .
6. Jay doesn't like the new .

3 (SPEAKING) Look at Luke's room again.

a) Make sentences about the room. → ○ p. 125

19/2

There	+	is / are	+	a lamp / a wardrobe / comics / new posters / a shelf	+	on / above / in / next to	+	the bed. / the black boxes. / the desk. / the window. / the wall.

b) Make more sentences about Luke's room.

4 (LISTENING) Find out about Dave's bedroom.

a) Listen to Dave. Which is his room? → ○ p. 125

1, 19

b) Write five sentences about one of the pictures.

19/2

There is a football under …

5 (JUST FOR FUN) Ben's tidy room

I always tidy my room.

I say "There is a place for everything."

Ooops!

6 Make questions about Luke's room. → M Walking sentences, p. 158

a) Put the words in the right order. → ◯ p. 125

20/3a

1. ? • Where • the shelf • is
2. books • on • there • ? • the shelf • Are
3. above • ? • the desk • is • What
4. wardrobe • ? • Where • Luke's • is
5. behind • posters • there • Are • ? • the wardrobe
6. colour • the boxes • What • are • ?

b) Answer the questions in a).

20/3b

The Arsenal lamp. | No, there aren't. | Black. | Next to the window. | Yes, there are. | Above the bed.

7 (GAME) What's in the picture?

Partner A: Look at the picture for one minute. Then close your book.
Partner B: Ask A five questions about the picture.

Take turns. Who has got more correct answers?

Is/Are there …? • Where …? •
What colour …? • What is above/on/under …?

8 (TASK) My room → V At home, p. 164 → M Gallery walk, p. 155

20/4

a) Draw your dream room. Label the things in it.

b) Ask about your partner's room.

A: What's in your dream room?
B: There's a bed, a … and ….
A: What colour is/are the …?
B: It's/They're ….
A: Is/Are there … in your room?
B: Yes, there is/are …. • No, there isn't/aren't ….
A: Where is/are ….
B: It's/They're above the ….

c) Write a text about your dream room.

STUDY SKILLS

Schreibe die Wörter für Möbelstücke auf Klebezettel und hänge sie an die Möbel. Dann hast du sie immer wieder vor Augen.

Ich kann mich über mein Zimmer unterhalten. ✓

Hier lerne ich, Kleidung auszusuchen und zu kaufen.

In the sports shop

1 What clothes do you remember?

→ M Think – pair – share, p. 157

2 (READING) Read the dialogues.

1, 20
21/1

It was Luke's birthday and he got some money. Today Luke and Jay are in the new sports shop in Greenwich Shopping Park.

Shop assistant: Can I help you, boys?
Luke: Yes, I need some new trainers.
Shop assistant: What's your size?
Luke: Size 6. My feet are very big.
Shop assistant: Here. These trainers are size 6.
Luke: Yes, they're a nice colour but they're too small. Do you have them in a larger size?
Shop assistant: Yes, here you are.
Jay: They're £55. That's expensive! Here – these red trainers are cheaper than those.
Luke: Can I try them on, please?
Shop assistant: Here you are, then.
Luke: OK, thanks. They're great!

Next Luke needs a T-shirt.
Luke: Look at this grey T-shirt. It's really cool!
Jay: Yes, but it's too long. Do you like this pink T-shirt?
Luke: It's very pretty, Jay. Holly likes pink. It's also shorter than the grey T-shirt but a lot worse. I need something smaller than size L.
Jay: That blue T-shirt is better. It's shorter than the grey T-shirt too.

Luke: OK then. I'd like to buy the blue T-shirt, please.
Luke buys the red trainers and the blue T-shirt. Then they go to a snack bar.

3 Choose the right answers.

→ M Peer correction, p. 156

1. Luke and Jay are in a ___ .
   sports centre • sports shop • supermarket • stadium
2. Luke wants to buy ___ .
   new trainers and a T-shirt • an Arsenal scarf and a shirt • new trainers and a scarf • a T-shirt and jeans
3. Luke's shoe size is ___ .
   4 • 5 • 6 • 7
4. Luke buys ___ trainers.
   white • yellow • red • blue
5. Luke buys the ___ T-shirt.
   grey • blue • white • green

CULTURE

In Großbritannien werden Schuhgrößen anders als in Deutschland angegeben. Hier kannst du die Schuhgrößen für Kinder miteinander vergleichen:

UK:	1	2	2½	3	4	5	6
EU:	33	34	35	36	37	38	39

4 Find the opposites.

a) Put the letters in the right order. → ○ p. 126

1. expensive ⟷ p a c h e
2. good ⟷ d a b
3. old ⟷ e n w
4. large ⟷ l a m l s
5. short ⟷ g n o l
6. worse ⟷ r e t t e b

STUDY SKILLS

Wörter merkst du dir leichter, wenn du sie als Gegensatzpaare lernst.

b) Find more word pairs.

5 What do you think of these clothes?

21/2

Use the words from exercise 4.

This coat is too large.

This T-shirt is too ___

This ___

This ___

6 (SOUNDS) Listen, read and say.

1, 21

I think these clothes are pretty.
I think these three shirts are expensive.

I think those clothes are cool.
I think those three shirts are too small.

[θ] and [ð]

7 (SPEAKING) How much are they? → ○ p. 126

Look at the pictures and ask your partner.

A: How much is the T-shirt/scarf/...?
are the jeans/trainers ...

B: It's £20./They're ....

Bei den Wörtern „jeans" und „trainers" müsst ihr aufpassen! Sie stehen in der Mehrzahl. How much are the jeans? They're ....

Language detectives → G 4, p. 143

The red trainers are cheaper than the white trainers.
These trainers are a nicer colour than those.
The green T-shirt is longer than the grey T-shirt.
That blue T-shirt is better than the pink T-shirt.
The green T-shirt is worse than the grey T-shirt.

Welche Endung wird an die Eigenschaftswörter angehängt?
Nach den Eigenschaftswörtern kommt das Wort —— ?
Wie ist es im Deutschen?

22/3

8 Compare the clothes in the picture.

a) Complete the sentences.

1. The red T-shirt is —— than the yellow T-shirt. (short)
2. The white scarf is —— than the green scarf. (long)
3. The black jeans are —— than the blue jeans. (cheap)
4. The yellow T-shirt is —— than the white scarf. (cheap)
5. The black jeans are —— than the blue jeans. (short)
6. The green scarf is —— than the white scarf. (cheap)

b) Make more sentences about the clothes.

9 (SONG) I love your style

1, 22

Bildet drei Gruppen und singt jeweils eine der Strophen mit.

I really like your T-shirt,
I really like your dress.
No matter what the price is,
No one would ever guess.
I really like your tank top,
I really love your jeans.
No matter what the brand is,
Or what the logo means.

I love your style,
You look just great in everything you wear,
If you choose this suit, if you pick that dress,
If you spend a little more, or a little less.
I love your style,
It's just important to feel good.
It's not that high fashion thing,
Not the 'bling bling bling',
You do your own thing, your own thing!
I love your style!

You are in the spotlight, everywhere you go,
And you look great, don't you know?
You are in the spotlight everywhere,
You look great in everything you wear.
I love your style!

10 (SPEAKING) What do you think?

22/4

Compare the clothes in exercise 7. Make sentences.

I think the	+	dress shoes pullover trainers ...	+	is are	+	cooler nicer better worse prettier	+	than the ....

11 (TASK) Clothes shopping → V Buying clothes, p. 165

a) Bring or draw three pictures of clothes. You can bring/draw pictures of a T-shirt, a scarf, a pullover, trainers, shoes and jeans. Write prices on the pictures.

b) Make dialogues in groups of three.

You: Look, do you like this T-shirt? It's cool.
Your friend: Really? I think this T-shirt is cooler than that T-shirt.
You: Yes, but it's size XL. It's too big for me.

You: I'd like to buy this T-shirt, please.
Shop assistant: That's £15, please.
You: Here you are.
Shop assistant: Here's your T-shirt. Bye!
You: Thank you. Bye!

pullover | scarf | trainers | shoes | jeans | ...

nice | pretty | good | cheap | ...

nicer | prettier | better | cheaper | ...

size M | size L | ...

small | long | short | ...

£10 | £20 | ...

Ich kann Kleidung aussuchen und kaufen.

Sherlock's story

1 What do you remember about Sherlock?

2 (READING) Read the story.

1, 23

Hello. I'm Sherlock. My family are the Elliots – Anna, Jack, Jamie, Irina and Luke. I love everyone in the family, but Luke is my pet. He's really great! We have a lot of fun together.

Luke and I have got a nice bedroom in our house. Every morning I get up at half past seven and wash Luke's face. Then he gets up and washes his face again. He always does that – I don't know why. After that he makes my breakfast in the kitchen. I love breakfast! Then Luke has his breakfast.

Jack usually goes to work early. Then at twenty past eight Luke, Irina and Jamie go to school. I always help Luke with his school bag. At quarter to nine Anna says goodbye too. She comes home at quarter past two. Then we have lunch together in the kitchen.

In the mornings I have to look after the house for the family. Sometimes there are cats in my garden. That's bad – it isn't their garden! The neighbour's cat Ross is the worst of all. So I always bark. Then they think I'm scary and they run away.

5

On Saturdays Luke and I go to dog school. Luke learns new tricks. One trick is: I listen for the word "Sit!". But I run away. Then the teacher always says, "You've got a lot more to learn!" Yes, Luke has got a lot more to learn.

6

On Sundays I sometimes go to Greenwich Park with my family. My family likes picnics. I like picnics too because there is no table. Sometimes Jamie puts his food next to me and I eat it. Yummy!

7

In the evenings my family often sits in the living room and watches TV. Then we play a game. I watch TV too, and they throw shoes to me. I take the shoes to my room. I like shoes!

8

At nine o'clock Luke and I go to our room. He's a good pet so he can sleep in my bed. I always sleep well. After my busy day I'm very tired.

3 Match the headings with the right pictures.

23/1

At dog school | Luke and Sherlock get up in the morning | Sherlock and his family | Games in the evening | Cats in the garden | Picnic in the park

4 (TASK) Choose one of the tasks.

P

a) Choose a new time or day in Sherlock's life. Draw a picture and write a text for it.

At night / At lunchtime / In the afternoon / …

OR

b) Have you got a pet? Write a funny story about its day. Draw pictures too.

Ich kann eine Geschichte über einen Hund verstehen. ✓

A new room

1 Lies die Seite aus einem Möbelkatalog.

2 (MEDIATION) Worum geht es hier?

23/2

Erkläre diese Katalogseite einem Freund / einer Freundin, der/die kein Englisch spricht.

3 Finde alle Wörter, die du kennst oder erschließen kannst.

Zeichne eine Tabelle und schreibe die Wörter mit ihrer deutschen Bedeutung in die Tabelle. Erkläre, warum du sie verstehst.

Englisches Wort	Bedeutung im Deutschen	Wieso ich es verstehe
lamp	Lampe	es ist ähnlich

Ich kann Informationen aus einem Katalog weitergeben. ✔

How to be polite

1 What words do you use in English to be polite?

Which words are polite? Which words are not polite? Make a table.

Please. | Sorry! | You again?! | Thank you. | Excuse me! | What do you want?

polite	not polite

2 (VIEWING) Watch the film.

4 a) Put the pictures in the right order.

A

B

C

D

b) Answer the questions.

1. When Laura opens the door
   - she says “Please!”
   - the woman says “Thank you!”
   - the man is happy.
2. The woman in the queue says to Laura
   - “Excuse me! There’s a queue.”
   - “Don’t do that, please!”
   - “Are you crazy?”
3. The man on the escalator says
   - “Good morning!”
   - “Wake up!”
   - “Excuse me!”
4. Who says sorry at the end?
   - Laura
   - The woman
   - Laura and the woman

VIEWING SKILLS

Bevor du den Film noch einmal anschaust, lies die Möglichkeiten durch. Was erscheint dir logisch oder wahrscheinlich? Achte dann genau auf diese Stellen im Film.

Ihr müsst gar nicht viel sagen. Schaut euch die Bewegungen und den Gesichtsausdruck der Personen im Film an und spielt eine der Szenen nach.

3 Act the scene.

Choose one of the four situations and act the scene.

Ich kann einen Film zum Thema „Höflich sein“ verstehen. ✓

Checklist

Find more online: 6ag9ry

✔ **Ich kann sagen, wo ich wohne.**

I live in a flat with .... • Our house is in .... • My favourite room is .... • We live opposite ....

24

✔ **Ich kann über Aufgaben im Haushalt sprechen.**

I often empty the dishwasher. • I have to tidy my bedroom. • I clean our kitchen and bathroom every week.

24

✔ **Ich kann mich über mein Zimmer unterhalten.**

The wardrobe is next to the window. • There's a new shelf above the bed.

24

✔ **Ich kann Kleidung aussuchen und kaufen.**

The pink T-shirt is shorter than the grey T-shirt. • The trainers are too small. • I'd like to buy this T-shirt.

25

✔ **Ich kann eine Geschichte über einen Hund verstehen.**

25

✔ **Ich kann Informationen aus einem Katalog weitergeben.**

25

✔ **Ich kann einen Film zum Thema „Höflich sein" verstehen.**

(UNIT TASK)

A survey

Step 1

Get into groups of six.

Step 2

Find out what students in your group do in a typical day and take notes.

What do you do every day?

take out the rubbish · do homework · watch TV · empty the dishwasher · feed a pet · talk to friends · ...

Sophie: feeds her cat, does her homework
Max: plays computer games, takes out the rubbish, helps in the garden

Step 3

Make a chart about your everyday activities. → V Free-time activities, p. 174

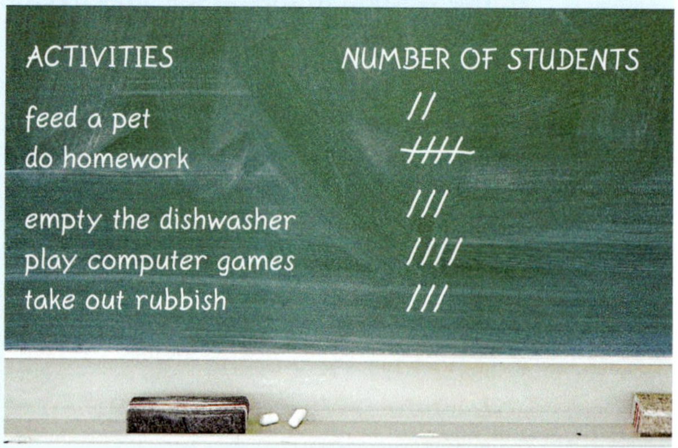

Step 4

Make a graph.

a) Draw a graph.

OR b) Use a computer for your graph.

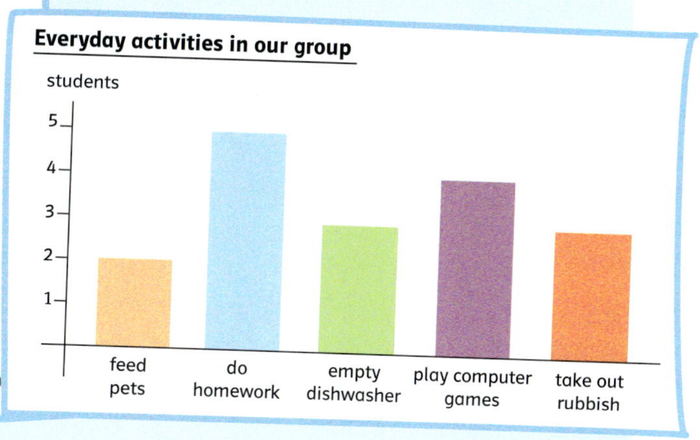

Step 5

Present your survey to your class.

- In our group two students feed their pets.
- Five students do their homework.
- Three students empty the dishwasher.
- Four students play computer games.
- Three students take out the rubbish.

SPEAKING SKILLS

Wenn eine Gruppe alles deutlich erklärt und eine übersichtliche Grafik präsentiert hat, könnt ihr sagen: "Thank you. That was very clear."

Just for fun

Ben's typical day

We all have to do jobs in my family.

Mum hoovers the tree.

Dad feeds Incey, our pet.

Everyone has to do something.

The United Kingdom

Schau auf der Karte hinten im Buch nach, wenn du bei 1b und 1c Hilfe brauchst.

1 Look at the map.

a) Aus wie vielen Ländern besteht das United Kingdom?

b) Finde für jedes Land die richtige Hauptstadt. Edinburgh Cardiff London Belfast

c) Welche der Städte hat die meisten Einwohner?

Entdecke auf diesen Bildern Großbritannien und schaue dir die Fragen an. Du kannst sie bestimmt gleich beantworten.

2 Look at the pictures.

1. In welchem Land wird nicht nur Englisch gesprochen?
2. Welches Instrument wird in Schottland gespielt?
3. Wo kann man als Tourist in England z. B. übernachten?

CULTURE

Auch in Deutschland machen viele Leute Urlaub. Wo kann man hier übernachten?

5 1, 24

Unit 3 Intro

London life

INTERNET

Home About me My friends

Dominik's blog

<1>
Hi everyone at home in Poland! I'm in London with my cousin Luke. Today we visited some famous sights here. London is one of the best cities.

<2>
The London Eye is a big wheel. Germans helped to build it.

1 What are they?

28/1

a) Match the words.

The London Eye Big Ben St Paul's Madame Tussauds	is	a museum. a big wheel. a tower. a church.

b) Say the right place.

1. Germans helped to build it. That's the ....
2. There are a lot of wax figures there.
3. It's about 300 years old.

2 (LISTENING) Listen to the dialogue.

1, 25
28/2

a) What do they talk about?

Westminster Bridge • Tower Bridge

b) Choose the right answers.

1. The bridge **often / never** opens.
2. It opens for **big ships / small ships**.
3. You can find **on the internet / in a book** when it opens.
4. They **can / can't** all go and see the bridge open.

Am Ende dieser Unit kann ich ...
- über Sehenswürdigkeiten in London sprechen.
- Sehenswürdigkeiten miteinander vergleichen.
- sagen, was jemand gerade tut.
- jemandem den Weg beschreiben.

<3>
Big Ben, or the Elizabeth Tower, is a very famous tower with a clock near Westminster Bridge. People clean the clock every five years.

<4>
Madame Tussauds is a famous museum. It's about 180 years old and lots of people go there every day. It has wax figures of stars and kings and queens.

<5>
St Paul's is a famous old church. It's about 300 years old. It's 111 metres high.

<6>
Listen!

3 (TASK) London sights → V London sights, p. 166 → M Milling around, p. 156

Which sights in London would you like to see? Talk to your partner.

A: I would like to visit the London Eye.
It looks really cool.
I like big wheels.
They're very exciting.
What would you like to visit?
B: I would like to visit ....

Madame Tussauds | Big Ben | ...
very interesting | great | very old | ...
old towers | museums | ...

Ich kann über Sehenswürdigkeiten in London sprechen. ✓

Hier lerne ich, Sehenswürdigkeiten miteinander zu vergleichen.

Up high on the London Eye

1 (READING) Read the fact cards.

1, 26

Sight: The London Eye
Built: 1999
Height: 135 metres
Interesting fact:
The diameter of the wheel is 120 metres.

Sight: Big Ben
Built: 1858
Height: 96 metres
Interesting fact:
The tower has 334 steps.

Sight: The Shard
Built: 2012
Height: 310 metres
Interesting fact:
It has 44 lifts.

2 (READING) Read the dialogue.

1, 27
29/1

Luke, Dominik and Luke's mum are on the London Eye.

Dominik: Look, is that Big Ben? I always thought it was bigger.

Luke: No, Big Ben is really only the bell in the tower. The name of the tower is the Elizabeth Tower but everyone calls it Big Ben. It's smaller than the London Eye.

Luke's mum: Yes, the London Eye is the largest big wheel in Europe. It's 135 metres high – the same as 64 red telephone boxes. But look, can you see that really tall building, Dominik?

Luke: That's the Shard and it's taller than the London Eye.

Dominik: I think it's the tallest building in London.

Luke's mum: Yes, I think it's the tallest building in Europe. It has 87 floors. Why don't we go to the city centre tomorrow?

Dominik: I'd like to visit Madame Tussauds. I'm sure it's very interesting.

Luke: Or visit the scariest place in London – the London Dungeon.

Luke's mum: Very good ideas, you two. Which is nearest? Here's the map for more information.

3 Put the sights in the right order.

29/2–3a

Year: 1. Big Ben 2. …

Height: 1. The Shard 2. …

Interesting facts: 1. For me number 1 is ….

So sagst du die Jahreszahlen auf Englisch:
1999 – nineteen ninety-nine
1858 – eighteen fifty-eight
1701 – seventeen oh one

4 (WRITING) Complete the fact cards from exercise 1.

Find three more interesting facts about the three sights in the dialogue on page 50.

1, 28
29/4
5 (LISTENING) Find out about Madame Tussauds.

a) What can you see at Madame Tussauds? → ○ p. 126

kings and queens | sports stars | old trains | film stars | old cars

b) Find the numbers.

29/3b

1. There are —— wax figures at Madame Tussauds in London.
2. Madame Tussauds has museums in —— different countries.
3. The museums are in —— cities.

29/4
6 Find out more about Madame Tussauds on the internet.

1. Where in London is Madame Tussauds?
2. How much is it to visit Madame Tussauds?
3. Is there a Madame Tussauds in Germany?

STUDY SKILLS

Wenn du etwas im Internet suchst, gibst du am besten in eine Suchmaschine ein passendes Schlagwort ein. Du könntest mit Madame Tussauds beginnen.

7 (SPEAKING) Places in your town

a) Name the places. → ○ p. 127

b) Talk to a partner. Where would you like to take a visitor to in your town? Say why.
→ M Double circle, p. 154

A: I'd like to take a visitor to the market, because ….
B: I'd like to take a visitor to ….

8 (LISTENING) Listen to the dialogue.

1, 29
30/5

a) Listen and write the heights of the buildings in London.

b) Put the buildings in order from tallest to smallest.

The Gherkin | The BT Tower | The Bishopsgate Tower | One Canada Square

Language detectives → G 5, p. 144

Vergiss das Wort „the" nicht!

The Shard is the tall<u>est</u> building in Europe.
The London Eye is the larg<u>est</u> big wheel in Europe.
The London Dungeon is the scari<u>est</u> place in London.

Welche Endung haben die Eigenschaftswörter?
Was kannst du damit ausdrücken?

Language → G 5, p. 144
big → the biggest
good → the best
bad → the worst

9 Make sentences. → M Bus stop, p. 154

30/6

I think	+	August the Shard the London Eye London Madame Tussauds England	+	is	+	the largest big wheel the biggest country the coolest museum the tallest building the best time the prettiest city	+ in London. in Great Britain. in Europe. of the year.

10 (TASK) My town → V Comparing places, p. 167

30/7

a) Write the name of an interesting sight or building in or near your town.

b) Write a fact card for it like in exercise 1 on page 50. Try and think of interesting facts.

c) Now say why it is special:
The ... is/has the nicest ... /
the largest ... / the coolest ...

STUDY SKILLS

Wenn du dir Notizen machst, schreibe nur Stichwörter auf. Überlege dir zuerst die Oberbegriffe und schreibe sie untereinander. Zähle dann hinter jedem Begriff weitere Informationen auf.

OR

a) Think of three sights or buildings in or near your town that are interesting for visitors. Say why they are interesting, like this:

park: pretty
tower: tall
church: old

b) Now write a short text about your town.

Come to Kaufbeuren. It has the prettiest parks, the tallest towers and the oldest churches.

Ich kann Sehenswürdigkeiten miteinander vergleichen. ✔

In the city centre

1, 30
31/1

1 (READING) Look at the picture and read the sentences.

2 Make sentences about the people.

Finish the sentences.

1. A woman is taking ....
   A woman is taking photos.
2. A little boy is talking to ....
3. A boy is playing on ....
4. A woman is listening to ....
5. A man is eating ....
6. The people are buying ....

3 (LISTENING) Who is it?

a) Look at the picture. Find the people in the picture.

A The boy in the red T-shirt.
B The woman in the blue dress.
C The man in the green shirt.

1, 31

b) Listen and look at the picture. Who is it?

1. That's B. 2. ...

Language detectives → G 6, p. 145

I'm taking photos now.
I often take photos on holiday.

Look! That man is eating a burger.
He usually eats sandwiches.

They're all waiting to buy that new computer game today.
People often wait here.

Vergleiche die Sätze:
Wann verwendest du die -ing Form (present progressive), wann das simple present?
Welche Wörter zeigen dir, dass du die -ing-Form benutzen musst?

4 (SPEAKING) What are the people doing at the café?

31/2

Make sentences about the picture. → ○ p. 127 → M Peer correction, p. 156

eat	listen
read	drink
wear	wait

1. A girl is —— a blue dress.
   A girl is wearing a blue dress.
2. Two boys are —— chips.
3. A woman is —— a magazine.
4. Two girls are —— to music.
5. A boy is —— water.
6. A woman: "I'm —— for a friend."

32/3 5 (WRITING) **Make sentences.** → M Peer correction, p. 156

a) What are Luke and Sherlock doing now? → ○ p. 128

1. Luke is taking Sherlock for a walk.
2. He is writing ….
3. He …

Luke • take Sherlock for a walk
He • write a message
He • listen to music
Luke • eat a sandwich
Sherlock • eat a sandwich
Sherlock • make a mess
Luke • think about a concert

b) Write sentences about students in your class. The other students guess who it is.

A: He is wearing a … / She's looking at ….
B: That's ….

Language detectives → G 7, p. 146

What are you doing?
What is Luke doing?
Are you watching TV?
Is the woman playing the trumpet?

Wie bildest du die Fragen?

32/4 6 (SPEAKING) **Act the phone call.** → ○ p. 128

Luke's mum is visiting an old friend in another town. Act her phone call with Luke's dad. Make questions for Luke's mum and answers for his dad.

Is Are	Luke Irina you	doing cleaning tidying taking	the bathroom? his/her homework? his/her bike? his/her room? Sherlock for a walk?

Yes, he/she is. | No, he/she isn't. | Yes, I am. | No, I'm not.
…'s playing with a friend. | …'s watching TV. | …'s playing computer games.

7 (GAME) Who is it?

Look at the pictures. Choose one of the people but don't say who it is.
Your partner then asks you questions.

A: Is it a girl?
B: No, it isn't.
A: Is he dancing?
B: No, he isn't.
A: Is he playing with his cat?
B: Yes, he is.

8 (TASK) Charades

Think of an activity. Act the activity. Your friends guess what you are doing.

Ich kann sagen, was jemand gerade tut.

On a treasure hunt

1 Look at the picture.
Which things can you buy in a souvenir shop?

2 (READING) Read the dialogue.

1, 32
33/1a

Jay and Dave are on a treasure hunt with their youth club in London. They can't find the next clue so they go into a souvenir shop and ask somebody.

Suddenly, Dave's phone rings.

Dave: Hello? Oh, hi Olivia! … No, we aren't hanging about in a snack bar and we aren't reading comics. We can't find the next clue. We're standing in a souvenir shop. … Bye!

Jay: (to shop assistant) Excuse me, we're on a treasure hunt and we can't find the next clue. It's not easy.

Shop assistant: Oh, hi. OK. Do you have a picture on your phone?

Dave: Yes, here it is.

Shop assistant: Oh, I think that's on the right, near the newspaper kiosk in Oxford Street.

Jay: Can you tell us the way there please?

Shop assistant OK. Go out of the shop. Turn right and go across the street. Then take the second street on the left and go straight on. Then you take the third street on the right and it's on the left.

Dave: Thank you for your help.

Shop assistant: No problem. Goodbye.

Jay and Dave: Bye.

3 Check the sentences.

a) Are the sentences right or wrong? → ○ p. 129

1. Dave and Jay are on a treasure hunt in London.
2. They go into a snack bar and ask a shop assistant.
3. Dave talks to Olivia on his phone.
4. Jay has a picture of the clue on his phone.
5. The next clue is in Bond Street.
6. The next clue is near a newspaper kiosk.

b) Correct the wrong sentences.

Language detectives → G 7, p. 146

I'm not hanging about in the snack bar.
We aren't reading comics.
She isn't dancing in the street.
They aren't running in the classroom.

Was drücken die Wörter
'm not, aren't und isn't aus?
Wo müssen sie stehen?

33/2–3

4 Say what they aren't doing.

a) Complete the sentences. → ○ p. 130 → M Bus stop, p. 154

1. Holly —— in the kitchen. (sing)
   Holly isn't singing in the kitchen.
2. Olivia —— netball. (play)
3. Luke and Jay —— their homework. (do)
4. Dave —— in a queue. (wait)
5. Amber —— cola. (drink)
6. Olivia and Holly —— on the phone. (talk)

b) Make more sentences.

1. Holly (ride)  now.
2. Jay and Shahid (take)  today.
3. Luke (write)  now.
4. Olivia (watch)  today.

5 (LISTENING) Match the street plans with the dialogues.

1, 33
33/4–5

a) Listen to the four dialogues and point to the right street plan.

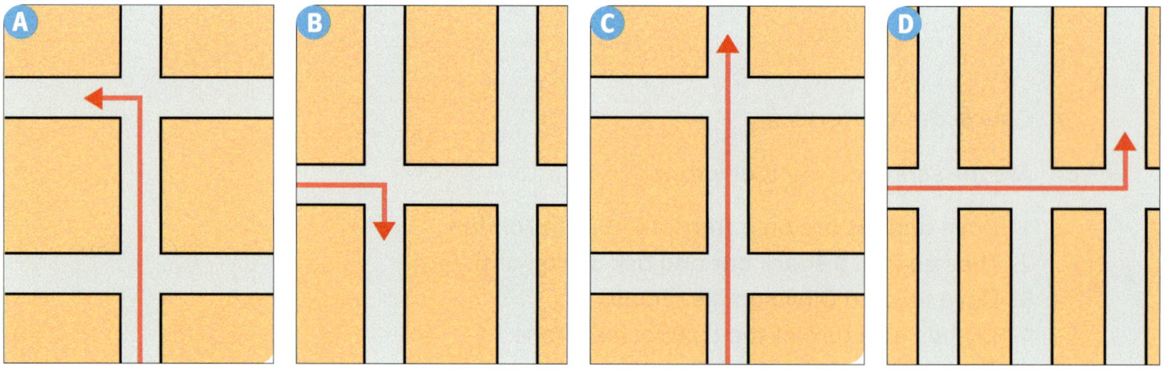

b) Listen again and match the street plans (A–D) with the right places.

Oxford Street | wax museum | Rick's snack bar | church

6 Look at the street map and complete the sentences. → ○ p. 130

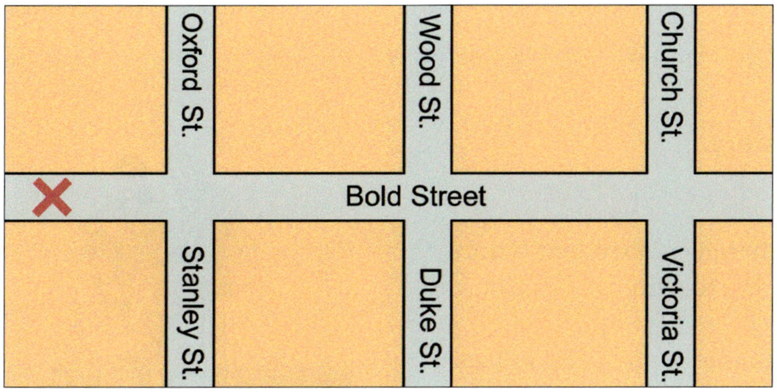

1. The first street on the left is Oxford Street.
2. The second street on the left is ___ .
3. The ___ street on the right is Stanley Street.
4. The third street on the ___ is Victoria Street.
5. The ___ street on the ___ is Church Street.
6. The ___ street on the ___ is Duke Street.

7 (SPEAKING) Use the street map and then ask your partner.

34/6–7

A: Excuse me, where is Oxford Street?
B: It's the first street on the left.

Duke Street | Bold Street | ...
second | third
on the right

8 (TASK) Giving directions → V Directions, p. 168

You and your partner are at the souvenir shop. Ask your partner the way to different places in his/her town.

> Excuse me, can you tell me the way to the cinema?

> Yes. ...

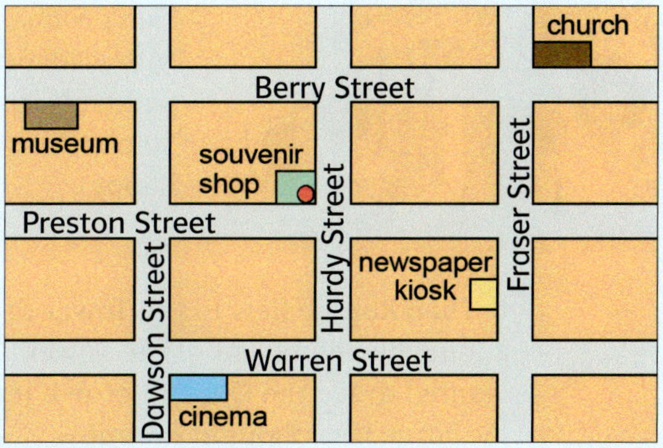

Ich kann jemandem den Weg beschreiben.

The Wizard of London

1 Look at the pictures first. Guess: What is the story about? → M Think – pair – share, p. 157

2 (READING) Read the story.

1, 34

A Once upon a time, there was a student wizard. His name was Ronnie. His teacher was Hector, the Wizard of London.
One day Hector took Ronnie to the London Eye. They saw all of London from the Eye.
Hector looked across the city and then said to Ronnie, "I'm 214 years old now, Ronnie, and I'm too old to work. You're my best student, so you can be the new Wizard of London."
"Me? Great!" said Ronnie.
"Yes, but don't forget." Hector looked at him and said, "It's a lot of work too. Look after the city! The people of London and their computers need you!"

B Ronnie was very busy. He checked all the famous sights in London for Hector.
He started with Big Ben. He flew from the London Eye to the top of Big Ben. Ronnie arrived at ten o'clock.
"Bong, Bong, Bong."
That's boring, thought Ronnie. He wanted to do magic and have fun.
"Abracadabra!" shouted Ronnie.
Suddenly, the big clock started to play the loudest pop song in London! Some tourists started to dance. *That's better,* thought Ronnie. He was happy.

C Then Ronnie flew to the Tower of London. He saw a long queue in front of the Tower. A lot of people wanted to see the Queen's crown jewels.
I've got an idea, thought Ronnie.
"Shazaam!"
The tourists found the crown jewels around their necks and in their hands.
Ronnie was very happy. *I like my job. It's fun and it's easy!*

D Whoosh! Hector the Wizard arrived at the Tower.
"Ronnie, what are you doing?" Hector was not happy.
"What's the problem?" asked Ronnie. "Everyone in London is having a good time."
"Oh, Ronnie. This is not London. London is fun without dancing and crown jewels on tourists."
"Sorry. It wasn't a good idea but I can correct everything," said Ronnie.
Umm, I was the same when I was a student wizard, thought the old wizard and said, "OK, Ronnie, but don't forget the Queen!"
"The Queen?"
"Yes, you know," said the older wizard. "She wants the crown jewels back!"

3 Match the sentence parts. Ein Satzteil bleibt übrig.

1. One day Hector took Ronnie
2. Ronnie wanted
3. Ronnie saw a long queue of people
4. Hector was not happy

a. in front of the Tower.
b. when he met Ronnie at the Tower.
c. in Hyde Park.
d. to the top of the London Eye.
e. to do magic.

4 Take notes about Ronnie's story.

35/1

- What? (Was geschieht? Worum geht es?)
- When? (Wann passiert es?)
- Who? (Wer ist beteiligt?)
- Where? (Wo geschieht es?)

STUDY SKILLS

Wenn du eine Geschichte verstehen willst, kannst du versuchen, auf Fragen mit den Fragewörtern Antworten zu finden. So kannst du dir die Geschichte Abschnitt für Abschnitt durchlesen und anhand der Fragewörter zu jedem Abschnitt Notizen machen.

5 Choose one of the tasks.

a) Make freeze frames of Ronnie's day as the new Wizard of London.
→ M Freeze frame, p. 154

OR

b) Ronnie tells his mother about his day. Write a short dialogue. → M Writers' conference, p. 158

Ronnie's mum: How was your day, Ronnie?
Ronnie: It was fantastic! …

Hector took me to …

I wanted to …

There was a long queue …

Hector was not happy …

Ich kann eine Geschichte über London verstehen. ✔

The London Dungeon

What is the London Dungeon?

The Dungeon brings together amazing actors and special effects in an exciting show that you can see, hear, touch, smell and feel. It's really funny and sometimes scary.

We love it. You will love it too. Here's why:

- 18 shows, 20 actors, 1000 years of history
- special effects
- 2 fantastic underground rides
- exciting storytelling

Yes, but how does it work?

You have to see the London Dungeon. It's a 90-minute trip through 1000 years of London's dark history. You and your friends walk through the Dungeon from show to show, guided by professional actors.

We show REAL history (but without the boring bits).

DUNGEON TICKETS

	Walk-up price	Online price
Adult (16+)	£28.95	£19.95
Child (4–15 years)	£24.45	£18.50

35/2

1 Beantworte diese Fragen einer deutschen Touristin, die kein Englisch spricht.

1. Was kann man im London Dungeon sehen?
2. Ist es spannend?
3. Wie lang dauert die Tour?
4. Was ist der Unterschied zwischen „walk-up price“ und „online price“?
5. Was kostet der Eintritt?

MEDIATION SKILLS

Du musst nicht jedes Detail verstehen, nur die Informationen, die du wirklich brauchst.

Ich kann touristische Informationen über eine Sehenswürdigkeit weitergeben.

A day out in London

In diesem Film triffst du Marley, Nick, Jinsoo und seine Schwester Mina.

1 What do you know about London?

CULTURE

Mit der „Oyster Card“ können englische Schülerinnen und Schüler bis 16 Jahre alle Busse in London umsonst nutzen. Welche Angebote für Schüler gibt es bei euch?

2 (VIEWING) Watch the film.

6

a) Put the pictures in the right order.

A

B

C

D

b) Who is it?

1. He eats food at a market stall.
2. He has a present for Jinsoo.
3. She wants to look at another stall.
4. He's from Taunton in the southwest of England.
5. He phones Mina.
6. He wants ice cream.

3 (SPEAKING) Make a dialogue. → V London sights, p. 166

A: I want to see the sights of London. Let's go to Camden Market.
B: Oh, I don't know. Why don't we go to Madame Tussauds?
A: OK. Meet you at two o'clock.
B: Cool. See you then.

The Shard | St Paul's | ...

The London Dungeon | The London Eye | Tower Bridge | ...

2:30 | 3:00 | 3:15 | ...

Ich kann einen Film über London verstehen. ✓

Checklist

Find more online: 6ag9ry

✔ **Ich kann über Sehenswürdigkeiten in London sprechen.**

I would like to visit …. • It looks really …. • I like …. • They're very ….

36

✔ **Ich kann Sehenswürdigkeiten miteinander vergleichen**

The London Eye is the largest big wheel in Europe. • The Shard is the tallest building in London.

36

✔ **Ich kann sagen, was jemand gerade tut.**

I'm reading this message. • Are you watching TV? • What are you doing? • She's playing the saxophone.

36

✔ **Ich kann jemandem den Weg beschreiben.**

Take the second street on the left. • Go straight on.

37

✔ **Ich kann eine Geschichte über London verstehen.**

37

✔ **Ich kann touristische Informationen über eine Sehenswürdigkeit weitergeben.**

37

✔ **Ich kann einen Film über London verstehen.**

(TASK)

Audio guides for kids

Ein Audioguide ist wie ein Reiseführer als Hörbuch.

Arbeitet in Vierergruppen. Jede Gruppe macht einen Audioguide über einen interessanten Ort in eurer Stadt. Nehmt eure Texte auf und spielt sie eurer Klasse vor.

Step 1

What's interesting about your town?

→ M Think – pair – share, p. 157

What do kids like in your town or city?
Where do kids like to go?
Make a list.
What are your six favourite places?

Step 2

Get into groups of four.

a) Each group makes an audio guide for one interesting place from Step 1.

b) Collect information about your place. You can ask friends. You can also use the internet or go to the tourist information centre in your town.

Step 3

Write about your place.

Write short sentences. Talk to your listeners or ask them questions. Check your texts.

- (Tim:) Hello. Welcome to the Munich audio guide. We are Anne, Lea, Luca and Tim. Today we are at Hellabrunn Zoo.
- (Anne:) The Hellabrunn Zoo is one of the biggest German zoos. It has 771 different kinds of animals.

Step 4

Practise and record.

a) Practise your texts.
b) Record your texts. You can use your phones or a computer with a microphone.

LISTENING SKILLS

Hört euch die Aufnahme an. Ist sie so in Ordnung oder müsst ihr den Text noch mal aufnehmen?

Step 5

Present your audio guides.

a) Play your audio guides to the class.

b) Give feedback to each group. → M Tip top, p. 158
- Did you understand everything?
- Does the audio guide have the important facts?
- What is interesting about the audio guide?

Just for fun

Finding the way with Ben

Excuse me, can you tell me the way to the London Dungeon?

Yes, take the first street on the left, then the third street on the right.

Why walk when flying is much easier?

Special days in Great Britain

13

On Pancake Day British people traditionally make pancakes and eat lots of them. In some cities pancake races take place. People race with a frying pan, flipping the pancake while they are running. There is a famous race in London each year.

Pancake Recipe

1. Ingredients:
   100 g flour
   2 eggs
   300 ml milk
   1 tbsp oil
   some salt
2. Put the flour and milk into a bowl.
3. Add the eggs.
4. Mix everything together.
5. With help from an adult person pour some of the mixture in the frying pan.
6. Cook until brown.
7. Eat them with sugar and lemon.

1 Look at the photos and texts about Pancake Day.

1. Wann ist Pancake Day?
2. Was machen die Teilnehmer im Foto?
3. Womit isst man *Pancakes* in Großbritannien?

CULTURE

Pancake Day – oder Shrove Tuesday – ist am gleichen Tag wie Faschingsdienstag in Deutschland. Traditionell wurden *Pancakes* gebacken, um Eier und Mehl vor der Fastenzeit (Lent) aufzubrauchen. Welchen Brauch gibt es in deiner Gegend an diesem Tag?

Entdecke hier Interessantes zu Großbritannien. Schaue dir zuerst die Fragen an – du kannst sie bestimmt gleich beantworten.

1

2

2 Look at the posters.

1. Um wie viel Uhr fängt die Ostereiersuche an?
2. Wie / Als was sollst du dich bei dem Children's Book Day verkleiden?
3. Was kostet der Eintritt zum Children's Book Day?
4. Wofür kannst du am 2. und am 21. April einen Preis gewinnen?

The school year

The Thomas Tallis school year has lots of big events. They are all in our school planner.

September

Lantern procession

The school year always starts in September and the first big event is the lantern procession at the end of the month. Every student in Years 7 and 8 makes his or her own lantern.

2

April

School trip

At the end of April, Year 8 students go on a school trip to a youth hostel. They usually do activities like canoeing and rock climbing. They sometimes visit local museums.

3

1 Find out about the school year.

40/1

a) Match the words with the photos.

canoeing | long jump | lanterns | play games

Canoeing is photo number ....

b) Ask questions.

It's in September. What is it?
Students make/do/help ... What is it?

2 (LISTENING) Listen and choose the right answers.

2, 2

1. The students must meet at
   a) 4:30.
   b) 5:30.
2. The students must wear
   a) black or white.
   b) their school uniform.
3. After the procession there is
   a) no food.
   b) lots of food.
4. At the end the students give their lanterns to
   a) their teachers.
   b) their parents.

Am Ende dieser Unit kann ich …
- mein Schuljahr beschreiben.
- über ein Schulfest berichten.
- einen Plan für ein Sportfest erstellen.

June

Summer fair

The summer fair is on the third Saturday in June. Students, teachers and parents always help at the fair. We raise money for charities and school projects. You can buy or sell lots of things at different stalls. You can play games too.

July

Sports day

I'm good at the long jump. That's why I like sports day. We can invite our friends and families to school. It is at the beginning of July. This year it's on 7th July. And we never have homework the next Monday.

3 Ask questions about the events.

When is the school trip? – It's in April.
What do the students do? – They usually ….

4 (TASK) Your school year → V School year, p. 169

40/2

Write about your school year.

At Scholl-Schule there is a … in ….
There isn't a … in ….
Our … is usually in ….
My favourite event is the …. It's in ….

sports day | lantern procession | Christmas market | flea market | summer fair | school trip | …

December | March | May | …

Ich kann mein Schuljahr beschreiben. ✔

Hier lerne ich, über ein Schulfest zu berichten.

A stall at the fair

Beim Datum musst du aufpassen. Du schreibst „16th June", aber du sprichst „the sixteenth of June".

1 (READING) Read the dialogue.

2, 3
41/1

This year the Thomas Tallis School summer fair was on 16th June. Holly was not at the fair. She had a bad cold and stayed in bed.

Holly: Hello?
Olivia: Is that you, Holly? It's Olivia here.
Holly: Oh hi Olivia.
Olivia: Are you feeling better now?
Holly: Yes, a little bit. What did you do at the summer fair?
Olivia: I helped with the car wash. We made a lot of money.
Holly: What other stalls did they have?
Olivia: There was a cake stall, face painting, a barbecue, a table football game and a raffle.
Holly: A raffle? What was the first prize?
Olivia: Two tickets for a football match on 24th September. Luke's dad won the first prize.
Holly: Cool! What did they sell at the barbecue?
Olivia: They sold hot dogs, burgers and salads.
Holly: That's great. I'm sad that I missed it all.
Olivia: Yes, but at the end of the summer fair we tidied the playground and the classrooms. Jay took photos of everyone.

2 Finish the sentences.

a) Fill the gaps. → ○ p. 130

1. Holly had a ___ ___ and didn't go to the fair.
2. Olivia helped with the ___ ___.
3. Luke's dad won the ___ ___ in the raffle.
4. They sold burgers, ___ ___ and ___ at the barbecue.
5. Holly missed it, but Jay ___ ___ of everyone.

CULTURE

In Großbritannien wird bei Schulfesten oft Geld für wohltätige Zwecke gesammelt. Es werden Wettbewerbe veranstaltet oder Kuchen verkauft. Wie ist das an eurer Schule?

b) Answer the questions.

1. How many different stalls were there at the summer fair?
2. When is the football match?

3 Find the names of the stalls.

41/2 a) Find the names of the activities and match them with the right pictures.

A 
B 
C 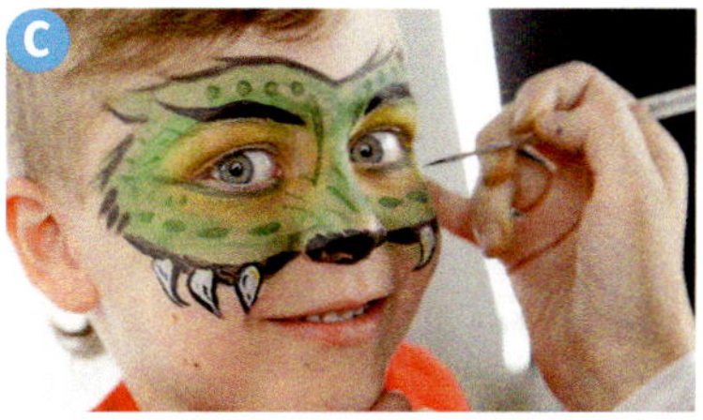
D 
E 

1. A is car wash.

wash | cake | painting | cue | car | game | table | stall | football | barbe | face

b) What other activities can you do/find at a school fair?

Wenn du eine Frage stellst, dann geht deine Stimme am Ende hoch.

4 (SOUNDS) Listen, read and say.

2, 4
41/3

1. Is that you, Holly?
2. Are you feeling better now?
3. What did you do at the fair?
4. A raffle?
5. That's great.

5 (SPEAKING) What are the dates?

2, 5

a) Say these dates. → p. 131

1. It's the eleventh of January.

first	1st	seventh	7th	thirteenth	13th
second	2nd	eighth	8th	twentieth	20th
third	3rd	ninth	9th	twenty-first	21st
fourth	4th	tenth	10th	twenty-second	22nd
fifth	5th	eleventh	11th	thirtieth	30th
sixth	6th	twelfth	12th	thirty-first	31st

b) Say the dates for your birthdays. → M Double circle, p. 154

My birthday is on the ninth of May.

6 (LISTENING) Luke's planner

2, 6
42/4

Which is Luke's planner – A, B or C?

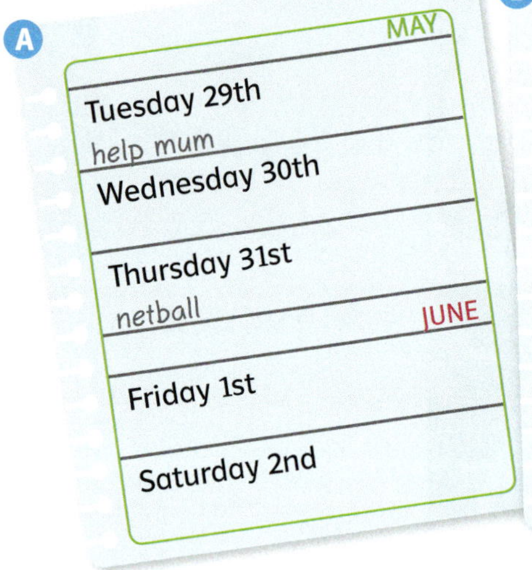

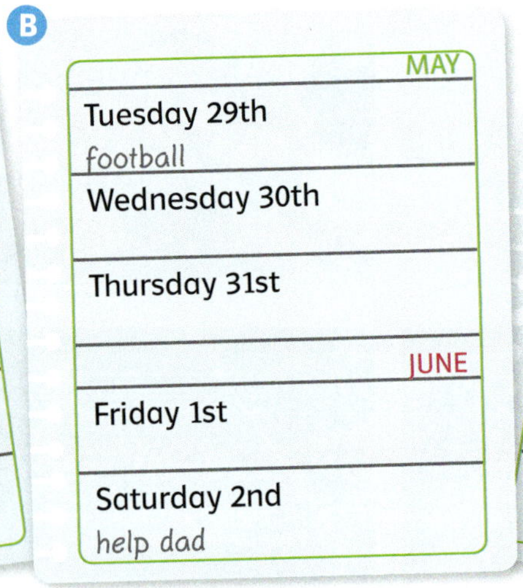

7 (WRITING) When are the events?

42/5

a) Write the dates of the events in the Thomas Tallis school year. → p. 131

The lantern procession is on the thirtieth of September.

Our school trip is on the twenty-third of April.

Our band plays on the twelfth of May.

Our summer fair is on the sixteenth of June.

Our sports day is on the seventh of July.

1. The lantern procession is on 30th September.
2. The ….

b) Write when events in your school year are.

This year our school trip is on …. Our flea market is on ….

8 What happened at the fair? → M Bus stop, p. 154

42/6

Make sentences.

Luke's dad was the winner	+ of +	the summer fair.
The students made a lot		everyone.
They tidied the classrooms at the end		May.
Jay took photos		the first prize in the raffle.
Our sports day is usually at the end		money for charity.

Language → G8, p. 147

The winner of the first prize was Luke's dad.
Jay took photos of everyone.

9 Complete the sentences with in, at or of.

43/7

1. Holly wasn't —— the fair.
2. She stayed —— bed.
3. She drank a lot —— water.
4. Holly felt better at the end —— the day.

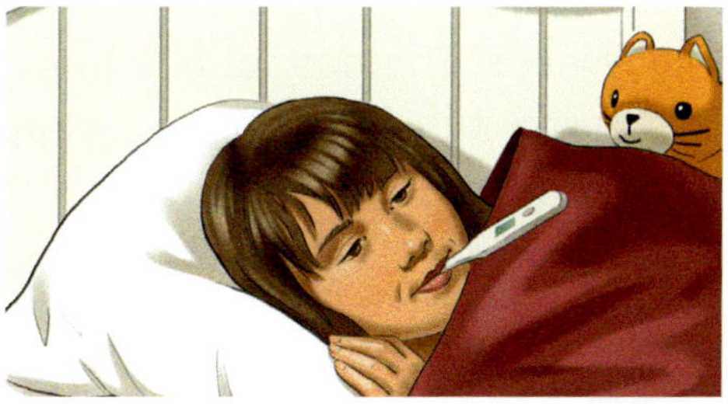

10 (TASK) A report about the summer fair → V Summer fair, p. 170 → M Read and look up, p. 157

43/8

Tell a new student about your school's summer fair last year.

Our summer fair was on 2nd July.

We did face painting.

We also made some money for our school.

At the end of the summer fair we tidied the playground.

The summer fair was great!

31st August | 5th September | 12th July

made cakes | organized a game | had a raffle | ...

class | club | ...

tidied the classroom | helped our teachers | ...

fun | hard work | ...

SPEAKING SKILLS

Du kannst deinem Partner oder deiner Partnerin beim Erzählen helfen. Höre zu, nicke und sage „That's nice." oder „Really?" usw.

Ich kann über ein Schulfest berichten. ✓

Hier lerne ich, einen Plan für ein Sportfest zu erstellen.

Sports day at Thomas Tallis

Erinnerst du dich noch an die Uhrzeit?
11:00 eleven o'clock
11:15 quarter past eleven

1 (READING) Read about sports day at Thomas Tallis School.

2, 7
44/1

Come to our THOMAS TALLIS SCHOOL **SPORTS DAY**

When? On 7th July at 11:00
Where? Thomas Tallis school playing field
Who? All students and families are welcome!

9:00	warm-up
11:10	long jump
12:15	cricket game
BREAK	
1:20	200 metre race
2:25	sack race
MEDALS FOR THE WINNERS	

Sports day is always a lot of fun. It starts on the playing field at 11:00 and usually lasts about six hours. Students take part in the long jump, the 200 metre race, the sack race or a cricket game. After the races and games the students eat lots of fruit and ice cream. They drink water and juice too. But not everyone is doing sport. A lot of parents are watching the events – it's a lot of fun. Oh look! Some Year 8 students are running in the 200 metre race now and Emma Brooks is winning!

2 Choose the right answers.

44/2

1. Sports day starts at ___.
   10:30 • 11:00 • 11:30 • 12:00
2. Students take part in ___.
   football • netball • horse riding • races
3. The students eat ___.
   ice cream • sandwiches • salad • cake
4. Some students are playing ___.
   cricket • tennis • netball • football
5. A lot of parents are ___.
   eating ice cream • running in a race • watching the events • talking on their phones
6. Emma Brooks is winning in ___.
   the sack race • the 200 metre race • the long jump • football

Bei der Uhrzeit im Englischen sagt man vormittags a.m. und nachmittags p.m. 15 Uhr wäre also zum Beispiel 3 o'clock p.m. Wie viel Uhr wäre 10 o'clock p.m. im Deutschen?

3 What are the words?

remember

44/3

a) Find more words. → M Think – pair – share, p. 157

1. sports: netball, …
2. food: salad, …
3. places: park, …

STUDY SKILLS

Du kannst dir Wörter leichter merken, wenn du sie nach Oberbegriffen sortierst.

b) Find the right heading.

1. January • March • July • October → months
2. Sports • Art • Maths • German
3. water • juice • tea • cola
4. netball • football • tennis
5. Tuesday • Thursday • Sunday • Monday

4 (LISTENING) Listen to the announcement about sports day.

2, 8
45/4

Some times are wrong here. Listen and write the correct times.

EVENTS

11:10 long jump
11:15 cricket game
11:20 200 metre race
11:25 sack race

CULTURE

An englischen Schulen gibt es bei Sportfesten z. B. 100-Meter-Läufe oder auch Sackhüpfen. Wie ist es an eurer Schule?

45/5 **5** (WRITING) **Look at these words.**

a) Place or time? Put the words in the right list. → ○ p. 132

Place	Time
at school	on 7th July

on 7th July ✓ · on Saturday · at home · at school ✓ · at the playing field · at the flea market · at 11 o'clock · next to the window · today · next week · in the playground

b) Find more words for each list.

Language detectives → G 9, p. 148

The sports day starts on the playing field at 11:00.
Some Year 8 students are running in the 200 metre race now.

Schau dir die Sätze an. Es gibt Angaben des Ortes und der Zeit. Was kommt im Satz zuerst: Ort oder Zeit?

45/6 **6** **Word order**

a) Make sentences. → ○ p. 132 → M Peer correction, p. 156

1. in the race • is running • at the moment • Luke → Luke is running in the race at the moment.
2. in the playground • Olivia • isn't playing • now • netball
3. has to stay • today • Sherlock • at home
4. to the flea market • on Saturday • can't go • Holly
5. Dave • at 11 o'clock • wants to be • at the sports day
6. Jay • at the weekend • sings • at home
7. today • Is Gwen • at the sports day • drinks • selling • ?

Merke dir: Ort vor Zeit – das ist gescheit!

b) Make sentences.

on Saturday afternoon

on Sunday afternoon

on Saturday morning

at lunchtime

1. Dave went to the swimming pool on Saturday afternoon.

7 (SPEAKING) Can you come?

46/7

Act a phone call. You want to go to a game with your partner.

A: Hello?
B: Hi, it's … here. There's a football match in the park on Saturday. Can you come?
A: On Saturday? What time?
B: At 2:30.

A: Yes, I can.
B: Great!

A: No, sorry. I can't.
B: Oh no.

netball game | cricket game | football match

at the sports centre | at the playing field | at our school

Sunday | Monday afternoon | Thursday afternoon

3:00 | 3:30 | 4:00

8 (TASK) A sports day

46/8

You want to plan a sports day. → V Sports day, p. 171

Work with a partner. Make a list.

The sports day

Where: at Otto-Hahn-Schule
When: on Saturday, 8th May

Warm-up	10:00
Long jump	12:00
200 metre race	12:30
Break	
Football	2:15

Medals for the winners

the playing field | sports centre | …

on Wednesday | on Friday | …

3rd October | 22nd June | …

sack race | football | …

1:20 | 2:15 | 3:45 | …

cakes | …

Check your times and spelling carefully.

Ich kann einen Plan für ein Sportfest erstellen. ✓

The school trip to Windmill Hill

1 (READING) Read the story.

2, 9

It's the end of April and Class 8RS are going on their school trip to the Windmill Hill Hostel.

STUDY SKILLS

Wenn du ein Wort in der Geschichte nicht kennst, können dir oft die Bilder helfen.
Auf dem Bild kannst du sehen, was passiert ist.

1

2

On the first day the class visits a transport museum.

3

The next morning …

4

2 Put the sentences in the right order.

47/1

A Luke and Jay hear scary noises outside their tent.
B The class visits a transport museum.
C They all laugh about their tricks at the party.
D The class arrives at the Windmill Hill Hostel.
E The girls can't put their shoes on.
F Luke and Jay tell the others about the noises in the night.

3 (TASK) Choose one of the tasks.

47/2

a) What did Dave write in his diary about the week at Windmill Hill?
→ M Writers' conference, p. 158

We went to ….
On the first day we ….
The next day ….

STUDY SKILLS

Schreibe zuerst nur Stichwörter auf. Überlege dir die Oberbegriffe und schreibe sie mit Spiegelstrichen untereinander. Zähle dann hinter jedem Oberbegriff weitere Informationen auf.

OR

b) You are on a school trip with your class. Make a list of all the interesting activities you want to do. → V Activities on a trip, p. 172

Make a plan for the week. Present it to your class.

	morning	afternoon
Monday	treasure hunt	
Tuesday		

On Monday morning I'd like to do a treasure hunt.

Ich kann eine Geschichte über eine Klassenfahrt verstehen. ✓

School clubs

INTERNET

<1> Home <2> About <3> News <4> Info

Thomas Tallis School clubs – Open day

Do you want to try something different?

Do you want to make new friends?

Do you have some free time after school?

yes!

football

Then come to the Main Hall at 4 o'clock on Monday, 15th September.

You can …
- find one of our sports clubs and get some exercise.
- join one of our art clubs and be creative.
- meet people with the same interests.

badminton

dance club

art

1 (MEDIATION) **Beantworte die Fragen auf Deutsch.**

47/3

Du bist im Internet auf der Website der Thomas Tallis School. Dein kleiner Bruder möchte wissen, was du da gerade liest.

1. Um was geht es auf der Website?
2. Wann und wo findet die Veranstaltung statt?
3. Welche AGs werden angeboten?

2 **Welche AGs gibt es bei euch? Wo kann man das erfahren?**

Ich kann Informationen über Schul-AGs weitergeben. ✔

A picnic in the park

In diesem Film triffst du Laura, Marley und Jinsoo sowie Mrs Thompson, die Mutter von Marley.

1 What can you do in a park? Complete the mind map. → M Think – pair – share, p. 157

2 (VIEWING) Watch the film.

8

a) Put the pictures in the right order.

b) Who says it?

1. Would you like a sandwich, Jinsoo?
2. I really want to watch it too.
3. Can you pass me some water, please?
4. It's Korean. Typical snack food, usually for picnics.

3 (SPEAKING) Make a picnic dialogue.

A: Can you pass me some water, please?
B: Sure.
A: Thanks.
C: Help yourselves!
A: Mmm! Delicious.
C: Would you like a sandwich?
B: Yes, please!
A: Can I have some salad, please?
C: Yes, of course.

some juice | some tea
That's nice. | Great!
some salad | some fruit
some pizza
No, thanks. | I'm fine.

Ich kann einen Film über ein Picknick verstehen.

Checklist

Find more online: 6ag9ry

✔ **Ich kann mein Schuljahr beschreiben.**

The lantern procession is at the end of September. • It is on the third Saturday in June. • The sports day is at the beginning of July.

48

✔ **Ich kann über ein Schulfest berichten.**

I helped with the car wash. • We made a lot of money. • Luke's dad won the first prize. • Jay took photos of everyone.

48

✔ **Ich kann einen Plan für ein Sportfest erstellen.**

It starts at 11:00 and usually lasts about six hours. • Students take part in the long jump. • After the races and games the students eat lots of ice cream.

48

✔ **Ich kann eine Bildergeschichte über eine Klassenfahrt verstehen.**

49

✔ **Ich kann Informationen über Schul-AGs weitergeben.**

49

✔ **Ich kann einen Film über ein Picknick verstehen.**

(UNIT TASK)

A news programme

Arbeitet in Vierer- oder Sechsergruppen.
Jede Gruppe schreibt einen Bericht für eine Nachrichtensendung über eure Schule.
Spielt die Sendung eurer Klasse vor.

Step 1

Choose one of these topics for your group's report.

A A report with information about a **school club.** You can use the simple present.
Example: The school band is on Tuesday.

B A report about a **special event** at school (yesterday, last week, …). You can use the simple past.
Example: Last week was the school trip.

C A report with live **sports news** at your school. You can use the present progressive.
Example: Marc is running very well.

Step 2

Collect facts and words for your report.

Make a mind map.

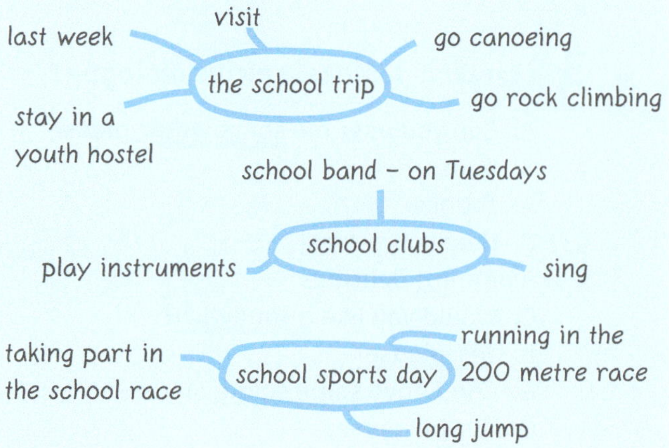

Step 3

Write your report and find pictures. Check your report.

Are you happy with it?

School trip
Last week was our school trip. We did lots of exciting things. We stayed in a youth hostel. Some of us went canoeing or rock climbing. Other students …

School band
Our report is about the school band. The band is on Tuesdays at 4 p.m. with Mr Ross. Students can play instruments and sing.

School sports day
Welcome to the school sports day. Lots of students are running in the 200 metre race or taking part in the sack race and long jump! Look, there's Marc from Year 8. He's running very well. Way to go, …

Step 4

Plan the news programme.

Who would like to present which part?

a) Talk with the other groups. Find the best order for the reports.

b) You can add sentences like these:
"Now here is Julia with the sports news."
"Now over to David. He has a report about the school trip."

c) Practise your report. → M Read and look up, p. 157

Step 5

Act out your class news programme and show your pictures. You can also film your programme. Then give feedback to other groups. → M Tip Top, p. 158

Just for fun

Ben and sport

Sport isn't always easy …

Netball is OK, but sometimes I'm faster than the ball …

My favourite sport is ba-T-minton.

Welcome to the youth hostel!

1 (LISTENING) Listen and answer the questions.

2, 10
52/1

You are at the youth hostel with your class. There are a lot of English-speaking tourists. They need your help.

1. Look at note number 1. Listen and answer the tourists' questions.
2. Look at note number 2. Listen and answer the tourists' questions.

2 (SPEAKING) Look at notes 1 and 2 and act. → M Double circle, p. 154

One of you is the English tourist and the other answers his questions.

Can I have breakfast at 11 o'clock?
Can I play tennis here?
What can I visit here?
What is "Schwimmbad" in English?
How can I get to Bavaria Filmstadt?

lunch | dinner | ...
two | three | ...
go swimming | play football | ...
nur Montag bis Freitag | ...
Olympiapark | ...

Hier wiederholst du,
- wie du jemandem Auskunft geben kannst.
- wie du erzählen kannst, was du erlebt hast.

3 (LISTENING) Listen to Dave's phone call.

52/2

Dave is at the youth hostel and tells his parents what he did yesterday.

a) Put the pictures in the right order and find the word.

2, 11

s  e  h  l 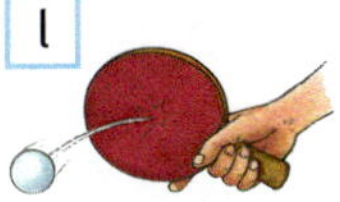 t 

o 

b) Look at a) and speak about Dave's day. → ○ p. 132

breakfast | bike tour | snack bar | souvenir | swimming pool | table tennis

First he …. / Then he ….

4 (LISTENING) Listen again.

2, 11
53/3

Right or wrong?

1. Dave likes his trip to Munich.
2. He wants to go on a bike tour on Sunday.
3. He visited the Bavaria Filmstadt and then he went to the swimming pool.
4. He found a red T-shirt at the swimming pool.
5. He played table tennis with two German boys.

5 You were at the youth hostel. Tell your partner what you did there.

53/4–5

1. I always got up at/around 8 o'clock. — 8:30 | 9 o'clock | …
2. I had breakfast with my friends. — with some English boys and girls | …
3. In the morning I often played table tennis. — went to the swimming pool | went to the skater park | …
4. I also visited Munich. — went on a bike tour | visited the Olympiastadion | …
5. There I lost my phone. — bought a souvenir | found a green scarf | …

Language → G 1, p. 140

So bildest du die Vergangenheit.

I visit**ed** Bavaria Filmstadt.
I play**ed** table tennis yesterday.

Do you remember?
aber: I was – I had – I did – I made – I went

Everyone's a star

football player
happy

singer
stage
famous

1 (SPEAKING) Talk about the photos.

54/1

a) What can you see in photos 1 and 2?

I can see a ….
There is/are ….
They are …./ She is ….

b) Read Olivia's text. Is she a star too? What makes a star? Talk with a partner.

Yes, she is, because ….
No, she isn't, because ….

2 (READING) Read the stories about the charity projects (A–C).

a) What do or did the people do? Make a list of all the activities.

b) Which project do you like best? Talk to your partner and say why.

I like text A because it's about …

c) Who is a star for you? And why?
→ M Bus stop, p. 154

is good at sport/music …
works a lot
helps others
…

Am Ende dieser Unit kann ich …
- über Stärken sprechen.
- eine E-Mail über meinen Alltag schreiben.
- sagen, wie es mir geht.

A Let's clean the streets!
Students from Year 8 at a school in Manchester helped the caretaker and cleaned their playground. After that they cleaned the streets near their school. Neighbours and people in shops gave them money and said "thank you". In the evening the students were happy about £265 and gave the money to charity.

B Don't talk!
Emily and Grace from Belfast didn't talk on Red Nose Day because they wanted to raise money for charity! They wrote what they wanted. They only opened their mouths to eat and drink. Their family and friends raised £54.

C Jane Goodall
Jane Goodall loves chimpanzees. She fights for them and wants to stop animal experiments.
Children can work in Jane Goodall's projects all around the world and help to save the environment.

3 (TASK) You're a star for me! → V People's qualities, p. 173

54/2

Why is your partner a star? Tell him or her.

A: You're a star for me because you're good at football.
B: Really? Thanks.
A: Yes. And you often help your little sister with her homework.
B: Oh! That's nice of you! You're a star for me because …

you can dance | you're funny | you help me | …
always | sometimes | …
go to the sports club | help your friends | help other people | help at home | …

Ich kann über Stärken sprechen. ✔

Hier lerne ich, eine E-Mail über meinen Alltag zu schreiben.

An e-mail from Joe

1 (READING) Read Joe's e-mail to Jay.

2, 13

Joe lives in Manchester and is a friend of Jay's. Joe and Jay stay in contact by e-mail.

E-MAIL

Dear Jay,

Thanks for your last e-mail.

How are you?

I've got to tell you something. I'm in a cooking project at school. It's really good. I'm very lucky that my dad has a restaurant and that I can sometimes help him in the kitchen. My favourite food is chocolate cake.

Stella (my older sister) watches the chefs too. They show us things and we sometimes help them. Now I'm quite good at cooking different meals. Somebody at school wanted chicken fried rice and nobody cooked it faster than me! It's really easy. You only need four cups of rice, some pieces of chicken and a bottle of oil.

On Saturday I went skating. I'm still learning, but it's my new hobby. I went with my friends and we skated for about two hours. We had a fantastic time. Everyone wore helmets of course. I have to skate with you when I see you next time!

I have to be quiet at the moment because my dad is sleeping. He finished work in the restaurant at three o'clock this morning.

I must stop now. I've got to do my homework. Stella often helps me. She's a star! I must take her skating next time ...

See you soon.

Yours,

Joe

CULTURE

Chinesisches Essen ist in Großbritannien beliebt. Welche ausländischen Spezialitäten kann man in deinem Ort essen?

2 Choose the right answer.

55/1

1. Joe is in a **band / cooking project** at his school.
2. Joe's dad has a **snack bar / restaurant**.
3. Joe really likes **chocolate cake / chocolate bread**.
4. **Joe and his dad / Joe and his sister** sometimes watch the other chefs.
5. Joe went skating **on Sunday / on Saturday**.
6. Joe has got to **make a cake / do his homework**.

55/2 2, 14

3 (LISTENING) Listen to the interviews with other students in the cooking project.

a) Say which is the first interview, the second, the third, the fourth.

Name: Nicola
How old: 12
Special cooking talent: salads
Hobbies: dancing

Name: Brad
How old: 13
Special cooking talent: cakes
Hobbies: swimming

Name: Emily
How old: 12
Special cooking talent: burgers
Hobbies: skating, singing

Name: Simon
How old: 12
Special cooking talent: fish and chips
Hobbies: computer games

b) Make a card about your partner.

4 (SPEAKING) What are you good at?

a) What can you say about Nicola, Emily, Brad and Simon? → ○ p. 133

- Simon is good at cooking fish and chips. He plays computer games.
- Emily is good at ….
- ….

b) What are you good at?

I'm quite good at ….
I'm not very good at ….

c) Ask other students and then tell the class. → M Double circle, p. 154

2, 15

5 (SONG) Chinese food

Bildet drei Gruppen (A–C): A singt Zeile 5–6, B Zeile 11–12 und C Zeile 17–18

After balling, I go clubbing,
Then I'm hugging,
Then I'm hungry and I'm
walking on the street,
And I'm getting getting getting
Getting grumpy, grumpy …
I see chow, by my right,
I smell food in the air.
It's Chinese food, my
favourite,
So I'm getting getting getting
getting hungry …
(Chorus:) I love Chinese food,
You know that it's true.
I love fried rice,
I love noodles,
I love chow mein,
Chow mo-mo-mo-mo mein!

Language detectives → G 10, p. 149

Worauf beziehen sich die unterstrichenen Wörter in Satz 2 und 3?
Was bedeuten *me*, *him* und *them* im Deutschen?

I've got to do my homework. Stella often helps me.
My dad has a restaurant and I can help him in the kitchen.
I went with my friends and I skated for about two hours with them.

6 Complete the sentences. → ○ p. 133 → M Peer correction, p. 156

56/3

me | him | her | it | us | them

1. Some people like tomatoes but I don't like ___.
2. Ice cream is different. I really love ___.
3. Where is Joe? I can't find ___.
4. Joe's sister is nice. Do you like ___?
5. We are the new chefs. Joe's dad really likes ___.
6. I'm Joe. Do you know ___?

7 Questions and answers

56/4

a) Match the sentences. → ○ p. 133

1. A: Do you like apples?
2. A: Holly is very busy in the kitchen.
3. A: I'd like to cook with you.
4. A: Where's the new restaurant on this map?
5. A: Who's that boy there?
6. A: Do you like this food?

B: Joe's good at cooking. Maybe he can help us.
B: I know him. He's in my class.
B: Yes, I love it.
B: No, I don't like them.
B: OK. I can help her.
B: Maybe I can help. Show me the map.

b) Answer the questions about their weekends.

Did Olivia see her mother on Saturday?
No, she saw her on ___.

Did Holly meet Luke on Sunday?
No, she met ___ on ___.

Did Holly play with her guinea pigs on Sunday?
No, she played with ___ on ___.

8 (WRITING) Write the e-mail.

57/5

Jay got this e-mail from his cousin Amir in Manchester. Put the sentences in the right order.

See you soon, Amir
Dear Jay,
It's not long now before the summer holidays.
Maybe we can go to a cricket match when I visit you in London. What do you think?
How are you?
Thank you for your last e-mail.

WRITING SKILLS

Wenn du jemandem eine E-Mail schreibst, solltest du wie folgt vorgehen:

1. Mit einer Anrede beginnen:
   Dear Jane, / Hi Terry,
2. Dich bedanken für die letzte E-Mail:
   Thank you for …
3. Deinen Partner fragen, wie es ihm geht:
   How are you?
4. Den Hauptteil deiner E-Mail schreiben.
5. Deine Mail beenden:
   Yours, Simon. / See you soon, Simon

9 (WRITING) Jay's e-mail to Joe

57/6

Make sentences.

Dear Joe,

Thanks for	at home.
My uncle Hamid has	me some new ideas.
He showed	your e-mail.
I'm not very good at cooking	a restaurant too.
I sometimes sing	but I'm quite good at singing.

Yours, Jay

10 (TASK) Write your own e-mail to Joe. → V Free time activities, p. 174 → M Writers' conference, p. 158

57/7

Say hello to Joe. Say thank you for his e-mail.

Tell him
- how you are at cooking:
  I'm very good / not very good at cooking.
- about things you are good at:
  I'm very/quite good at dancing.
- who helps you:
  … helps me with feeding my pets.
- how often you do things:
  I often/sometimes play …

Close the e-mail.

Say goodbye.

playing football | reading | …
singing | writing stories | …
tidying my room | my homework | …
go to the cinema | go swimming | …

STUDY SKILLS

Prüfe die Texte. Hast du alle Wörter richtig geschrieben? Hast du überall die richtige Zeitform verwendet? Wenn du dir nicht sicher bist, schlage hinten im Buch oder in einem Wörterbuch nach.

Ich kann eine E-Mail über meinen Alltag schreiben.

Olivia's accident

1 (READING) Read about Olivia's accident.

2, 16
58/1

Olivia had an accident on her bike and is at the doctor's.

Doctor: Hello, Olivia. How are you today?
Olivia: Hello, Doctor Hardy. Not very well. I had an accident on my bike this morning.
Doctor: What happened?
Olivia: I was on my way to school. A little boy ran in front of me. I fell off my bike and fell on my face. But I didn't run into the boy.
Doctor: Did you hurt anything else?
Olivia: My teeth and my nose are OK. But I hurt my right arm a little.
Doctor: Let me see. Does that hurt?
Olivia: Ouch! Yes, it does.
Doctor: What about your head and your legs? Did you wear a helmet?
Olivia: Yes, I did. I think my head and legs are OK.
Doctor: Do you have a headache?
Olivia: Yes, I do, but it isn't too bad. I was lucky because my friend Dave was with me. He went with me back to my house.
Doctor: OK. I think it's nothing serious. Stay at home today and tomorrow. You can go to school on Thursday.
Olivia: Oh, OK. Thank you. Goodbye.
Doctor: Goodbye.

2 Find out about Olivia's accident.

58/2

a) Match the sentence parts. → ○ p. 134

1. Olivia had an accident
2. A little boy ran
3. She fell off
4. Her teeth and her nose
5. Olivia hurt
6. Her headache isn't
7. Olivia has to

a. are OK.
b. stay at home today and tomorrow.
c. on her bike.
d. too bad.
e. in front of her.
f. her bike.
g. her arm.

b) Answer the questions.

1. When did the accident happen?
2. What did Olivia have on her head?
3. When can she go back to school?

3 (LISTENING) What are the callers' problems?

2, 17
58/3

Listen to the four phone messages and point.

1. 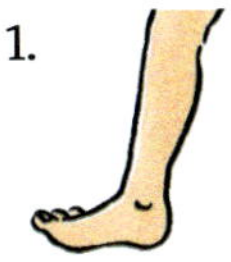
2. 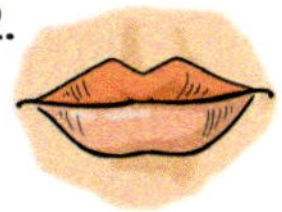
3. 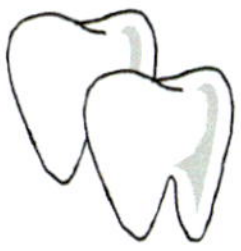
4. 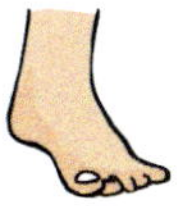
5. 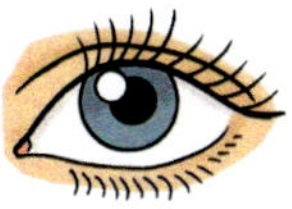
6. 

4 Accident words

a) Make sentences.

1. I fell off my  and hurt my 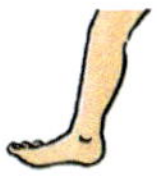 .
2. I fell off my  and hurt my  .
3. I fell off a  and hurt my  .
4. I fell off a  and hurt my  .

b) Make mind maps. → M Think – pair – share, p. 157

arm | bike | eye | head | hand | ladder | kitchen | teeth | nose | skateboard | foot | chair | garden

STUDY SKILLS

Ordne den Wortschatz in Mind maps, dann kannst du dir die Wörter besser merken.

1 

2 

3 

5 (SOUNDS) Listen, read and say.

2, 18

[æ]: accident, happen, ran, at, had

[ʌ]: uncle, bus, lucky, front, under

[æ] and [ʌ]

6 Who says it?

59/4

Who says the sentences? Olivia or the doctor?

1. Stay at home today and tomorrow.
2. I had an accident.
3. Does that hurt?
4. I think it's nothing serious.
5. Ouch!
6. Did you wear a helmet?
7. Let me see.
8. I think my head is OK.

7 Answer the doctor's questions.

1. How are you today? — a. Not very well. — b. Nice homework today.
2. What happened? — a. I was at home. — b. I had an accident.
3. How did that happen? — a. Yesterday. — b. I don't know.
4. Did you hurt anything else? — a. No, I didn't. — b. Yes, I went by bike.
5. Do you have a headache? — a. Yes, I do. — b. No, I didn't.

8 Look at the questions and answers.

59/5

Put in do, does or did. → ○ p. 135
→ M Peer correction, p. 156

1. ___ you have a headache? – Yes, but it's not too bad. → Do you have a headache?
2. ___ you wear a helmet? – Yes, I did.
3. ___ your leg hurt? – Yes, it does a little.
4. ___ your feet hurt? – I think they're OK.
5. ___ you only hurt your foot? – No, I hurt my arm too.
6. When ___ the accident happen? – It happened on the way home from school.
7. Where ___ it hurt? – My head hurts.
8. How ___ the accident happen? – A little girl ran into me.

Language → G 11, p. 150

Do your teeth hurt? – Yes, they do.
Does your arm hurt? – Yes, it does a little.
When did the accident happen?
– It happened yesterday.

9 Holly's accident

a) 60/6 Holly had an accident with Jay outside a shop in Greenwich. Match questions for the doctor and ask Holly about her accident.

1. What
2. Did you only
3. Does that
4. Do you have
5. Did you wear
6. When did it

a. hurt?
b. happen?
c. a headache?
d. a helmet?
e. hurt your leg?
f. happened?

b) Match Holly's answers with the questions in a).

Yes, but the headache isn't too bad. | This afternoon. | No, I hurt my arm too. | Ouch! Yes. | I skated into a friend and hurt my leg. | Yes, I wore a helmet.

I always wear a helmet!

10 (WRITING) Write the story of an accident.

Look at the photos. Write about Holly's and Jay's accident.

WRITING SKILLS

So schreibst du eine Geschichte:

- Was passiert im ersten Foto? Schreibe dir dafür Stichpunkte auf. Du kannst die Wörter auch in einer Tabelle mit folgenden Fragen auflisten: *who – when – where – what – why.*
- Wenn du nicht weißt, wie ein Wort auf Englisch heißt, dann schaue in deinem deutsch-englischen *dictionary* ab Seite 218 nach.
- Versuche nun, die Geschichte zu erzählen, indem du ganze Sätze schreibst. Lies die Geschichte am Ende noch mal durch.

11 (TASK) At the doctor's

60/7

Act a dialogue at the doctor's. A had an accident and goes to the doctor, B.

A: Hello, doctor. I had an accident this morning.
B: What happened?
A: I fell off my bike and hurt my arm.
B: Did you only hurt your arm?
A: No, I hurt my leg too.
B: Let me see. Does that hurt?
A: A little.
B: I think it's nothing serious. Stay at home today. You can go back to school tomorrow.
A: OK. Thank you.

my bike | a ladder | a chair | ...
hand | foot | ...
head | mouth | ...
today and tomorrow | this week
on Friday | ...
on Tuesday | on Friday | on Thursday | ...

Ich kann sagen, wie es mir geht. ✓

Teen Times

1 Look at the pictures. What can you see?

2 (READING) Read the news reports.

2, 19
61/1

STUDY SKILLS

Wenn du wissen willst, wie ein englisches Wort auf Deutsch heißt, kannst du es im *English-German dictionary* ab S. 199 nachschlagen. Die Wörter sind alphabetisch gelistet. Manchmal musst du auch auf den zweiten, dritten oder vierten Buchstaben in einem Wort achten. Das Wort *sports* steht z. B. vor *spy*.

Teen Times

1 English boy wins dream job

An eleven-year-old boy has his dream job. He is testing roller coasters for a day. He has to go on 60 rides at a theme park near Manchester. Then he has to tell people how much fun the rides are. For lots of people this is a very scary job! But this boy loves roller coasters. He is very happy!

2 The amazing Emma

Emma Moore from Hampshire, England, or 'The Amazing Emma', is the UK's youngest magician. When she was eleven, Emma started to do magic in front of people all over Britain. She won many prizes and raised thousands of pounds for different charities. She gave lots of the money to a local children's charity.

3 Which report is it?

61/2

1. It's about a girl. Her sister is in a wheelchair. That's story number ….
2. It's about a boy. He climbed seven mountains.
3. It's about a very young magician.
4. It's about a boy. He likes roller coasters.

4 Use your dictionary.

Put the words in alphabetical order:

give – girl | busy – build | detective – desk | young – your | change – charity | month – money | mountain – mouse

girl – give; …

Teen Times

3 15-year-old climbs seven mountains

When Jordan Romero from Salt Lake City, Utah was 13, he became the youngest person to climb Mount Everest, the world's highest mountain. Jordan and his team climbed to the top of Mount Everest from the Chinese side. Jordan climbed the highest mountains on all seven continents. He was 15, when he climbed the last mountain – in Antarctica.

4 An amazing sister

Sally's younger sister Lily is in a wheelchair. Her parents have to spend a lot of time with her because she is often in hospital. Sally helps her parents and holds Lily's hand when she visits the doctor. Lily likes the skateboard park and Sally always takes her. She is really fast in her wheelchair. Sally's parents think that she does a fantastic job and that she's an amazing sister for Lily.

5 Choose one of the tasks.

a) Did you like the stories? Talk about each story to a partner.

I liked / didn't like story 1 because ….

interesting | boring | funny | exciting | not nice | awful | cool | …

Present your dialogue to the class.

OR

b) Write a text about a day in your dream job.

I worked for my favourite football team. I helped at football practice and looked after the balls. I watched the game every Saturday and talked to the stars. It was great!

at the animal rescue shelter | in a big shop | …

meet lots of people | see interesting things | learn about animals | …

Ich kann Berichte über außergewöhnliche Menschen verstehen. ✓

What's on TV?

THIS WEEK'S TV TIPS

<< Tuesday, 6–8 p.m. >>

Escape to Chimp Eden

BBC2, Sunday 6:00–6:30 p.m.

Mr Cussons works for the Jane Goodall Institute in South Africa. He is the local director for Chimp Eden and helps to prepare chimpanzees for the wild.

Home and Away

Channel 5, 6:00–6:30 p.m.

Soap opera from the east coast of Australia. The programme follows the lives of the people there.

Help! My dad is an alien.

Channel 4, 6:00–7:20 p.m.

Science fiction film. Alice is a young girl who has a dad with some funny talents.

Teens in the kitchen

BBC1, 7:00–8:00 p.m.

A new cooking game show starts this weekend. Four fantastic teenage chefs are in our studio kitchen. The judges look at the teen chefs' skills with fish and fruit.

1 (MEDIATION) **Beantworte die Fragen.**

61/3

Auf der Suche nach Sendungen für Jugendliche in deinem Alter in Großbritannien stößt du auf diese Seite. Deine kleine Schwester interessiert sich dafür, sie spricht aber kein Englisch. Beantworte ihre Fragen.

1. Welche verschiedenen Arten von Sendungen gibt es?
2. Worum geht es in den Sendungen?

2 **Welche Sendung würdest du gerne sehen? Warum?**

Ich kann Informationen aus einer Programmübersicht weitergeben.

The film star

In diesem Film triffst du Laura, ihre Freunde, den Lehrer Mr Nair und die Schauspielerin Polly McCane.

1 Talk about stars.

Which star would you like to meet?
Say why.

VIEWING SKILLS

Ihr könnt den Film mit englischen oder deutschen Untertiteln ansehen. Dann könnt ihr besser verstehen, was die Personen sagen.

2 (VIEWING) Watch the film.

10 a) Put the pictures in the right order.

A

B

C

D

b) Choose the right answer.

1. Mr Nair has three tickets for …
   an acting workshop. • a Shakespeare play.
2. At the Drama Club Laura says she practised …
   on Saturday. • all weekend.
3. Laura tells Polly that at the Drama Club …
   she forgot her text. • she saw Polly's film.
4. Mr Nair says Laura can go …
   and meet Polly McCane. • to the acting workshop.

3 (SPEAKING) Make a dialogue with a star.

A: Excuse me, are you the actor Polly McCane?
B: Yes, that's right.
A: I can't believe you're here. I love your new film!
B: Thanks! It's nice to meet you!
A: Bye!

the football player | the singer | …

…

I think you are the best football player in the world.

I know all your songs. | …

Goodbye now. | See you! | …

Ich kann einen Film über einen Star verstehen. ✓

Checklist

Find more online: 6ag9ry

✔ **Ich kann über Stärken sprechen.**

You're a star for me because …. • You can …. • You often ….

62

✔ **Ich kann eine E-Mail über meinen Alltag schreiben.**

Dear Jay, • I'm quite good at …. • … helps me with …. • I sometimes …. • See you soon • Yours, ….

62

✔ **Ich kann sagen, wie es mir geht.**

I hurt my arm. • My teeth are OK. • Does that hurt? • It's nothing serious. • Do you have a headache?

62

✔ **Ich kann Berichte über außergewöhnliche Menschen verstehen.**

63

✔ **Ich kann Informationen aus einer Programmübersicht weitergeben.**

63

✔ **Ich kann einen Film über einen Star verstehen.**

(UNIT TASK)

A presentation

In dieser Aufgabe bereitest du eine Präsentation über einen Star vor. Lies zuerst alles durch und arbeite dann mit deiner Partnerin / deinem Partner.

Step 1

Who is your favourite star?

→ M Milling around, p. 156

Do you like sports stars, music stars or film stars? Find a partner who likes the same star.

Step 2

Collect information about your star.

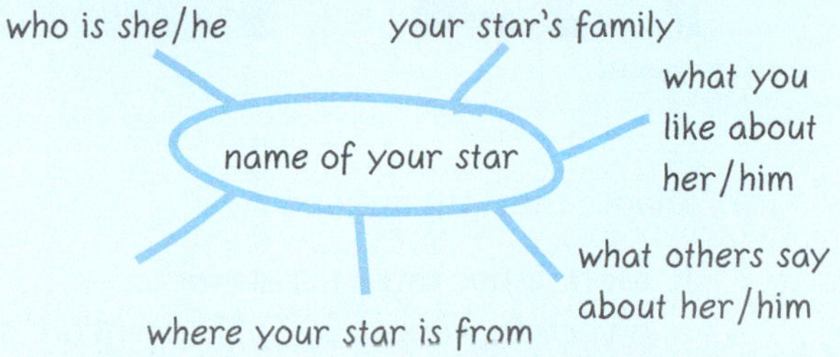

Find photos, songs, interviews, video clips … for your presentation. You can look at magazines or use the internet.

Step 3

Make a plan for your presentation.

How can you start and end your presentation?

1. Introduction: Hello. Our presentation is about ….
2. What the star does
3. Why the star is famous
4. More information about the star
5. Photo(s) and/or video clip(s)
6. Conclusion: Thanks. Do you have any questions?

Step 4

Write your presentation.

You can put your information on transparencies or on a computer.
Write headings and keywords.
Which photos, songs … do you want to show?

STUDY SKILLS

Lege pro Punkt bzw. Unterpunkt deiner Gliederung (Step 3) eine Folie an. Schreibe für jede Folie eine Überschrift und die wichtigsten Stichwörter auf. Wähle aus, welche Fotos, Poster, Songs, Videoclips etc. du in deiner Präsentation zeigen willst.

Step 5

Practise your presentation.

→ M Read and look up, p. 157

Who presents which part?

SPEAKING SKILLS

Du kannst für jede Folie das, was du sagen willst, auf einer Karteikarte in Stichwörtern aufschreiben. Übe den Vortrag, bis du ihn (fast) auswendig kannst.

Step 6

Present your star.

a) Present your star to your class.

b) Ask for feedback.
- Was it interesting?
- Did you understand everything?

c) The others give feedback. → M Tip top, p. 158

Your presentation was very interesting because it was new to me!

I didn't understand everything because you were too quiet/fast.

Just for fun

Ben's cousin

My cousin is a famous star … *Every bat wants to meet him …* *because he's an amazing acro-Bat!*

What do you know about the USA?

1 Answer the questions.

1. Welche Stadt ist die Hauptstadt der USA?
   A Washington, D.C. B New York C Los Angeles
2. Wie viele Staaten gibt es in den USA?
   A 10 B 50 C 100
3. Welches Land grenzt nördlich an die USA, welches südlich?
   A Grönland B Kanada C Mexiko

Wenn du Hilfe brauchst, schau auf der Karte hinten im Buch nach.

Entdecke auf diesen Bildern die USA und schaue dir die Fragen an. Du kannst sie bestimmt gleich beantworten.

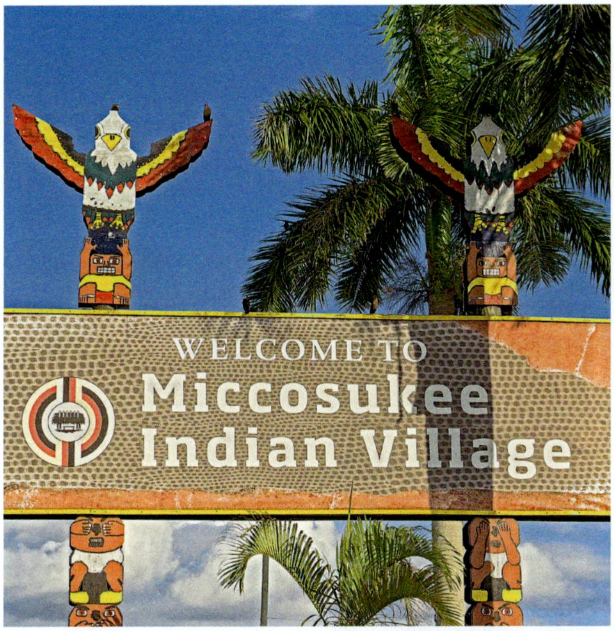

CULTURE

Die Flagge der USA wird auch *Stars and Stripes* genannt. An der Anzahl der Sterne kannst du abzählen, wie viele Staaten es gibt. Wie sieht die Flagge in deinem Land aus?

4. Mit welcher Währung bezahlt man in den USA?
   A Pfund B Euro C Dollar
5. Auf welcher Straßenseite fahren die Autos in den USA?
   A rechts B links
6. Welche typischen amerikanischen Sportarten kennst du?
7. Wer lebte ursprünglich in Nordamerika?
8. Wie heißen die typischen amerikanischen Restaurants?
   A Tapas Bar B Burger Van C American Diner

Goodbye Greenwich

1 Look at the pictures.

→ M Think – pair – share, p. 157

What can you see in the pictures of Chicago?

park • buildings • people •
pier • stadium • bridge

2 Who is it?

66/1

1. She'll miss Dave.
   That's **Holly**.
2. They have to move to Chicago.
   That's ....
3. She thinks the same as Luke.
4. He hopes Dave will visit his friends again.
5. He's surprised.

Am Ende dieser Unit kann ich …
- eine Kurznachricht schreiben.
- über das Wetter berichten.
- Hoffnungen und Wünsche ausdrücken.

3 (TASK) A message → V Messages, p. 175

66/2

a) Choose a topic and write a message.

don't feel well | had an argument with my brother/sister | won a football match

b) Write an answer to a message in your group.

Message:
Hi everyone. Guess what? I won a football match.
I'm really happy.

Answer:
Congratulations! Where are you? …

I have good news. | Oh no!
I can't believe it. | …
I feel awful. | I'm angry!
I'm really excited. | …
That's too bad. | Well done! | …

Ich kann eine Kurznachricht schreiben. ✔

Hier lerne ich, über das Wetter zu berichten.

What's the weather like?

1 (READING) Read these blog entries about the weather in the United States.

2, 21

Hi, I'm Kimi and I live in Anchorage in Alaska. It is often rainy here and there is snow in winter. It is often cloudy here in winter too. Winter is the coldest season. Then everyone wears hats and gloves outside. There are many bears around Anchorage.

Hi, I'm Pablo and I live in Phoenix, Arizona. The weather here is usually really warm and sunny. The summer is very long and it doesn't rain very much. You can wear a T-shirt and shorts outside nearly all summer. The wettest month of the year is July. Lots of mountain lions live near here.

Hi, I'm Jordan and I live near Chicago. We have four seasons here. The summer is often hot and sunny. The winter is cold and snowy and there isn't much sun. The weather in spring and autumn is usually mild. It's not very hot or very cold. It is often windy here in spring and summer.

Hi, I'm Linda and I live near Miami, Florida. Here the weather is hot and rainy in summer. The summer is sunnier than the rest of the year. The winters are not very cold and are quite dry. We have a lot of alligators here in Florida.

2 Find out where the children live.

67/1

a) Read what the children write and find the towns on the map on the inside cover of the book.

b) What's the place?

1. It's hot and it rains a lot here in the summer.
2. It's windy here in the spring and summer and not very sunny in winter.
3. Here it's usually very hot and dry.
4. There are often a lot of clouds here in winter.

3 (LISTENING) What's the weather like?

a) Before you listen, what's the weather like today?

2, 22 b) Listen and point.

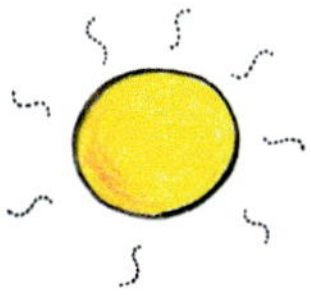

1. sunny

2. wet

3. cold

4. windy

5. hot

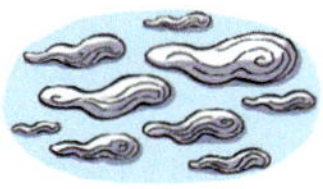

6. cloudy

4 Find the words. → M Bus stop, p. 154

67/2

Wow! It's so hot!

It's — today.

It's —.

It's — today.

It's very —.

Brrr! It's —!

windy | cold | hot ✓ | sunny | cloudy | wet

5 (SPEAKING) Talk about the weather.

67/3

a) Make dialogues. → ◯ p. 135

A: It's sunny today. Let's have a picnic.
B: That's a good idea! Let's do that!

OR

A: It's wet today. We can't have a picnic.
B: OK. Let's watch TV.

cold | hot | ... | play football | play frisbee | ...

stay at home | play a computer game | ...

b) Make more dialogues.

dry | mild | snowy | windy

68/4

6 Complete the table with the months for each season.

spring	summer	autumn	winter
April	August	…	…

68/5

7 (SPEAKING) What clothes do you wear where you live?

a) What do you wear in spring / in summer / in autumn / in winter?

b) Say what you wear in different weather.

I	+	usually never always	+	wear	+	a T-shirt and shorts a scarf and gloves jeans a coat a hat	+	on	+	rainy snowy sunny windy hot cold	+ days.

68/6

8 (WRITING) Write a diamond poem about the weather. → M Gallery walk, p. 155

Write a poem like this.

Winter (1 word)
cold snow (2 words)
I can make (3 words)
a snowman (2 words)
Fantastic! (1 word)

9 Compare these things.

69/7

a) Make sentences with -er. → p. 136

1. Summer is (warm) winter.
   Summer is warmer than winter.
2. February is (cold) August.
3. July is (sunny) December.
4. Phoenix is (hot) Anchorage.
5. Winter is (snowy) autumn.
6. Chicago is (wet) Phoenix.

Don't forget!
hot → hotter than → the hottest
sunny → sunnier than → the sunniest

b) Ask your partner questions about the weather where you live.

Which is sunnier, August or November?
Which is colder, summer or autumn?

69/8 10 Complete the sentences. → M Peer correction, p. 156

a) Fill in the words about weather in the United States. Use -est. → ○ p. 136

1. Pablo: I think Phoenix is the —— place in the United States.
   I think Phoenix is the hottest place in the United States.
2. Jordan: I think Chicago is the —— place in the United States.
3. Kimi: I think Anchorage is the —— place in the United States.
4. Linda: I think Miami is the —— place in the United States.
5. Jordan: I think January is the —— month in Chicago.
6. Kimi: I think December is the —— month in Anchorage.

b) Make sentences about where you live.

11 (TASK) Write a blog entry about the weather where you live.

P
69/9

1. What is the weather like in your town?
   Think about the coldest and hottest times of the year.
2. Make a mind map.

Schau auf S. 108 und hole dir ein paar Ideen!

3. Write a draft of your blog entry.
4. Check your draft.
5. Write your blog entry.
   Hi, my name's Tim and I live near Straubing in Bavaria/Germany.
   The weather here is …

WRITING SKILLS

Schreibe auf jeder zweiten Zeile. Dann kannst du deinen Text in den anderen Zeilen korrigieren.
Gib deinem/deiner Partner/in deinen Entwurf. Kann er/sie den Entwurf verstehen?

Ich kann über das Wetter berichten. ✓

Hier lerne ich, Hoffnungen und Wünsche auszudrücken.

The leaving party

1 What do you need for a leaving party?

Look at the photo for help.

2 (READING) Read the dialogue.

2, 23
70/1

Dave: The food looks great! I love American food. Muffins are my favourite. But …
Holly: Is something wrong?
Dave: Well, I am a little bit worried. Maybe I won't like our new house or make friends in Chicago.
Olivia: I'm sure you'll love your new house and the big garden. Sid will love it too.
Jay: Don't worry, Dave. You'll make lots of good friends. Of course they won't be best friends like us!

Dave and his friends laugh.

Olivia: You can visit us in the summer. Then we'll have lots of fun.
Dave: Of course I'll visit you. I won't forget you. And I hope you won't forget me.
Olivia: Don't be silly! I hope we'll always be friends.
Luke: And we can chat online or send e-mails.
Jay: Or we can play a game online and talk at the same time.
Holly: Yes, and you can upload photos of your house and new friends for us. Then we can keep in touch.

3 Choose the right answers.

1. Dave is …
   excited • worried.
2. Dave thinks he won't like his new …
   house • school.
3. Dave thinks he won't …
   make friends • miss his old friends.
4. Dave says he won't …
   visit his friends • forget his friends.
5. Dave's new house has a big …
   kitchen • garden.
6. Dave's friends say they can …
   send him postcards • keep in touch by e-mail.

4 (LISTENING) Listen to the dialogue.

2, 24
70/2

Look at the pictures. What did Dave get from his friends? One picture is wrong.

1

2

3

4

5 What media can you use? → ◯ p. 137

70/3a

Match the words with the pictures.

talk on the phone | write a message | chat online | write an e-mail | watch TV

1. A is 'write a message'.

A

B

C
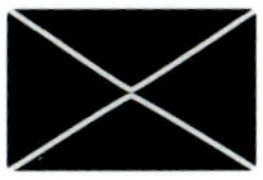

D

E

6 (SPEAKING) Interview a partner. → M Double circle, p. 154

70/3b
71/4

A: How often do you …
- write messages to your friends?
- watch TV?
- read books?
- play …?
- chat online?
- talk on the phone?
- write e-mails?

B: I often write messages to my friends.
I always watch TV after school.
I sometimes chat online.
I never play computer games.

7 (SOUNDS) Listen, read and say.

2, 25

a)
1. Is something wrong?
2. You'll love your new house.
3. We'll have lots of fun.
4. Of course I'll visit you.

b)
1. We'll have lots of fun.
2. I live in Anchorage in Alaska.
3. It is often cloudy here in winter too.
4. It is a long way away.

Language detectives
→ G12, p. 151

Olivia: I'm sure you'll love your new house.
Jay: You'll make lots of good friends.

Dave: I hope you won't forget me.
Olivia: I hope we'll always be friends.

I'm sure Dave will like the USA.

Wie kannst du über Hoffnungen und Wünsche für die Zukunft sprechen?

8 Complete the sentences.
→ M Peer correction, p. 156

71/5

1. Dave hopes his friends ___ keep in touch by e-mail.
   Dave hopes his friends will keep in touch by e-mail.
2. Dave's dad: I hope I ___ like my new job.
3. Dave hopes Sid ___ love the big garden.
4. His mum hopes they ___ forget to take the barbecue.
5. His parents hope Dave ___ miss his friends too much.
6. His friends hope Dave ___ visit them in Greenwich next summer.

will | won't

9 (SPEAKING) Make dialogues.
→ ○ p. 137

a) What are you worried about? Put in the words and talk to your partner. → ○ p. 137

71/6

A: I'm worried about the Biology lesson.
B: It ___ be a problem. You worked a lot for it.
A: Maybe I ___ have a bad day.
B: Of course you ___ ! You will be OK!

English | Maths | ...
won't | will

b) Make another dialogue. Here are some ideas.

I won't be in the team. | I like ... but does he or she like me? | ... | I won't finish all my homework for tomorrow. | I won't like the food in the cafeteria.

72/7

10 Make sentences.
→ M Walking sentences, p. 158

a) What does Luke say? → ○ p. 137

I hope I'm sure	+ Dave he	+ will won't	+ like be make keep forget	+ happy in the USA. in touch with us. new friends in the USA. us. his new school.

● b) Put the words in the right order and make more sentences for Luke.

1. miss • will • Dave • I
2. again • I • visit Greenwich • will • hope • he
3. we'll • hope • be • always • I • friends
4. will • say goodbye • we • be unhappy • when we

11 What jobs do the friends hope for?

72/8

a) Match the pictures of jobs with the friends.

1

2

A

B

3

4

C

D

1. Holly hopes she'll be ___ .
2. Olivia hopes ....

a teacher | a football player | a singer | a shop assistant

b) What jobs do you hope for? → M Double circle, p. 154

I hope ....

12 (TASK) A leaving card → V Messages, p. 175

72/9

Make a leaving card for a friend, somebody in your class or your teacher.

Hi ...,
We hope you'll like the USA and your new school. We hope you won't forget us.
We'll miss you. You're a good friend.
We had a great time with you.
Send us a photo of your new flat.
See you in August.

Holly Luke
Olivia Jay

Tim | Jana | ...

Landshut | Bamberg | Salzburg | ...

teacher | ...

house | school | ...

at Christmas | next summer | next year | ...

Ich kann Hoffnungen und Wünsche ausdrücken. ✓

A new life in the USA

1 Look at the pictures on these pages.

What will Dave tell his friends about the USA?

2 (READING) Read Dave's e-mails to his friends in Greenwich.

2, 26

73/1

E-MAIL

Hi Olivia,

Thanks for your e-mail. We arrived in Chicago three weeks ago. The neighbours are great. They organized a barbecue for us.

I made friends with Nick. He's in my class at school. He loves computer games too. He sometimes plays games on the internet with kids from Canada!

Our new house is bigger than our old house in Greenwich. The garden is big too and Sid is very happy here. He caught his first American mouse last week and brought it into our kitchen.

Did you have a good holiday? Where did you go?

See you soon, Dave

E-MAIL

Hi Holly,

You asked about the shops. There are no shops here where we live. People go everywhere by car and there aren't many buses. Everyone goes to a big shopping centre not far from our house. The Americans call them *malls*. They sell everything there. Malls have all kinds of shops as well as cinemas, sports centres and snack bars.

There's an underground in Chicago. It's like the London Underground but I only travelled on it once.

The weather is quite windy here. People call Chicago the 'Windy City'. I can understand that! It can also be very hot here sometimes.

How was your horse riding holiday?

Write back soon, Dave

E-MAIL

Hi Luke,
I'm in eighth grade here at the junior high school. They have interesting clubs here – like square dance and wall painting. Maybe I'll go to the wall painting club. They work as a team and paint walls in the school. They have to make their own designs first. Some of the walls in the school here look really amazing. They don't play football – or soccer – very much. They like American football and basketball here.
Did you have a good time with Dominik in Poland? What did you do?
All the best, Dave

3 Match the questions from Dave's friends with Dave's e-mails.

73/2

- Is there a football team at the school? → That was in Luke's e-mail.
- Does the school have good clubs?
- What are the shops like?
- What is your new house like?
- How's the weather?
- Did you make new friends?
- Does Sid like his new home?

4 Answer the questions.

1. When did Dave arrive in Chicago?
2. What did the new neighbours organize for Dave's family?
3. What can you buy in a mall?
4. What's the weather like there?
5. What year is Dave in at his new school?
6. What does the wall painting club do?

5 Choose one of the tasks.

a) Work in groups of three. One of you is Olivia, Holly or Luke.
Act a dialogue between them.
Tell the other two partners about your e-mail from Dave.
Write the information from your e-mail on a card and practise with your group.

Olivia: arrived in Chicago 3 weeks ago / …
Holly: no shops there / city centre / cars / …

Present your dialogue to your class.

OR

b) Imagine you are Olivia or Holly or Luke.
Write an answer to Dave's e-mail to you.
Answer his questions and tell him your news.
→ M Writers' conference, p. 158

Hi Dave,
Thanks for your e-mail. I had a great time in …

Ich kann eine Nachricht verstehen. ✓

An adventure holiday in Britain

INTERNET

Home | Tickets | Plan your visit | Contact

Do you want to do lots of fun activities in a short time?

From raft building to orienteering, you'll never be bored on one of our adventure holidays at Barton Hall! The centre has something for everyone. There are activities and tennis, board games and the heated swimming pool. In the evenings you can enjoy our programme of activities or just relax and chat with friends.

Who can come? Young people between 10 and 18.
Where is Barton Hall? We are not far from the coast in South Devon.

Orienteering

This is a great way to explore our centres. You will learn map reading skills first. Later you will use the skills to find special places around the centre.

Aeroball

This is like trampolining and volleyball at the same time. You bounce up and down and try to stop the other team from scoring goals. At the same time you try to score goals for your team.

1 Beantworte die Fragen deiner Mutter.

73/3

Du interessierst dich für die Ferienaktivitäten in Barton Hall. Deine Mutter möchte etwas darüber wissen. Beantworte ihre Fragen.

1. Welche Aktivitäten kann man dort machen?
2. Wie alt muss man sein?
3. Wo befindet sich Barton Hall?
4. Gibt es auch ein Angebot für abends?
5. Welche Angaben muss man im Anmeldeformular eintragen?

Holiday programme registration form

Name of child: Claire Bennett
Date of birth: 14th May 2004
Address where child lives:
18, Oaklands Drive, London SE 3
Home phone number: 0208-728-843
Any medical conditions: nut allergy
Parents' names: Isabel & Tom Bennett

Ich kann Informationen zu Freizeitveranstaltungen weitergeben.

The caves

In diesem Film triffst du die Freunde Marley, Jinsoo, Alicia, Laura und Lauras Großvater.

1 Would you like to visit a cave?

Are there caves near where you live?

2 (VIEWING) Watch the film.

12 a) Put the pictures in the right order.

A

B

C

D

b) Complete the sentences.

1. Laura's grandad is called ....
2. Marley doesn't want to go to the adventure ....
3. Laura's grandad tells them to stay away from ....
4. Laura says the caves aren't ....
5. Marley and Alicia have to hold ....
6. Grandad says it's time ....

VIEWING SKILLS

Achte darauf, welche Stimmung durch die Musik erzeugt wird. Sie hilft dir, den Film zu verstehen.

3 (SPEAKING) Talk about the film.

What scared the kids? Was it really a ghost? Talk about your ideas.

I think it was ... | I'm sure it was ... | I think so too. | I don't think so.

Ich kann einen Film über ein Abenteuer verstehen. ✔

Checklist

Find more online: 6ag9ry

✔ **Ich kann eine Kurznachricht schreiben.**

Guess what? • I can't believe it. • I'm really excited.

74

✔ **Ich kann über das Wetter berichten.**

It's sunny/hot/... today. • It doesn't rain very much. • It's the coldest place in the United States. • Everyone wears hats and gloves.

74

✔ **Ich kann Hoffnungen und Wünsche ausdrücken.**

I hope we'll always be friends. • I'm sure you'll .... • We'll have lots of fun. • I won't forget you.

74

✔ **Ich kann eine Nachricht verstehen.**

75

✔ **Ich kann Informationen zu Freizeitveranstaltungen weitergeben.**

75

✔ **Ich kann einen Film über ein Abenteuer verstehen.**

(UNIT TASK)

A poster about the United States

Step 1

Get into groups of two or three.

Step 2

Make a poster about the USA.

First you need a map of the USA.
Cut out a flag of the USA.
Then write the names of the capital city and other towns and cities on the map.

Step 3

Find out more facts about the USA and write them on your poster.

- What is the name of the money in the USA?
- How many states are there in the USA?
- How many people live in the USA?
- What is the name of the highest mountain? And the longest river? Put them on your map.
- What typical food do Americans eat?
- What famous stars from the USA do you know?
- What are the Americans' favourite sports?

STUDY SKILLS

Überprüft immer die Informationen, die ihr im Internet findet. Informationen dort stimmen nicht immer. Prüft daher auf weiteren Websites oder fragt Erwachsene.

Step 4

Find pictures for your information.

Can you find pictures of American people/food/sports in magazines or on the internet? Add the pictures to the information from Step 3.

Step 5

Check your poster.

Are you happy with it?

STUDY SKILLS

Achtet auf folgende Punkte:

- Inhalt: Sind alle wichtigen Informationen enthalten?
- Sprache: Habt ihr alle Wörter richtig geschrieben? Wenn ihr nicht sicher seid, schlagt hinten im Buch oder in einem Wörterbuch nach.
- Gestaltung: Ist das Plakat schön gestaltet?

Step 6

Organize a gallery walk. → M Gallery walk, p. 155

Put your poster on the wall. Then look at the posters of the other groups. Give feedback to other groups. Listen to their feedback.

Just for fun

Ben on the weather

My feet are really wet now!

What do bats sing when it's raining?

"Raindrops keep falling on my feet."

Unit 1, p.12

7 What did Olivia do in her holidays?

a) Put in the verbs.

1. It was Olivia's mother's birthday, so Olivia helped (help) Janet with the party.
2. She —— (ask) her friends for ideas.
3 At the party she —— (play) with her sister.
4. Later she —— (talk) to her friends.
5. At the end they all —— (dance).

Weißt du noch?
help-ed
like-d

Unit 1, p.13

8 (GAME) Last weekend

b) Put the cards on the table. Take a card (e.g. organized). Say what you did.
Your partner takes a card and answers.
The game is over when there are no more cards on the table.

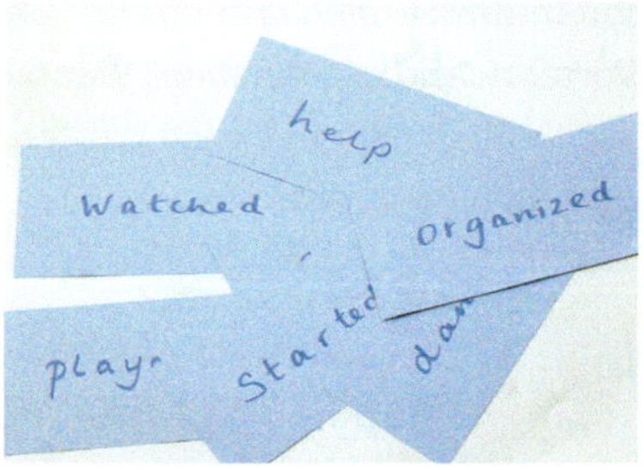

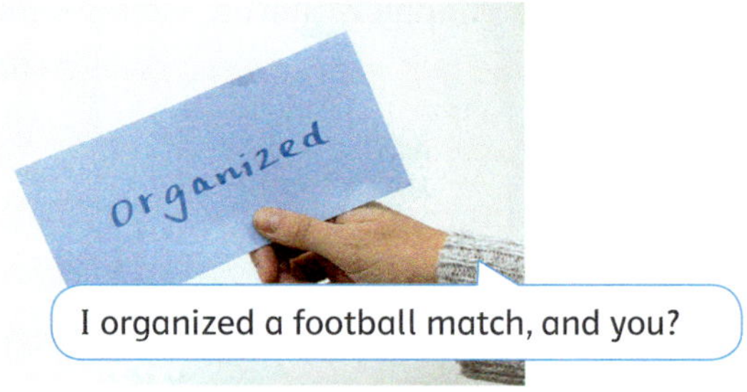

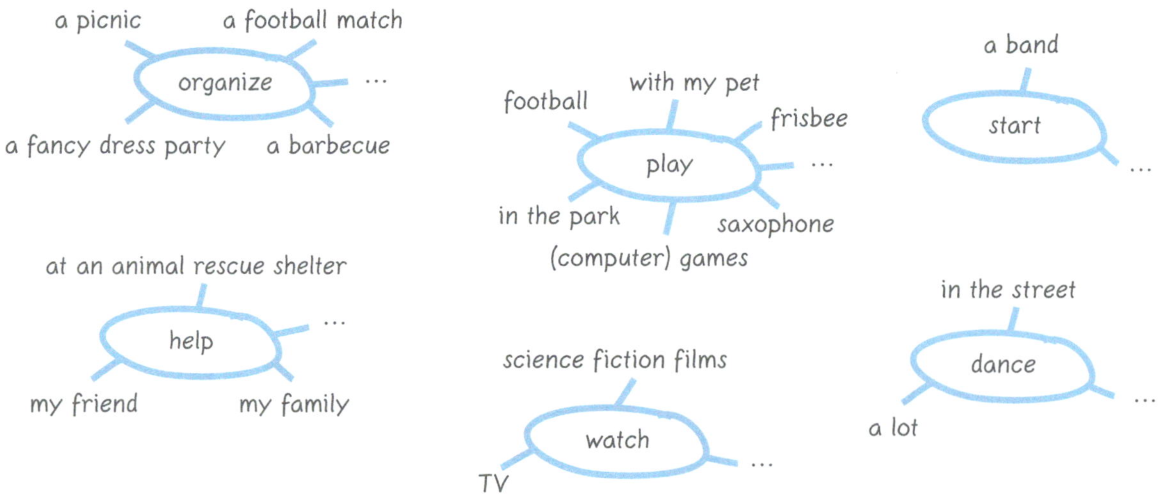

Unit 1, p.14

○ 12 (WRITING) Write about Jay's holidays.

a) Complete the sentences.

went | had | saw | bought | make | tell

1. Jay had a great time in Manchester! (have)
2. He —— a cool poster at a music shop. (buy)
3. Jay and his brother —— to a concert. (go)
4. They —— some famous bands (see).
5. Jay —— breakfast for his grandparents. (make)
6. His cousins —— him about cool places in Manchester. (tell)

Schau auf Seite 153 nach. Dort findest du alle unregelmäßigen Verben aufgelistet. Du brauchst die Form in der zweiten Spalte.

Unit 1, p.15

○ 3 Find the right order.

Holly: Hi Olivia, can I have my new scarf, please?
Olivia: The blue scarf?
Holly: Yes, you borrowed it last week. Did you bring it to school?
Olivia: Yes, I did. You weren't here so I put the scarf in your black bag.
Holly: It wasn't there. Did you lose it?
Olivia: No, I didn't lose it.
Holly: I have to go. Can you find it, please?

Gwen: Hi Olivia. Here's your scarf.
Olivia: Oh thank you! It's Holly's scarf. I put it in her bag. How did you find it?
Gwen: I looked in my bag and was surprised. There it was!

Olivia: Oh! Your bag looks like Holly's. That's what happened. I put the scarf in the wrong bag. I was really worried! Let's give it back to her. She was very unhappy.

Olivia: Holly! Gwen found your scarf. Here it is.
Holly: Where was it?
Olivia: It was in Gwen's bag. She has the same bag as you. I'm so sorry I lost your scarf, Holly!
Holly: I'm very sorry I was angry.
Olivia: Never mind.

Read the sentences. Then put the pictures in the right order.

Gwen: Here's your scarf.
Olivia: It's Holly's scarf.

Holly: Where was it?
Olivia: It was in Gwen's bag.

Holly: Did you lose it?
Olivia: No, I didn't lose it.

Diff corner

Unit 1, p.16

4 (WRITING) What are the words?

a) Find the words.

Unit 1, p.16

7 Say how you feel.

a) Match the sentences with the words from exercise 6.

1. Your friend is not happy because you ate his/her last sandwich.
   I am surprised • sorry.
   I am sorry.
2. Your cat doesn't come home. Where can he be?
   I am happy • worried.
3. You had an argument and your friend doesn't want to talk to you.
   I am unhappy • surprised.
4. You find some money.
   I am worried • happy.
5. Your little sister loses your phone.
   I am angry • happy.
6. You find your friend's book in your bag.
   I am surprised • unhappy.

Unit 1, p.17

○ 9 What didn't you do in your last holidays?

a) Make sentences about yourself with didn't.

I didn't play cricket.

visit

sing

watch

do

take

photos | a band | homework | a farm | cricket ✓ | a film

Unit 1, p.18

○ 11 (LISTENING) What happened?

1, 10

Listen to the three dialogues and answer these questions:

Dialogue A
1. What happened?
2. Where did Luke lose it?

Dialogue B
1. What happened?
2. Where did Olivia lose it?

Dialogue C
1. How was Jay's weekend?
2. What happened?
3. Where did Jay and his cousins sing?
4. Did people like it?

At school. | Jay sang with his band. | Luke lost his phone. | Not so good. | In the park. | No, they didn't. | Olivia lost Holly's new scarf. | At his uncle's birthday party.

Unit 1, p. 19

Beginne die Sätze mit den Fragewörtern: What? When? Why? Where? How?

○ 14 What did Olivia's mum ask?

a) Put the words in the right order.

1. did • What • borrow? • you
   What did you borrow?
2. you • it? • borrow • When did
3. did you • Where • put the scarf?
4. didn't you • the scarf to Holly? • give • Why
5. get her scarf back? • Holly • How • did

Revision, p. 26

○ 1 (LISTENING) Listen to the dialogues and find the answers.

Haruki. | I'm five. | Yes, I do. (3x) | I don't know. | I'm from Munich.

Unit 2, p. 31

○ 3 (LISTENING) Look at the pictures.

1, 16

Listen to the sounds in Holly's flat and put the pictures in the right order. Write the names of the rooms.

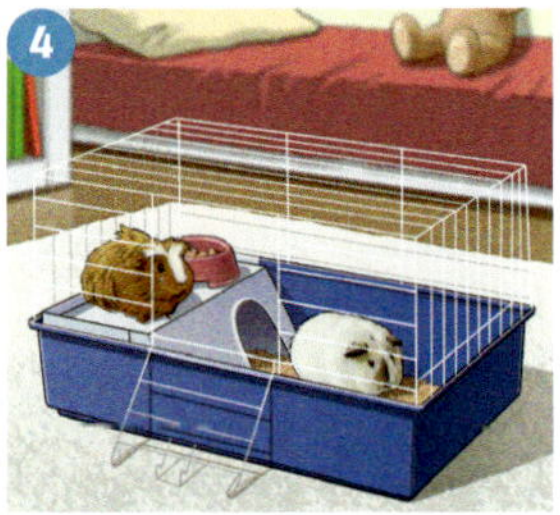

bedroom | living room | bathroom | kitchen

Unit 2, p. 32

○ 7 (WRITING) How often do they do it?

a) Put the right words in the sentences.

1. Amber —— loads the dishwasher. (++)
2. Dave —— takes out the rubbish. (+)
3. Olivia —— makes her bed in the morning. (++++)
4. Luke —— tidies the living room. (–)
5. Holly —— feeds her guinea pigs chocolate. (–)
6. Dave —— hoovers the living room on Saturday. (++++)

– = never
+ = sometimes
++ = often
+++ = usually
++++ = always

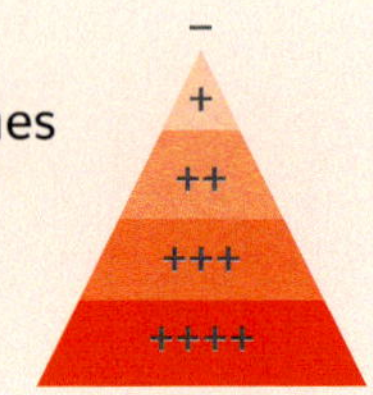

always | often | never | sometimes

Unit 2, p. 34

○ 3 (SPEAKING) Look at Luke's room again.

a) Make sentences about the room.

There +	is are +	a lamp a wardrobe a shelf comics new posters +	in the black boxes. above the desk. on the wall. above the bed. next to the window.

Unit 2, p. 34

○ 4 (LISTENING) Find out about Dave's bedroom.

1, 19 a) Listen to Dave. Which is his room?

a desk | a chair | an Arsenal scarf
two shelves ✓ | a bed | a car poster
laptop is on the bed | a football

Schreibe die Liste links ab. Dann höre dir den Text genau an. Wenn etwas erwähnt wird (z. B. two shelves), hake es ab.

Unit 2, p. 35

○ 6 Make questions about Luke's room.

a) Put the words in the right order.

1. ? • the shelf • Where is
2. books • ? • the shelf • on • Are there
3. above • the • ? • desk • What is
4. wardrobe • ? • Where is • Luke's
5. behind • posters • Are there • ? • the wardrobe
6. the boxes • What colour • are • ?

Unit 2, p. 37

○ 4 Find the opposites.

a) Put the letters in the right order.

1. expensive ⟷ p a c h e	c___	4. large ⟷ l a m l s	s___
2. good ⟷ d a b	b___	5. short ⟷ g n o l	l___
3. old ⟷ e n w	n___	6. worse ⟷ r e t t e b	b___

Unit 2, p. 38

○ 7 (SPEAKING) How much are they?

Look at the pictures and ask your partner.

A:

How much +	is / are +	the T-shirt? / the scarf? / the pullover? / the dress? / the jeans? / the trainers?

B:

It's £20. They're £39. It's £34.
It's £5 They're £35. It's £14.

Bei den Wörtern „jeans", „trainers", „shoes" müsst ihr aufpassen! How much are the jeans? They're ....

Unit 3, p. 51

○ 5 (LISTENING) Find out about Madame Tussauds.

1, 28 a) What can you see at Madame Tussauds?

kings and queens ✓ sports stars old trains
film stars old cars

Schreibe die Liste links ab. Dann höre dir den Dialog genau an. Wenn etwas erwähnt wird (z. B. kings and queens), hake es ab. Zwei Dinge werden nicht erwähnt.

Unit 3, p. 51

7 (SPEAKING) Places in your town

a) Name the places.

museum | park | shopping centre | tower
market | cinema | stadium | church

Unit 3, p.54

4 (SPEAKING) What are the people doing at the café?

Make sentences about the picture.

eating | listening
reading | drinking
wearing | waiting

1. A girl is —— a blue dress.
   A girl is wearing a blue dress.
2. Two boys are —— chips.
3. A woman is —— a magazine.
4. Two girls are —— to music.
5. A boy is —— water.
6. A woman: "I'm —— for a friend."

Unit 3, p. 55

○ 5 (WRITING) Make sentences.

a) What are Luke and Sherlock doing now?

- Luke • take Sherlock for a walk
- He • write a message
- He • listen to music
- Luke • eat a sandwich
- Sherlock • eat a sandwich
- Sherlock • make a mess
- Luke • think about a concert

Luke He Sherlock	+	is	+	taking .... writing .... listening .... eating .... making .... thinking ....

1. Luke is taking Sherlock for a walk.
2. He is writing ....
3. He ...

Unit 3, p. 55

○ 6 (SPEAKING) Act the phone call.

Luke's mum is visiting an old friend in another town. Act her phone call with Luke's dad. Make questions for Luke's mum and answers for his dad.

Is Are	+	Luke Irina you	+	doing his/her homework? cleaning the bathroom? tidying his/her room? cleaning his/her bike? taking Sherlock for a walk?

Yes, he/she is. | No, he/she isn't. | Yes, I am. | No, I'm not.
...'s playing with a friend. | ...'s watching TV. | ...'s playing computer games.

Unit 3, p. 57

3 Check the sentences.

1, 33

Jay and Dave are on a treasure hunt with their youth club in London. They can't find the next clue so they go into in a souvenir shop to ask somebody.

Suddenly, Dave's phone rings.

Dave: Hello? Oh, hi Olivia! … No, we aren't hanging about in a snack bar and we aren't reading comics. We can't find the next clue. We're standing in a souvenir shop. … Bye!

Jay: (to shop assistant) Excuse me, we're on a treasure hunt and we can't find the next clue. It's not easy.

Shop assistant: Oh, hi. OK. Do you have a picture on your phone?

Dave: Yes, here it is.

Shop assistant: Oh, I think that's on the right near the newspaper kiosk in Oxford Street.

Jay: Can you tell us the way there please?

Shop assistant: OK. Go out of the shop. Turn right and go across the street. Then take the second street on the left and go straight on. Then you take the third street on the right and it's on the left.

Dave: Thank you very much for your help.

Shop assistant: No problem. Goodbye.

Jay and Dave: Bye.

a) Are the sentences right or wrong?

1. Dave and Jay are on a treasure hunt in London.
2. They go into a snack bar and ask a shop assistant.
3. Dave talks to Olivia on his phone.
4. Jay has a picture of the clue on his phone.
5. The next clue is in Bond Street.
6. The next clue is near a newspaper kiosk.

Unit 3, p. 58

4 Say what they aren't doing.

a) Complete the sentences.

1. Holly isn't ___ in the kitchen. (sing)
   Holly isn't singing in the kitchen.
2. Olivia isn't ___ netball. (play)
3. Luke and Jay aren't ___ their homework. (do)
4. Dave isn't ___ in a queue. (wait)
5. Amber isn't ___ cola. (drink)
6. Olivia and Holly aren't ___ on the phone. (talk)

Unit 3, p. 59

6 Look at the street map and complete the sentences.

1. The first street on the left is Oxford Street.
2. The second street on the left is ___.
3. The ___ street on the right is Stanley Street.
4. The third street on the ___ is Victoria Street.
5. The ___ street on the ___ is Church Street.
6. The ___ street on the ___ is Duke Street.

left | second | Wood Street | right | right | first | third

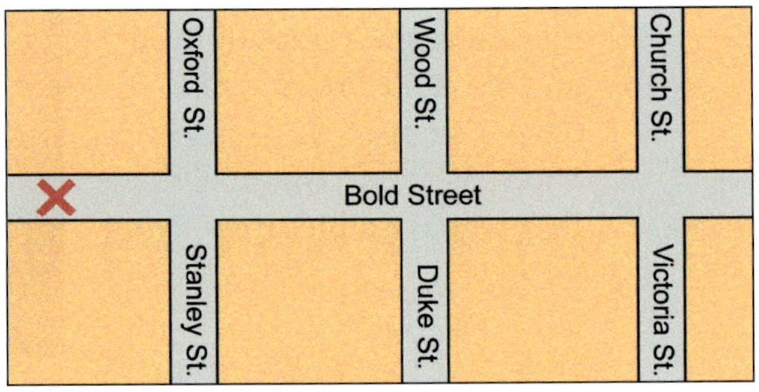

Unit 4, p. 70

2 Finish the sentences.

a) Fill the gaps.

1. Holly had a ___ ___ and didn't go to the fair.
2. Olivia helped with the ___ ___.
3. Luke's dad won the ___ ___ in the raffle.
4. They sold burgers, ___ ___ and ___ at the barbecue.
5. Holly missed it, but Jay ___ ___ of everyone.

took photos | hot dogs | car wash | salads | first prize | bad cold

Unit 4, p. 71

○ 5 (SPEAKING) What are the dates?

2, 5 a) Say these dates.

1. It's the eleventh of January.

2. It's the eighth			June.
3. It's the twenty-second	+	of +	July.
4. It's the thirtieth			October.
5. It's the sixteenth			December.

first	1st	tenth	10th
second	2nd	eleventh	11th
third	3rd	twelfth	12th
fourth	4th	thirteenth	13th
fifth	5th	twentieth	20th
sixth	6th	twenty-first	21st
seventh	7th	twenty-second	22nd
eighth	8th	thirtieth	30th
ninth	9th	thirty-first	31st

Unit 4, p. 72

○ 7 (WRITING) When are the events?

a) Write the dates of the events in the Thomas Tallis school year.

The lantern procession is on the thirtieth of September.

Our school trip is on the twenty-third of April.

Our band plays on the twelfth of May.

Our summer fair is on the sixteenth of June.

Our sports day is on the seventh of July.

1. The lantern procession is on 30th September.
2. The …

12th | 7th | 30th ✓ | 23rd | 16th

Unit 4, p. 76

○ 5 (WRITING) Look at these words.

a) Place or time? Put the words in the right list.

Place	Time
at school	on 7th July
in the kitchen	on Tuesday
at my house	at 9 o'clock
	yesterday

on 7th July ✓ · on Saturday · at home · at school ✓ · at the playing field · at the flea market · at 11 o'clock · next to the window · today · next week · in the playground

Unit 4, p. 76

○ 6 Word order

a) Make sentences.

1. in the race • is running • at the moment • Luke
   Luke is running in the race at the moment.
2. in the playground • Olivia • isn't playing • now • netball
3. has to stay • today • Sherlock • at home
4. to the flea market • on Saturday • can't go • Holly
5. Dave • at 11 o'clock • wants to be • at the sports day
6. Jay • at the weekend • sings • at home
7. today • Is Gwen • at the sports day • drinks • selling ?

Merke dir: Ort vor Zeit – das ist gescheit!

Revision, p. 85

○ 3 (LISTENING) Listen to Dave's phone call.

b) Describe Dave's day.

He went to a souvenir shop.

In the evening he played table tennis with a girl.

Then he went on a bike tour in Munich.

First he had breakfast at 7:30.

He had lunch in a snack bar.

He went to the swimming pool with Boris.

Unit 5, p. 89

4 (SPEAKING) What are you good at?

a) What can you say about Nicola, Emily, Brad and Simon?

- Simon is good at cooking fish and chips. He plays computer games.
- Emily is good at ....
- ....

Nicola Emily Brad Simon	is good at cooking/ making	salads. fish and chips. burgers. cakes.	She He	likes plays	computer games. skating and singing. dancing. swimming.

Unit 5, p. 90

6 Complete the sentences.

1. Some people like tomatoes but I don't like **her** • **them**.
2. Ice cream is different. I really love **it** • **us**.
3. Where is Joe? I can't find **them** • **him**.
4. Joe's sister is nice. Do you like **her** • **it**?
5. We are the new chefs. Joe's dad really likes **them** • **us**.
6. I'm Joe. Do you know **him** • **me**?

Unit 5, p. 90

7 Questions and answers

a) Match the sentences.

1. A: Do you like apples?
2. A: Holly is very busy in the kitchen.
3. A: I'd like to cook with you.
4. A: Where's the new restaurant on this map?
5. A: Who's that boy there?
6. A: Do you like this food?

B: Joe's good at cooking. Maybe he can help us.
B: I know him. He's in my class.
B: Yes, I love it.
B: No, I don't like them.
B: OK. I can help her.
B: Maybe I can help. Show me the map.

Diff corner

Unit 5, p. 92

○ 2 Find out about Olivia's accident.

Olivia had an accident on her bike and is at the doctor's.

Doctor: Hello, Olivia. How are you today?
Olivia: Hello, Doctor Hardy. Not very well. I had an accident on my bike this morning.
Doctor: What happened?
Olivia: I was on my way to school. A little boy ran in front of me. I fell off my bike and fell on my face. But I didn't run into the boy.
Doctor: Did you hurt anything else?
Olivia: My teeth are OK. But I hurt my right arm a little.
Doctor: Let me see. Does that hurt?
Olivia: Ouch! Yes, it does.
Doctor: What about your head and your legs? Did you wear a helmet?
Olivia: Yes, I did. I think my head and legs are OK.
Doctor: Do you have a headache?
Olivia: Yes, I do but it isn't too bad. I was lucky because my friend Dave was with me. He went with me back to my house.
Doctor: OK. I think it's nothing serious. Stay at home today and tomorrow. You can go to school on Thursday.
Olivia: Oh, OK. Thank you. Goodbye.
Doctor: Goodbye.

a) Match the sentence parts.

1. Olivia had an accident
2. A little boy ran
3. She fell off
4. Her teeth and her nose
5. Olivia hurt
6. Her headache isn't
7. Olivia has to

a. are OK.
b. stay at home today and tomorrow.
c. on her bike.
d. too bad.
e. in front of her.
f. her bike.
g. her face and arm.

Unit 5, p. 94

8 Look at the questions and answers.

Put in do, does or did.

Language → G 11, p. 155
Do your teeth hurt? – Yes, they do.
Does your arm hurt? – Yes, it does a little.
When did the accident happen? – It happened yesterday.

1. ___ you have a headache? – Yes, but it's not too bad.
   Do you have a headache?
2. ___ you wear a helmet? – Yes, I did.
3. ___ your leg hurt? – Yes, it does a little.
4. ___ your feet hurt? – I think they're OK.
5. ___ you just hurt your foot? – No, I hurt my arm too.
6. When ___ the accident happen? – It happened on the way home from school.
7. Where ___ it hurt? – My head hurts.
8. How ___ the accident happen? – A little girl ran into me.

Unit 6, p. 107

5 (SPEAKING) Talk about the weather.

a) Make dialogues.

A: It's sunny today. Let's have a picnic.
B: That's a good idea! Let's do that!

OR

A: It's wet today. We can't have a picnic.
B: OK. Let's watch TV.

A: It's sunny today. Let's have a picnic.
It's hot today. Let's play football.
It's wet today. We can't have a picnic.
It's cold today. We can't play frisbee.

B: That's a good idea! Let's do that!
B: OK. Let's watch TV.
B: OK. Let's stay at home.
B: OK. Let's play a computer game.

Diff corner

Unit 6, p. 108

9 Compare these things.

a) Make sentences with -er.

1. Summer is (warm) winter.
   Summer is warmer than winter.
2. February is (cold) August.
3. July is (sunny) December.
4. Phoenix is (hot) Anchorage.
5. Winter is (snowy) autumn.
6. Chicago is (wet) Phoenix.

Language → G 4, p. 143

warm	→	warmer
cold	→	colder
wet	→	wetter
hot	→	hotter
snowy	→	snowier
sunny	→	sunnier

Unit 6, p. 109

10 Complete the sentences.

a) Fill in the words about weather in the United States. Use -est.

1. Pablo: I think Phoenix is the ___ place in the United States. 
   I think Phoenix is the hottest place in the United States.
2. Jordan: I think Chicago is the ___ place in the United States. 
3. Kimi: I think Anchorage is the ___ place in the United States. 
4. Linda: I think Miami is the ___ place in the United States. 
5. Jordan: I think January is the ___ month in Chicago. 
6. Kimi: I think December is the ___ month in Anchorage. 

wettest | coldest | snowiest | hottest ✓ | sunniest | windiest

Unit 6, p.111

○ 5 What media can you use?

Match the words with the picture.

the phone | message | online | e-mail | TV

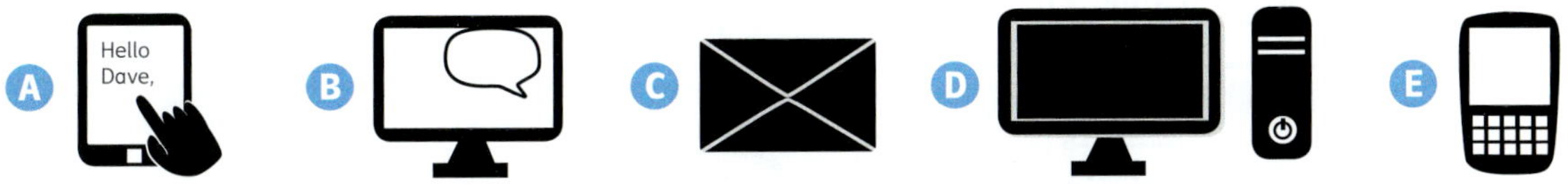

write ___ chat ___ write an ___ watch ___ talk on ___

1. A is 'write a message'.

Unit 6, p.112

○ 9 (SPEAKING) Make dialogues.

a) What are you worried about? Put in the words and talk to your partner.

A: I'm worried about the Biology lesson.
B: It won't be a problem. You worked a lot for it.
A: Maybe I will have a bad day.
B: Of course you won't! You will be OK!

English | Maths | ...

Unit 6, p.112

○ 10 Make sentences.

a) What does Luke say?

I hope I'm sure	+	Dave he	+	will like will be will make will keep won't forget	+	happy in the USA. in touch with us. new friends in the USA. us. his new school.

G2

Mit **G** sind die Grammatikkapitel gekennzeichnet und der Reihe nach durchnummeriert. Eine Übersicht über alle Themen findest du auf der nächsten Seite.

Beim Lupen-Symbol findest du Besonderheiten und Tipps.

(TEST YOURSELF)

Am Ende jedes Grammatikkapitels kannst du ausprobieren, ob du alles verstanden hast. Die Lösungen dazu findest du auf S. 152.

R = Revision (Wiederholen)

Unit 1

G1 R: Die einfache Vergangenheit: Aussagen

Revision: The simple past: statements

Um über Dinge zu sprechen, die in der Vergangenheit passiert und vorbei sind, verwendest du die **einfache Vergangenheit** (simple past).

Signalwörter	
yesterday	gestern
last year	letztes Jahr

Bei den meisten Verben hängst du dafür die Endung **-ed** an das Verb.

I play**ed** cricket yesterday.	Ich spielte gestern Kricket.
Jay visit**ed** his uncle last week.	Jay besuchte letzte Woche seinen Onkel.

Im Deutschen gibt es verschiedene Möglichkeiten, Vergangenes auszudrücken:

He play**ed** football.	Er hat Fußball gespielt. / Er spielte Fußball.

Achtung Schreibweise:
worry → worr**ied**

Einige Verben haben unregelmäßige Formen:
go → **went**, buy → **bought**, do → **did**, take → **took**, have → **had**

Eine Liste der unregelmäßigen Verben findest du auf Seite 153.

Die Formen von **be** in der Vergangenheit sind **was** und **were**. Es gibt Lang- und Kurzformen.

I **was**	I was **not**	I **wasn't**
you **were**	you were **not**	you **weren't**
he **was**	he was **not**	he **wasn't**
she **was**	she was **not**	she **wasn't**
it **was**	it was **not**	it **wasn't**
we **were**	we were **not**	we **weren't**
you **were**	you were **not**	you **weren't**
they **were**	they were **not**	they **weren't**

(TEST YOURSELF) Put in the verbs in the simple past.

1. I — (stay) at my grandparents' house.
2. She — (sing) songs with me.
3. We also — (go) tandem bike riding.
4. We — (worry) about him.
5. We — (have) a great time!
6. Olivia — (be) at home in the holidays.
7. The Frasers — (be) happy.
8. They — (not be) sad.

G2 R: Die einfache Vergangenheit: Fragen, Verneinung und Kurzantworten

Revision: The simple past: questions, negatives and short answers

Um zu sagen, was in der Vergangenheit **nicht passiert** ist, setzt du **didn't** (= did not) vor das Verb.

Olivia **didn't win** the game.	Olivia hat das Spiel nicht gewonnen.
They **didn't buy** a new book.	Sie haben kein neues Buch gekauft.

Verneinungen mit **be** in der Vergangenheit bildest du mit **wasn't** und **weren't**.

Holly **wasn't** at school.	Holly war nicht in der Schule.
We **weren't** late.	Wir sind nicht zu spät gekommen.

Bei **Fragen** in der Vergangenheit, auf die man mit **Ja** oder **Nein** antworten kann, steht **did** am Satzanfang, außer bei **be.** Du kannst diese Fragen mit Kurzantworten beantworten.

Did you **lose** your pen?	Hast du deinen Stift verloren?	Yes, I **did**.	No, I **didn't**.
	Habt ihr euren Stift verloren?	Yes, we **did**.	No, we **didn't**.
Did Olivia **ask** Gwen?	Hat Olivia Gwen gefragt?	Yes, she **did**.	No, she **didn't**.
Did Luke **play** football?	Hat Luke Fußball gespielt?	Yes, he **did**.	No, he **didn't**.
Did they **have** a party?	Haben sie eine Party gefeiert?	Yes, they **did**.	No, they **didn't**.

Bei **Fragen** mit **Fragewörtern** stellst du das Fragewort an den Satzanfang.

What did you **do** with the scarf?	Was hast du mit dem Schal gemacht?
When were they in the classroom?	Wann waren sie im Klassenzimmer?

(TEST YOURSELF) Use the correct form of the simple past.

1. Olivia — (not see) Holly in the classroom.
2. — Olivia — (put) the scarf in Holly's bag? No, she —.
3. — — you — (what; do) after school? We went swimming.
4. I — (not be) at home yesterday.
5. The boys — (not be) in their classroom. They were on the playground.
6. — (be) Olivia worried? No, she —.
7. — — you (where; be) last week? We were in Margate.

Unit 2

G3 Die einfache Gegenwart: Häufigkeitsadverbien

Adverbs of frequency

On Saturdays I usually clean my room.
I often help in the kitchen too.

Samstags putze ich normalerweise mein Zimmer.
Ich helfe auch oft in der Küche.

Wenn du ausdrücken willst, wie **häufig** etwas passiert, verwendest du **never**, **sometimes**, **often**, **usually** und **always**.

Diese Wörter (Häufigkeitsadverbien) stehen **vor** dem Verb:

I	**always**	load	the dishwasher.
Holly	**sometimes**	loads	
Amber	**often**	loads	
They	**never**	load	

Bei **am/is/are** (also einer Form von **be**) steht das Häufigkeitsadverb **nach** dem Verb.

I	**am**	**usually**	tired after sports.
The Richardsons	**are**	**often**	happy at home.

(TEST YOURSELF) **Put in never (–), sometimes (+), often (++), usually (+++) and always (++++).**

Don't forget:
he/she/it + Verb + -s

1. Holly (make +++) her bed in the morning.
2. Amber (visit ++) her friend on Saturdays.
3. They (empty –) the dishwasher.
4. Mr Richardson (be +++) happy.
5. Jay (hoover ++++) the living room.
6. Olivia (take out +) the rubbish.
7. Gwen (be –) worried about her friend.
8. The students (be +) very funny.

G4 Steigerung von Adjektiven mit -er (1. Steigerung)

Comparative form of adjectives

Sherlock is louder but I am nearer to the tree.

Sherlock ist lauter, aber ich bin näher am Baum.

Zum **Vergleichen** von Personen, Tieren oder Dingen brauchst du **Steigerungsformen**.
Bei einsilbigen Adjektiven hängst du für die **1. Steigerung** ein **-er** an.

Grundform	**1. Steigerung**	
cheap	cheap**er**	billig, billiger
large	large**r**	groß, größer

Achtung Schreibweise: nice – nic**er**, big – big**ger**

Bei zweisilbigen Adjektiven, **die auf -y enden**, sieht die 1. Steigerung so aus:

Grundform	**1. Steigerung**	
easy	eas**ier**	einfach, einfacher
pretty	prett**ier**	hübsch, hübscher

Die Adjektive **good** und **bad** haben eine unregelmäßige Steigerung:

Grundform	**1. Steigerung**	
good	**better**	gut, besser
bad	**worse**	schlecht, schlechter

(TEST YOURSELF) Compare these things.

1. This T-shirt is —— (long) than my blouse.
2. These trainers are —— (cheap) than these jeans.
3. I'm —— (happy) than you.
4. Jay's room is —— (nice) than Ben's room.
5. Ben is —— (pretty) than his sister.
6. The black jeans are —— (bad) than the blue jeans.
7. This dress is —— (cool) than this T-shirt.
8. The black pullover is —— (good) than the red pullover.

Unit 3

G5 Steigerung von Adjektiven mit -est (2. Steigerung)

Superlative form of adjectives

The London Eye is the largest big wheel in Europe!

Das London Eye ist das größte Riesenrad in Europa!

Bei einsilbigen Adjektiven hängst du für die **2. Steigerung** ein **-est** an.

Grundform	2. Steigerung	
small	the small**est**	klein, der/die/das kleinste
large	the larg**est**	groß, der/die/das größte

Achtung Schreibweise: nice – the nic**est**, big – the bigg**est**, hot – the hott**est**

Bei zweisilbigen Adjektiven, **die auf -y enden**, sieht die **2. Steigerung** so aus:

Grundform	2. Steigerung	
scary	the scar**iest**	gruselig, der/die/das gruseligste
pretty	the prett**iest**	hübsch, der/die/das hübscheste
crazy	the craz**iest**	verrückt, der/die/das verrückteste

Die Adjektive **good** und **bad** haben eine **unregelmäßige** Steigerung:

Grundform	1. Steigerung	2. Steigerung
good	better	the best
bad	worse	the worst

(TEST YOURSELF) Compare these things. Use -est, best or worst.

1. This is the — (old) church in the city.
2. The London Dungeon is the — (scary) place in London.
3. I think this is the — (bad) film of all.
4. Is this the — (large) museum?
5. I think Berlin is the — (good) city.
6. The — (cool) people live there.

G6 Die Verlaufsform der Gegenwart: Aussagen

The present progressive: statements

Look, I'm dancing.

Schau mal, ich tanze (gerade).

Mit dem **present progressive** kannst du ausdrücken, dass jemand **gerade dabei ist, etwas zu tun**. So bildest du **Aussagen** im present progressive:

am
are + **Verb** + **-ing**
is

Signalwörter

now	jetzt, nun
at the moment	im Moment
Look!	Schau mal!

Es gibt Langformen und Kurzformen.

Langform	Kurzform	
I **am** working.	I'**m** working.	Ich arbeite (gerade).
You **are** working.	You'**re** working.	Du arbeitest / Ihr arbeitet (gerade).
He/She/It **is** working.	He'**s**/She'**s**/It'**s** working.	Er/Sie/Es arbeitet (gerade).
We **are** working.	We'**re** working.	Wir arbeiten (gerade).
They **are** working.	They'**re** working.	Sie arbeiten (gerade).

Achtung Schreibweise: write – writ**ing**, take – tak**ing**, sit – sit**ting**, play – play**ing**

(TEST YOURSELF) Put the verbs in the present progressive.

1. The students —— (do) their homework.
2. We —— (wait) for the new computer game.
3. She —— (talk) to her friend at the moment.
4. Olivia —— (play) with her sister now.
5. I —— (write) a message at the moment.
6. Look, Luke —— (drink) a cola.
7. Holly —— (watch) a film.
8. Look! They —— (wear) funny T-shirts.

G7 Die Verlaufsform der Gegenwart: Fragen, Verneinung und Kurzantworten

The present progressive: questions, negatives and short answers

Are you watching me?
*I'm **not** playing computer games!*
I'm doing my homework.

Beobachtest du mich?
Ich spiele keine Computerspiele!
Ich mache gerade meine Hausaufgaben.

Sätze im **present progressive verneinst** du, indem du nach **am/are/is** ein **not** einfügst.

Langform	Kurzform	
I **am not** listening.	I'**m not** listening.	Ich höre (gerade) nicht zu.
You **are not** listening.	You **aren't** listening.	Du hörst / Ihr hört (gerade) nicht zu.
He/She **is not** reading.	He/She **isn't** reading.	Er/Sie liest (gerade) nicht.
We **are not** singing.	We **aren't** singing.	Wir singen (gerade) nicht.
They **are not** listening.	They **aren't** listening.	Sie hören (gerade) nicht zu.

Bei **Fragen** im present progressive werden **am/are/is** an den **Satzanfang** gestellt.
Achte auf die Kurzantworten!

Are you reading a book?	Yes, I **am**.	No, I'**m not**.	Liest du (gerade) ein Buch?
Is Jay singing well?	Yes, he **is**.	No, he **isn't**.	Singt Jay (gerade) gut?
Are they listening?	Yes, they **are**.	No, they **aren't**.	Hören sie (gerade) zu?

Bei Fragen mit Fragewort stellst du das **Fragewort an den Anfang.**

What are you doing? – I'm reading a comic.	Was machst du (gerade)? – Ich lese (gerade) einen Comic.

(TEST YOURSELF) Make questions. Give short answers. (☺ = Yes, ☹ = No)

1. you • sing a song? (☺)
2. she • play the saxophone well? (☹)
3. they • listen? (☹)
4. Jay and Luke, • you • read? (☹)
5. what • your friends • do? (play netball)
6. where • he • listen • to music? (at home)

Unit 4

G8 Besitzangaben mit of

The possessive form with of

The price of this T-shirt is £12.
The colours of the T-shirt are red and black.

Der Preis dieses T-Shirts ist £12.
Die Farben dieses T-Shirts sind rot und schwarz.

Die **Besitzangaben im 2. Fall** (**wessen?** → **Genitiv**) kennst du bereits. Mit ihnen kannst du ausdrücken, dass **etwas zu** einer oder mehreren **Personen** oder **Tieren gehört**.

Luke's dad	Lukes Papa
The Elliots' house	Das Haus der Elliots
Sherlock's balls	Sherlocks Bälle

Wenn du ausdrücken willst, dass **etwas zu** einer **Sache** oder einem **Gegenstand gehört**, benutzt du **of**.

The beginning	**of** the year	Der Anfang des Jahres
The colours	**of** the T-shirts	Die Farben der T-Shirts
Ben: "My birthday is on the eighteenth	**of** October."	Ben: „Mein Geburtstag ist am achtzehnten Oktober."

So wird das Datum geschrieben:
on 8th June – am 8. Juni
So wird das Datum gesprochen:
on **the** twenty-second **of** May – am 22. Mai

Überlege immer, ob etwas zu einer Person → **'s** oder zu einer Sache → **of** gehört.

(TEST YOURSELF) Make sentences. Use -'s or of.

1. the name • the street • is • Oxford Road
2. Olivia • sister • is • cool
3. the colours • books • are • green and yellow
4. Luke • favourite sport • is • football
5. Dave • school trip • is • at the end • April
6. the winner • first prize • is • Jay • brother

G9 Orts- und Zeitangaben: Satzstellung

Words of place and time: word order

I'm watching a film at the cinema.

Ich sehe gerade einen Film im Kino an.

Die **Satzstellung** im Englischen ist normalerweise **Subjekt + Verb + Objekt**. Wenn du ausdrücken willst, **wann** oder **wo** etwas stattfindet, benutzt du **Orts- und Zeitangaben**. Diese stehen normalerweise **am Ende des Satzes**.

Subjekt	Verb	Objekt	Ort/Zeit
Dave	plays	computer games	**in his room.**
Jay	listens	to music	**after school.**

Ort vor Zeit und O vor Z – genauso wie im Alphabet!

Achtung: Es gilt Ort vor Zeit!

Subjekt	Verb	Objekt	Ort	Zeit
Jay	listens	to music	in his room	**after school.**
Olivia	is riding	her bike	in the park	**now.**

Wenn du die Zeitangabe betonen willst, kannst du sie auch an den Satzanfang stellen.

Zeit	Subjekt	Verb	Objekt	Ort
Last Tuesday	I	didn't see	my friend	at school.

(TEST YOURSELF) Make sentences.

1. went • last weekend • to the swimming pool • Ben
2. a book • his sister • at the moment • is reading • in the living room
3. a comic • every day • buys • at the newspaper kiosk • Ben's father
4. is staying • Holly • today • at home
5. Luke • in the park • to a football match • goes • every Sunday
6. meets • Olivia and Gwen • he • every weekend • at the playground

Unit 5

G10 Personalpronomen: Objektform (me, you, him, ...)

Personal pronouns: object form (me, you, him, ...)

Hey, give me that banana, please!

Hey, gib mir bitte die Banane!

Personalpronomen können Nomen ersetzen. Du kennst sie schon als Ersatz für Nomen als **Satzgegenstand** (Subjekt): the **boy** sings → **he** sings; the **boys** play → **they** play

Personalpronomen können aber auch ein Nomen als **Satzergänzung** (Objekt) ersetzen:
I like Luke. → I like **him**. He often meets Jane and Tim. → He often meets **them**.

Subjektform		Objektform	
I	ich	me	mir/mich
you	du/Sie	you	dir/dich/Ihnen/Sie
he	er	him	ihm/ihn
she	sie	her	ihr/sie
it	es	it	ihm/es
we	wir	us	uns
you	ihr/Sie	you	euch/Ihnen/Sie
they	sie	them	ihnen/sie

(FÜR PROFIS)

You are lucky!	**Du** hast / **Ihr** habt / **Sie** haben Glück!
Jay, I want to send **you** a present.	Jay, ich möchte **dir** ein Geschenk schicken.
I like **you**.	Ich mag **dich**.
Can I ask **you** a question, Mr Fox?	Darf ich **Ihnen** eine Frage stellen, Herr Fox?

(TEST YOURSELF) Use him, her, you, us, them, me.

1. Jay sometimes makes ~~cakes~~ for his friends.
2. Jay wants to help ~~Olivia~~.
3. Sherlock shows ~~Luke~~ a lot of things.
4. Luke and Jay: "Can you give — a cake?"
5. Olivia: "I want to give — this present, Dad."
6. Dave: "Luke, can you help —, please?"

G11 R: Fragen, Kurzantworten

Revision: questions, short answers

Um in der **einfachen Gegenwart** (simple present) nach etwas **zu fragen**, benutzt du **do** oder **does**.

Do you **wear** a helmet?	Trägst du einen Helm?	Yes, I **do**.	No, I **don't**.
Does he **have** a headache?	Hat er Kopfschmerzen?	Yes, he **does**.	No, he **doesn't**.
Does she **ride** a skateboard?	Fährt sie Skateboard?	Yes, she **does**.	No, she **doesn't**.

Bei Fragen mit **Fragewort** stellst du das Fragewort einfach **vor do** oder **does**.

When do you **play** tennis?	Wann spielst du Tennis?
Why does he **do** this?	Warum macht er das?

Um in der **einfachen Vergangenheit** (simple past) nach etwas **zu fragen**, benutzt du **did**.

Did you **feel** good?	Habt ihr euch gut gefühlt?	Yes, we **did**.	No, we **didn't**.
Did your feet **hurt**?	Haben eure Füße wehgetan?	Yes, they **did**.	No, they **didn't**.

Bei **Fragen** mit Fragewörtern stellst du das **Fragewort immer an die erste Stelle**.

How do you **feel**?	Wie fühlst du dich?
When did the accident **happen**?	Wann ist der Unfall passiert?

(TEST YOURSELF) **Make questions and give (short) answers (positive and negative).**

1. you • ride • a skateboard • often • do • ?
2. a headache • does • have • Olivia • ?
3. hurt • your arms • do • ?
4. now • do • you • want • what • to do • ? (want to go to bed)
5. did • happen • the accident • when • ? (at 3 o'clock)
6. they • the girl • help • did • ?
7. on Tuesday • you • how • feel • did • ? (awful)
8. did • back to school • go • she • ?

Unit 6

G12 Die Zukunft mit will (Wünsche, Hoffnungen)

The will-future (wishes, hopes)

I hope you will come and visit me in the USA this summer.

Ich hoffe, ihr werdet mich in diesem Sommer in den USA besuchen.

Mit dem **will-future** kannst du **Hoffnungen** und **Wünsche** ausdrücken. Das **will-future** wird häufig in Sätzen benutzt, die mit **I think**, **I hope** oder **I'm sure** beginnen.

Aussagen mit **will/'ll + Verb (= Kurzform)**

I think I **will/'ll like** our new house.	Ich denke, ich werde unser neues Haus mögen.
I'm sure you **will/'ll miss** us.	Ich bin mir sicher, du wirst uns vermissen.

Verneinung: aus will + not + **Verb** wird: won't + **Verb**

I hope you **will not / won't forget** us.	Ich hoffe, du vergisst / ihr vergesst uns nicht.

Fragen im will-future beginnst du mit **will**. **Fragewörter** stehen am **Anfang**.

Will Dave **be** happy in the USA?	Wird Dave in den USA glücklich sein?
Yes, he **will**. / No, he **won't**.	Ja. / Nein.
When will you **visit** me?	Wann wirst du mich besuchen?

Im Deutschen kann über Zukünftiges mit der Zukunft oder der Gegenwart gesprochen werden. Vergleiche:

I'm sure it **won't rain**.	Ich bin sicher, dass es nicht regnet. Ich bin sicher, dass es nicht regnen wird.

(TEST YOURSELF) Write sentences in the will-future.

1. I hope you — (love) your new school.
2. I think he — (not have) a lot of money.
3. — you — (buy) a new car soon?
4. I don't think it — (be) a problem for you.
5. We — (not leave) England next week.
6. — Jay — (go) to the football match?

Lösungen

TEST YOURSELF

G1 1. stayed; 2. sang; 3. went; 4. worried; 5. had; 6. was; 7. were; 8. were not / weren't

G2 1. did not / didn't see; 2. Did … put, didn't; 3. What did … do; 4. was not / wasn't; 5. were not / weren't; 6. Was, was not / wasn't; 7. Where were

G3 1. usually makes; 2. often visits; 3. never empty; 4. is usually; 5. always hoovers; 6. sometimes takes out; 7. is never; 8. are sometimes

G4 1. longer; 2. cheaper; 3. happier; 4. nicer; 5. prettier; 6. worse; 7. cooler; 8. better

G5 1. oldest; 2. scariest; 3. worst; 4. largest; 5. best; 6. coolest

G6
1. are doing
2. are waiting
3. is talking
4. is playing
5. am writing
6. is drinking
7. is watching
8. are wearing

G7
1. Are you singing a song? Yes, I am.
2. Is she playing the saxophone well? No, she isn't.
3. Are they listening? No, they aren't.
4. Jay and Luke, are you reading? No, we aren't.
5. What are your friends doing? They are playing netball.
6. Where is he listening to music? At home.

G8
1. The name of the street is Oxford Road.
2. Olivia's sister is cool.
3. The colours of the books are green and yellow.
4. Luke's favourite sport is football.
5. Dave's school trip is at the end of April.
6. The winner of the first prize is Jay's brother.

G9
1. Ben went to the swimming pool last weekend.
2. His sister is reading a book in the living room at the moment.
3. Ben's father buys a comic at the newspaper kiosk every day.
4. Holly is staying at home today.
5. Luke goes to a football match in the park every Sunday.
6. Every weekend he meets Olivia and Gwen at the playground. / He meets Olivia and Gwen at the playground every weekend.

G10 1. them; 2. her; 3. him; 4. us; 5. you; 6. me

G11
1. Do you often ride a skateboard? / Do you ride a skateboard often? – Yes, I do. / No, I don't.
2. Does Olivia have a headache? – Yes, she does. / No, she doesn't.
3. Do your arms hurt? – Yes, they do. / No, they don't.
4. What do you want to do now? – I want to go to bed.
5. When did the accident happen? – It happened at 3 o'clock.
6. Did they help the girl? – Yes, they did. / No, they didn't.
7. How did you feel on Tuesday? I felt awful.
8. Did she go back to school? – Yes, she did. / No, she didn't.

G12
1. will / 'll love
2. will not / won't have
3. Will … buy
4. will / 'll be
5. will not / won't leave
6. Will … go

List of irregular verbs

Hier findest du unregelmäßige Verben aus dem Buch. Die Liste enthält jeweils die Formen des simple past, auch wenn sie noch nicht alle in den Units vorgekommen sind.

infinitive	simple past	German
to be [biː]	was, were [wɒz, wɜː]	sein
to become [bɪˈkʌm]	became [bɪˈkeɪm]	werden
to bring [brɪŋ]	brought [brɔːt]	(mit)bringen
to build [bɪld]	built [bɪlt]	bauen
to catch [kætʃ]	caught [kɔːt]	fangen
to do [duː]	did [dɪd]	machen; tun
to drink [drɪŋk]	drank [dræŋk]	trinken
to eat [iːt]	ate [eɪt]	essen
to feel [fiːl]	felt [felt]	(sich) fühlen
to fight [faɪt]	fought [fɔːt]	kämpfen; (sich) streiten
to find [faɪnd]	found [faʊnd]	finden
to fly [flaɪ]	flew [fluː]	fliegen
to forget [fəˈget]	forgot [fəˈgɒt]	vergessen
to go [gəʊ]	went [went]	gehen; fahren
to have [hæv]	had [hæd]	haben; besitzen
to hear [hɪə]	heard [hɜːd]	hören
to hold [həʊld]	held [held]	(fest)halten
to hurt [hɜːt]	hurt [hɜːt]	verletzen; wehtun
to keep [kiːp]	kept [kept]	halten
to leave [liːv]	left [left]	(ver)lassen; abfahren
to lose [luːz]	lost [lɒst]	verlieren
to make [meɪk]	made [meɪd]	machen; tun
to meet [miːt]	met [met]	(sich) treffen
to read [riːd]	read [red]	(vor)lesen
to ring [rɪŋ]	rang [ræŋ]	klingeln
to run [rʌn]	ran [ræn]	laufen; rennen
to see [siː]	saw [sɔː]	sehen
to sell [sel]	sold [səʊld]	verkaufen
to sing [sɪŋ]	sang [sæŋ]	singen
to sleep [sliːp]	slept [slept]	schlafen
to spend [spend]	spent [spent]	verbringen; ausgeben
to stand [stænd]	stood [stʊd]	stehen
to take [teɪk]	took [tʊk]	nehmen; (hin)bringen
to think [θɪŋk]	thought [θɔːt]	denken; glauben
to throw [θrəʊ]	threw [θruː]	werfen
to understand [ˌʌndəˈstænd]	understood [ˌʌndəˈstʊd]	verstehen
to win [wɪn]	won [wʌn]	gewinnen
to write [raɪt]	wrote [rəʊt]	schreiben

Bus stop
(Lerntempoduett)

Step 1
Bearbeite die Aufgabe zunächst allein.
Schreibe deine Lösungen auf.

Step 2
Wenn du fertig bist, gehe zum „bus stop“.
Entweder wartet dort schon jemand oder du wartest dort auf die nächste Person. Vergleicht und korrigiert eure Ergebnisse zu zweit.

Step 3
Gehe danach wieder zu deinem Platz zurück.
Bearbeite die nächste Aufgabe.

Double circle
(Kugellager)

Step 1
Teilt euch in zwei Gruppen A und B auf.
Gruppe A bildet den inneren Kreis. Gruppe B bildet den äußeren Kreis. Steht dabei so, dass ihr euch anseht.

Step 2
Wenn ein Signal ertönt, sprecht ihr mit der Person, die euch gegenübersteht.

Step 3
Beim nächsten Signal rückt der innere Kreis zwei Plätze weiter nach rechts. Wiederholt den Vorgang.

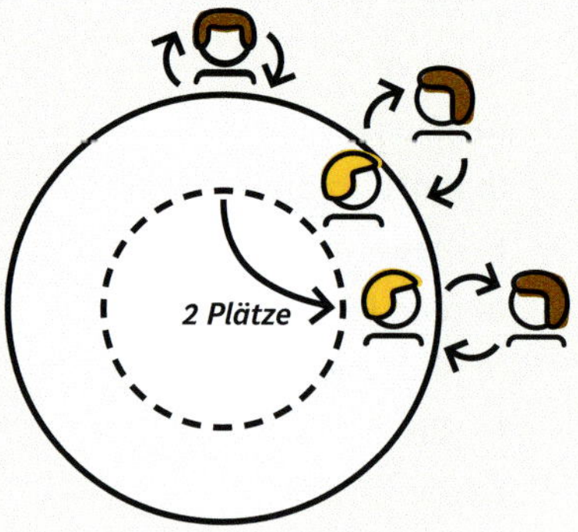

Freeze frame
(Standbild)

Step 1
Entscheidet euch in der Gruppe, welche Szene oder Personen ihr darstellen wollt. Verteilt die Rollen.

Step 2
Probiert verschiedene Standbilder aus und entscheidet euch dann für eines. Denkt daran: Ihr müsst euer Standbild eine Minute lang durchhalten. Keiner darf sich bewegen oder etwas sagen.

Step 3
Präsentiert der Klasse euer Standbild. Die anderen beschreiben, was sie sehen.

Gallery walk
(Galerierundgang)

Step 1
Hängt nach eurer Gruppenarbeit euer Produkt gut sichtbar im Klassenzimmer auf.

Step 2
Seht euch die Produkte der anderen an und bewertet sie.

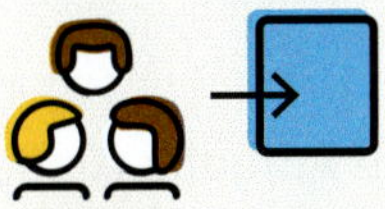

Step 3
Wertet dann eure Ergebnisse in der Klasse aus.

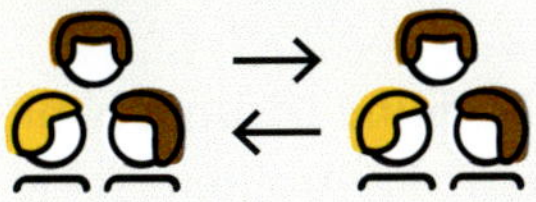

Milling around

(Marktplatz)

Step 1

Bearbeite die Aufgabe zunächst allein.

Step 2

Auf ein Zeichen von eurem Lehrer oder eurer Lehrerin steht ihr auf und geht durch den Raum. Vergesst nicht, die Aufgabe und einen Stift mitzunehmen.

Step 3

Wenn ein Signal ertönt, bleibt ihr stehen. Besprecht die Aufgabe mit der Person, die euch am nächsten steht.

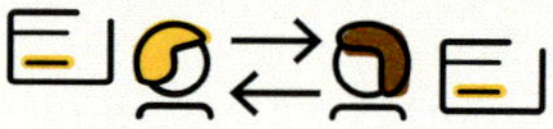

Step 4

Beim nächsten Signal trennt ihr euch und geht weiter durch den Raum. Wiederholt den Vorgang.

Peer correction

(Partnerkontrolle)

Step 1

Bearbeite die Aufgabe zunächst allein.

Step 2

Tausche deine Lösungen mit einem Partner / einer Partnerin. Kontrolliere seine oder ihre Lösungen.

Step 3

Vergleicht eure Lösungen und korrigiert sie dann gemeinsam.

Read and look up

(Lesen und Aufschauen)

Step 1

Schaue auf deinen Text und präge dir die erste Zeile oder den ersten Satz ein. Schaue hoch und sprich deine Zeile / deinen Satz lautlos oder leise vor dich hin. Nimm dir die nächste Zeile / den nächsten Satz vor.

Step 2

Übe nun mit einem Partner / einer Partnerin. Erzähle deinen Text, Zeile für Zeile oder Satz für Satz. Dazwischen schaust du immer wieder nach unten auf deinen Text.

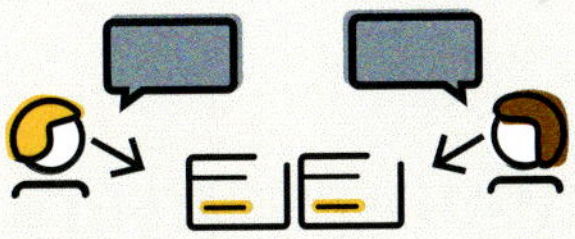

Step 3

Wiederhole alles, bis es gut klappt. Überlege dir, wo du stehen und wie du dich bewegen willst.

Think – pair – share

Step 1

Schreibe deine Ideen, Gedanken oder Lösungen zur Aufgabe auf.

Step 2

Tauscht euch zu zweit aus und besprecht eure Notizen.

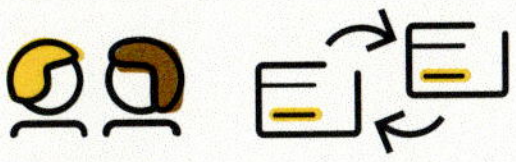

Step 3

Präsentiert euer Ergebnis anderen Paaren oder der gesamten Klasse.

Tip top

Step 1

Sage zunächst, was dir gut gefallen hat – was „top“ war.

Step 2

Sage nun, was noch nicht so gut war, und gib einen Tipp, was man noch verbessern könnte.

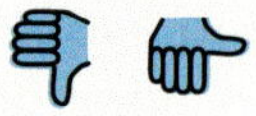

Walking sentences

Step 1

Nehmt eine Karte. Ihr findet darauf ein Wort und/oder ein Satzzeichen.

Step 2

Wenn ein Signal ertönt, geht durch die Klasse und bildet vollständige Sätze.
Stellt euch dazu in der richtigen Reihenfolge auf. Haltet eure Karten vor euch, so dass alle sie lesen können.

Step 3

Lest euren Satz vor und schreibt ihn auf.

Writers' conference

(Schreibwerkstatt)

Step 1

Bildet Vierergruppen.

Step 2

Lest euch eure Sätze/Texte gegenseitig vor.

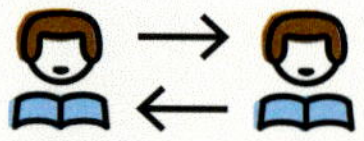

Step 3

Die Zuhörer sagen, was ihnen gefallen hat, und können Verbesserungsvorschläge machen.

Step 4

Jede Gruppe wählt den besten Text aus und liest ihn der Klasse vor.

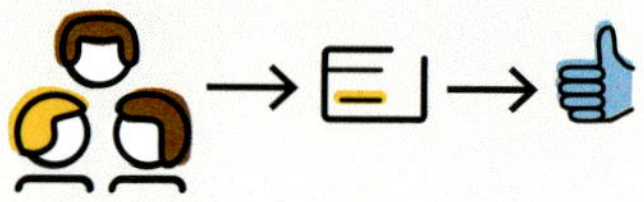

Du kennst schon einige Tipps und Tricks zum Vokabellernen. Erinnerst du dich? Hier gibt es weitere Tipps.

Vocabulary tips

Lernen mit Bewegung

Du kannst dir Wörter leichter merken, wenn du dich beim Lernen bewegst. Gehe dabei einfach umher und sprich die Wörter immer wieder laut aus. Oft hilft es auch, wenn du dabei bestimmte Bewegungen oder Gesten wiederholst.

Lernen mit Bildern

Stelle dir zu einem Wort, das du dir nicht so leicht merken kannst, ein Bild vor. Verbinde angenehme Erinnerungen damit. Das entspannt und hilft dir, das Wort zu behalten.

Lernen mit System

Du brauchst einen Karton mit drei Fächern und Karteikarten. Du kannst dir einen fertigen Karteikasten kaufen oder selbst einen basteln. Auf die vordere Seite der Karte schreibst du das englische Wort, auf die Rückseite das deutsche Wort.

1. Karten mit neuen Wörtern stellst du ins vordere Fach.
2. Wenn du ein Wort aus dem vorderen Fach kannst, kommt es in das zweite Fach.
3. Wörter im zweiten Fach wiederholst du nach ein paar Tagen. Kannst du sie noch? Dann kommen sie in das dritte Fach. Wörter, die du vergessen hast, müssen wieder zurück ins erste Fach.
4. Wiederhole ab und zu die Wörter aus dem dritten Fach.

Sounds

Dir ist die Lautschrift im vergangenen Schuljahr bereits an verschiedenen Stellen in deinem Buch begegnet. Erinnerst du dich?

Lies die folgenden Wörter laut:

1. [eg] 2. ['wɪnə] 3. [kæt] 4. [bʌs] 5. ['daɪəri] 6. ['wɪndəʊ]

Hinter manchen Symbolen für Vokale kann ein Doppelpunkt [:] stehen.
Das bedeutet, dass du diesen lang aussprechen sollst. Du kennst das auch aus dem Deutschen. Vergleiche die Wörter „Biene“ (lang) und „bin“ (kurz).

Im Englischen ist es sehr wichtig, die Vokale richtig auszusprechen, denn manchmal ergeben sich verschiedene Bedeutungen. Hier siehst du dafür Beispiele mit einem langen und kurzen „i“.

Substantive mit langem [i:]

[ʃi:p] – sheep

Substantive mit kurzem [ɪ]

[ʃɪp] – ship

Dieses Zeichen ['] findest du bei Wörtern, die aus mindestens zwei Silben bestehen.
Es zeigt dir an, welche Silbe betont wird.

['ʌndəgraʊnd] – **under**ground

[ˌʌndə'stænd] – under**stand**

Welche Silbe wird jeweils betont?

sixteen [ˌsɪk'sti:n], skateboard ['skeɪtbɔ:d]

Word banks

Online kannst du hören, wie man die Wörter ausspricht.

Word bank: **Everyday English**

→ Find more online 44jp78

How are you?
How was your weekend?
How was your holiday?
How was your party?
How was your trip?

OK.
I'm fine, thanks.
Brilliant.
Not bad.
Great.
Cool.

Awful.
Not so good.
Boring.

I like your ....
I love your ....

Thanks. It was a present.

What's new?

Not much.

I have a new ....

Really?

Sorry! I didn't understand.
Sorry! I was angry.
Sorry! I was worried.
Sorry! I was tired.
Can you say that again, please?
Can you repeat that, please?
Kannst du das bitte wiederholen?

No problem.
Never mind.
That's OK.
Of course. / Sure.
It doesn't matter.
Don't worry.
I'm not angry with you.

What's the problem?
What's wrong?
What do you mean?
What happened?

I lost my ....
Let's talk about the problem.

Word bank: **Holidays**

→ Find more online 44jp78

Word bank: **Jobs at home** → Find more online 44jp78

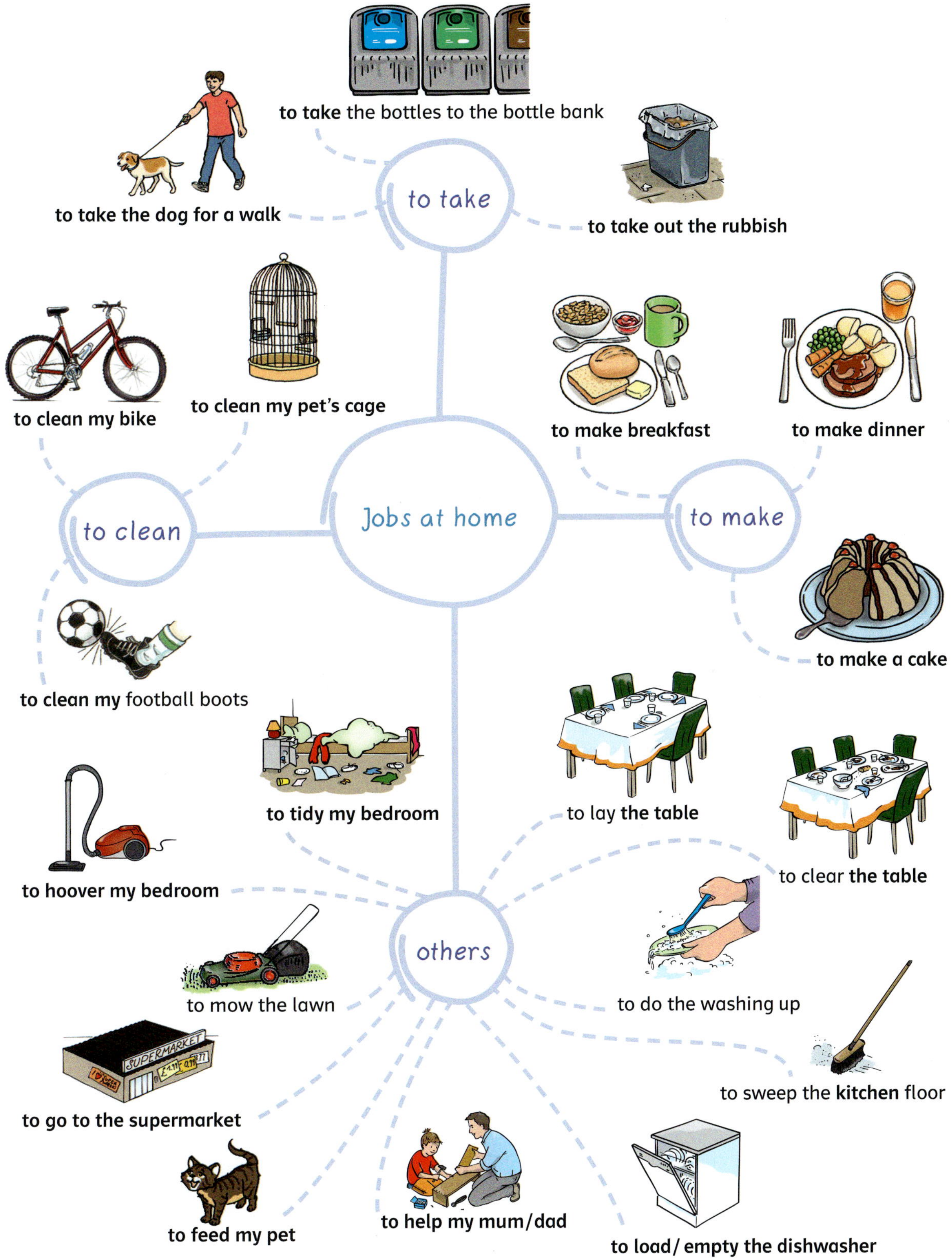

Word bank: **At home** → Find more online 44jp78

1. **table**	6. **carpet**	11. **poster**	16. **computer**
2. **chair**	7. **window**	12. **lamp**	17. **box**
3. **wardrobe**	8. **door**	13. alarm clock	18. **bag**
4. **bed**	9. **shelf**, **shelves**	14. **phone**	
5. floor	10. notice board	15. **book**	

Word bank: **Buying clothes**

→ Find more online 44jp78

1. **T-shirt**	5. pullover/ hoodie	8. **shoes**	12. socks	16. dress
2. **shirt**	6. top	9. **scarf**	13. baseball cap	17. jacket
3. trousers	7. shorts	10. blouse	14. hat	18. coat
4. tie		11. skirt	15. cardigan	

Sizes

XS extra small	S small	M medium	L large	XL extra large

The dress is very pretty.
The shirt looks cool.
The jacket **isn't very nice.**
The shoes are cheap.
The trousers **look good.**

Word bank: **London sights**

→ Find more online 44jp78

The O2

Red double decker **bus**

The London Eye

The Tower of London

Buckingham Palace

Camden Market

The London Dungeon

Big Ben

London taxi

Underground station

Westminster Abbey

Piccadilly Circus

Wembley Stadium

Look at the map of London at the front of your book for more famous London sights.

Word bank: **Comparing places**

→ Find more online 44jp78

1. castle	5. cathedral	9. monument	13. **market place**
2. **stadium**	6. synagogue	10. fountain	14. **river**
3. mosque	7. **church**	11. botanical garden	
4. **road bridge**	8. footbridge	12. gate	

The castle **in our town is the largest in Bavaria.**
Our botanical garden **is the prettiest in Germany.**
The church here is the oldest in Bavaria.

nice • **cool** • **cheap** • **tall** • **pretty** • **old** • **large** • **good**

Word bank: **Directions** → Find more online 44jp78

on the left

on the right

next to

opposite

Our house is on the right/left.

at the bus stop

The sports shop is near Rick's Café.

turn right
take the first street on the right

turn left
take the first street on the left

go straight on

go across the street

Asking the way:
Excuse me, please.
Can you tell me the way to ...?
Thank you for your help.

Giving directions:
I think that's near the ....
Go out of the shop and then ....
No problem.

Word bank: **School year** → Find more online 44jp78

School year

to visit

to visit a library

to visit a bakery

to visit the fire brigade

to visit a museum

to go

to go on a skiing trip

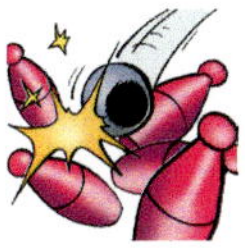

to go bowling

to go ice skating

others

to stay in a youth hostel

to take part in

to take part in a theatre festival

to take part in the **school cinema week**

to take part in a swimming gala

to take part in a painting competition

to take part in the school concert

to take part in a reading competition

Word bank: **Summer fair** → Find more online 44jp78

Summer fair

to have

to have a sack race

to have a potato and spoon race

to have a band

to have a climbing **wall**

to have a quiz

to play

to play knocking down the cans

to play boccia

to organize

to organize a raffle

to organize a cake sale

others

to make jewellery

to do karaoke

to design **T-shirts**

Word bank: **Sports day** → Find more online 44jp78

Sports day

to play

to play table football

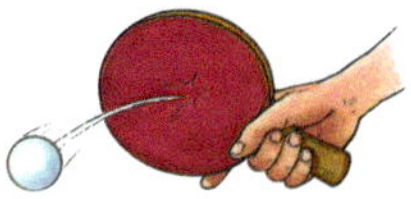
to play table tennis

to play basketball

to play beach volleyball

where?

in the gym

in the playground

in the hall

at the playing field

others

to **dance**

to do aerobics

to take part in

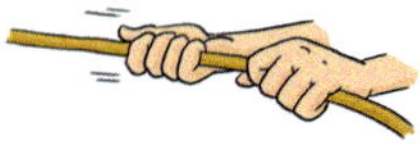
to take part in a tug of war

to take part in the long jump

to take part in a relay race

to take part in a hip-hop workshop

Word bank: **Activities on a trip** → Find more online 44jp78

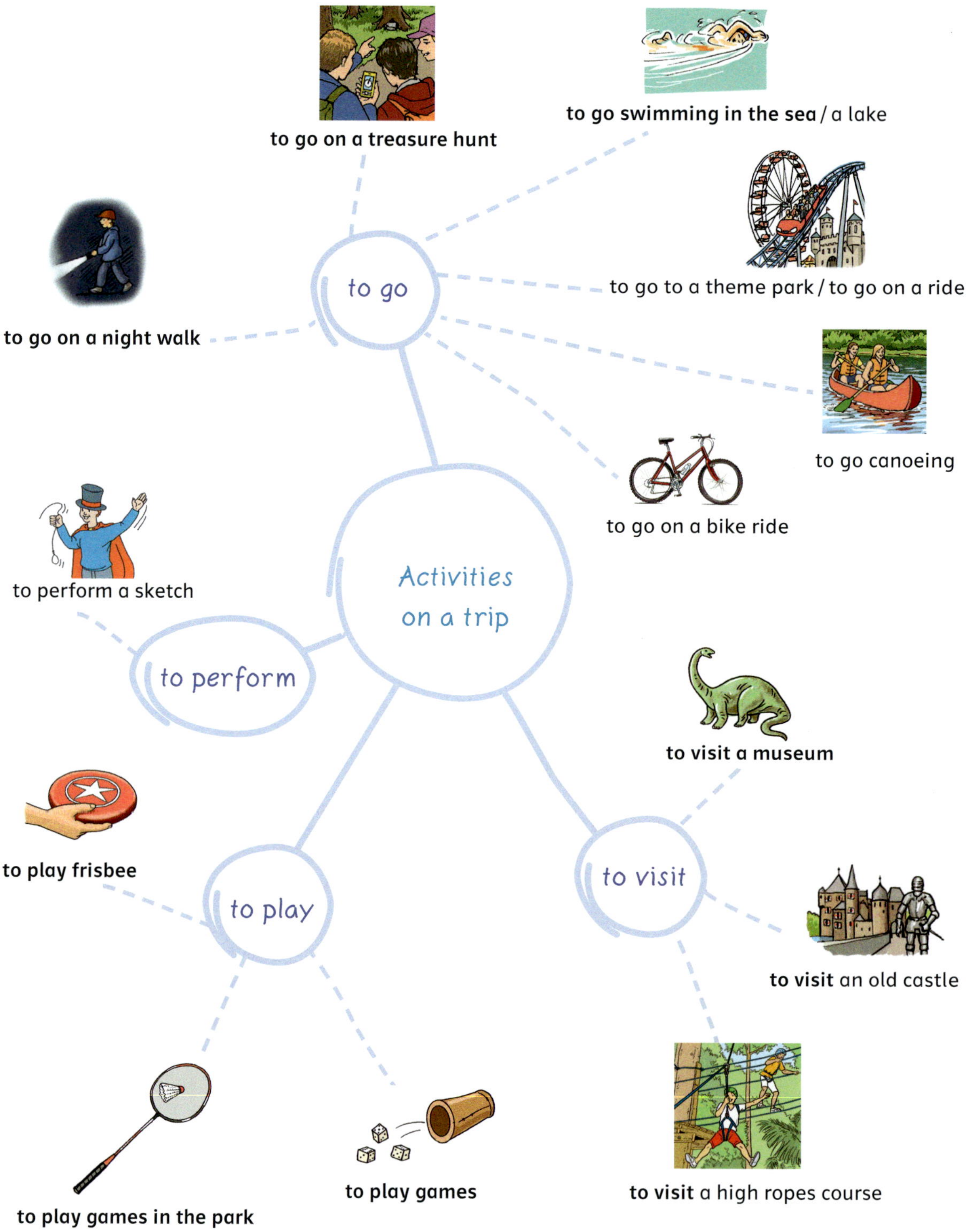

Word bank: **People's qualities** → Find more online 44jp78

You are good at …

music

football

sport

art

You can …

dance

sing

act

You …

help others

make me smile

do jobs at home

don't forget things

look after your sister/brother

look after your pet

You are …

funny

exciting

interesting

a good friend
always there for me

Word bank: **Free-time activities** → Find more online 44jp78

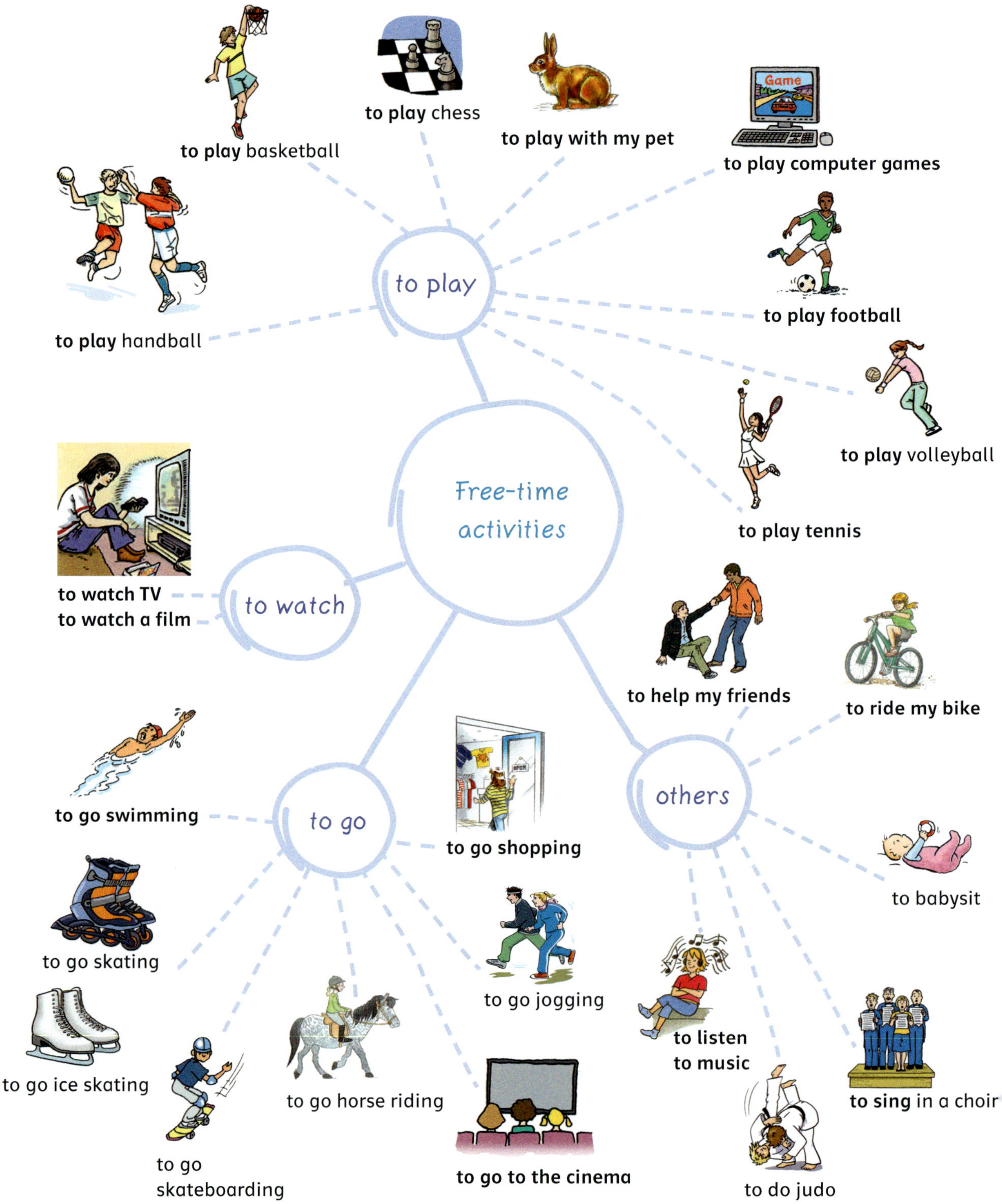

Word bank: **Messages** → Find more online 44jp78

Text message

thx

r u sure?

c u later

r u ☺?

Sorry ☹

Note

Thanks.

See you later.

I won't be long.

I'll be late.

I'm out shopping.

Don't forget to feed the cat.

Your lunch is in the fridge.

Do your homework.

E-mail

YOUR BIRTHDAY PARTY ON FRIDAY

Dear …,/Hi …,

Congratulations!

Well done!

Thank you!

Sorry!

I feel awful.

I have some good/bad news.

I can't believe it.

Thanks for your help.

I'm really excited/happy/sad.

Love, …/See you soon.

Farewell card

Vocabulary

Das vocabulary enthält alle neuen Wörter und Wendungen. Sie stehen in der Reihenfolge, wie sie im Buch vorkommen.

Die Wortliste ist in drei Spalten aufgeteilt:

Links findest du das englische Wort mit der Lautschrift in Klammern. (Die Lautschrift wird auf S. 160 und ganz unten auf jeder Seite im *Dictionary* erklärt.)

In der mittleren Spalte steht die deutsche Übersetzung.

Rechts findest du Beispielsätze, Hinweise und Tipps, die dir beim Lernen helfen.

Die **fett** gedruckten Wörter musst du lernen.

Symbole und Abkürzungen:

- 👄 Achte auf die Aussprache!
- ✎ Achte auf die Schreibung!
- ↔ ist das Gegenteil von
- → ist verwandt mit
- = entspricht
- *(sg)* Einzahl (Singular)
- *(pl)* Mehrzahl (Plural)
- [R] ähnlich wie im Russischen
- [T] ähnlich wie im Türkischen

Die *Word bank*-Seiten (S. 161 bis 175) helfen dir, die *task*-Aufgaben in den *Units* zu bearbeiten. Du findest dort nützlichen individuellen Wortschatz zum Thema der *Unit*, der dir hilft, über deine eigene Situation zu sprechen oder zu schreiben. Diese Wörter findest du auch im *Dictionary*.

Wenn du ein Wort nicht weißt und im Wörterbuch nachschlagen willst, schau auf den *Dictionary*-Seiten ab S. 199 nach. Oder bei den *Instructions* auf S. 229.

Unit 1 It's great to be back

p. 8	**back** [bæk]	zurück	We came **back** from our trip on Sunday.

Intro

	late [leɪt]	(zu) spät	It's **late**. Let's go.
p. 9	**Jamaica** [dʒə'meɪkə]	Jamaika	[R] Ямайка
	holiday ['hɒlədeɪ]	Ferien; Urlaub	My **holidays** were great.
	fantastic [fæn'tæstɪk]	fantastisch; großartig	Jay's holidays were **fantastic**.
	grandparents *(pl)* ['græn͵peərnts]	Großeltern	
	scarf *(sg)* [skɑ:f], **scarves** *(pl)* [skɑ:vz]	Schal; Tuch	
p. 8	**to be late** [bi: 'leɪt]	zu spät kommen	Dave doesn't want to **be late**.
	got up [͵gɒt‿'ʌp]	simple past von *to get up* (aufstehen)	I **got up** = ich stand auf/ich bin aufgestanden

Topic 1

p. 10	**summer** ['sʌmə]	Sommer	**summer** ↔ winter
	to **take photos (of)** [ˌteɪk 'fəʊtəʊz]	Fotos machen; fotografieren	Can I **take photos** of your house, please?
	took [tʊk]	simple past von *to take* (nehmen)	I **took** = ich nahm/ich habe genommen
	to **meet** [mi:t], **met** [met]	(sich) treffen	Luke **met** Dave in the park.
	cousin ['kʌzn]	Cousin; Cousine	R кузен T kuzen; kuzin
	sang [sæŋ]	simple past von *to sing* (singen)	I **sang** = ich sang/ich habe gesungen
	band [bænd]	Band; Musikgruppe	What's your favourite **band**?
	to **hear** [hɪə], **heard** [hɜ:d]	hören	When can we **hear** your songs?
	more [mɔ:]	mehr; weitere	I need **more** practice. 
	cricket ['krɪkɪt]	Kricket	
	grandfather ['grænˌfɑ:ðə]	Großvater	Your father's father is your **grandfather**.
	well [wel]	gut	Gwen can't see very **well**.
	to **feel** [fi:l], **felt** [felt]	(sich) fühlen	She can **feel** the ball.
	it [ɪt]	ihn; ihm	Where's the ball? I can't find **it**.
	What about ...? [ˌwɒt‿ə'baʊt]	Und ...?; Was ist mit ...?	I'd like to watch TV. **What about** you?
	to **go tandem bike riding** [ˌgəʊ 'tændəm ˌbaɪk raɪdɪŋ]	Tandem fahren	I **went tandem bike riding** with my cousin.
	in front [ɪn 'frʌnt]	vorn	She was **in front** on the tandem.
	made [meɪd]	simple past von *to make* (machen)	I **made** = ich machte/ich habe gemacht
	ate [eɪt]	simple past von *to eat* (essen)	I **ate** = ich aß/ich habe gegessen 
	ice cream [ˌaɪs 'kri:m]	Eis; Eiscreme	I like strawberry **ice cream**.
	It's Holly's turn. [ɪts 'hɒliz ˌtɜ:n]	Holly ist dran.	Thanks, Gwen. Now **it's Holly's turn**.
p. 14	**him** [hɪm]	ihm; ihn	Jay tells **him** the story.

Das kenne ich schon

family

uncle ['ʌŋkl]	Onkel	brother ['brʌðə]	Bruder
aunt [ɑ:nt]	Tante	daughter ['dɔ:tə]	Tochter
cousin ['kʌzn]	Cousin; Cousine	grandfather ['grænˌfɑ:ðə]	Großvater
mother ['mʌðə]	Mutter	grandparents *(pl)* ['grænˌpeərnts]	Großeltern
father ['fɑ:ðə]	Vater		
sister ['sɪstə]	Schwester		

Last summer

beautiful ['bju:tɪfl]	wunderschön	in the sun [ˌɪn ðə 'sʌn]	in der Sonne
we all slept in a tent [wi: ɔ:l ˌslept‿ɪn‿ə 'tent]	wir schliefen alle in einem Zelt	on the sand [ˌɒn ðə 'sænd]	im Sand
at the campfire [ˌæt ðə 'kæmpfaɪə]	am Lagerfeuer	I can't wait [aɪ ˌkɑ:nt 'weɪt]	ich kann es nicht abwarten
we counted stars [wi: ˌkaʊntɪd 'stɑ:z]	wir zählten die Sterne	to lie [laɪ]	liegen
sunshine ['sʌnʃaɪn]	Sonnenschein	When will summer come again? [ˌwen wɪl 'sʌmə kʌm ə'gen]	Wann wird es wieder Sommer sein?
good vibes [ˌgʊd 'vaɪbz]	gute Stimmung		

Topic 2

p. 15	**argument** ['ɑ:gjəmənt]	Auseinandersetzung; Streit	Achtung Aussprache!
	to **borrow** ['bɒrəʊ]	(sich) ausleihen	Can I **borrow** your bike, please?
	to **bring** [brɪŋ], **brought** [brɔ:t]	mitbringen; bringen	I can **bring** it to school on Monday.
	to **lose** [lu:z], **lost** [lɒst]	verlieren	**to lose** ↔ to find
	to **have (got) to** ['hæv (gɒt) tə], **had (got) to** ['hæd (gɒt) tə]	müssen	I'm late. I **have to** go.
	surprised [sə'praɪzd]	überrascht	I looked in my bag and was **surprised**.
	That's what happened. [ˌðæts wɒt 'hæpnd]	Das ist passiert.	What can I say? **That's what happened.**
	worried ['wʌrid]	beunruhigt; besorgt	I was really **worried**.
	unhappy [ʌn'hæpi]	unglücklich; traurig	She was very **unhappy**.
	found [faʊnd]	simple past von *to find* (finden)	I **found** = ich fand/ich habe gefunden
	the same [ðə 'seɪm]	der gleiche; derselbe; gleich; genauso	We have **the same** bag.
	as [æz]	wie; als	I have the same phone **as** you.
	I'm sorry. [aɪm 'sɒri]	Es tut mir leid.; Entschuldigung.	**I'm sorry** I lost your scarf.
	angry ['æŋgri]	wütend; zornig; verärgert; böse	I'm sorry I was **angry**.
	Never mind. [ˌnevə 'maɪnd]	Macht nichts.; Schon gut.; Mach dir nichts draus.	Sorry, I can't help you today. – **Never mind.**
p. 18	**dialogue** ['daɪəlɒg]	Dialog; Gespräch	Listen to the **dialogue**.
p. 19	**with** [wɪð]	bei	Jay stayed **with** his grandparents.

Das kenne ich schon

feelings

happy ['hæpi]	glücklich
unhappy [ʌn'hæpi]	unglücklich; traurig
worried ['wʌrid]	beunruhigt; besorgt
surprised [sə'praɪzd]	überrascht
angry ['æŋgri]	wütend; zornig; verärgert; böse
I'm sorry. [aɪm 'sɒri]	Es tut mir leid.; Entschuldigung.

Text

p. 20	**lucky day** [ˌlʌki 'deɪ]	Glückstag	Today is my **lucky day**!
	on the bus [ˌɒn ðə 'bʌs]	im Bus	Luke and Gwen were **on the bus**.
	to **answer** ['ɑ:nsə]	antworten; beantworten	Luke didn't **answer** Gwen.
	to **forget** [fə'get], **forgot** [fə'gɒt]	vergessen	I'm really sorry I **forgot** your birthday!
	everything ['evriθɪŋ]	alles	You forget **everything**, Luke.
	stop [stɒp]	Haltestelle; Halt	This is my **stop**. Bye.
	to **get off** [ˌget‿'ɒf], **got off** [ˌgɒt‿'ɒf]	aussteigen	Luke **got off** the bus at the stop.
	to **finish** ['fɪnɪʃ]	beenden; fertig machen; erledigen; enden; aufhören	Luke wanted to **finish** his game.
	to **put** [pʊt]	*hier:* stecken	He **puts** his phone in his bag.
	hand [hænd]	Hand	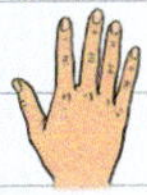
	to **phone** [fəʊn]	anrufen; telefonieren	I **phone** my friends after school.
	company ['kʌmpəni]	Unternehmen; Firma; Gesellschaft	R компания
	first ['fɜ:st]	zuerst; als Erstes	**First** I get up, then I have breakfast.
	rang [ræŋ]	simple past von *to ring* (klingeln)	I **rang** = ich klingelte/ ich habe geklingelt
	door [dɔ:]	Tür	
	hearing ['hɪərɪŋ]	Gehör	Your **hearing** is really good.

Film

penny *(sg)* ['peni], pence *(pl)* [pens]	Penny *(brit. Währungseinheit)*
lemon ['lemən]	Zitrone
battery ['bætri]	Batterie; Akku
wire [waɪə]	Draht; Kabel
nail [neɪl]	Nagel
experiment [ɪk'sperɪmənt]	Versuch; Experiment

Unit 2 Where I live

Intro

p. 28	**bedroom** ['bedrʊm]	Kinderzimmer; Schlafzimmer	My **bedroom** is green and it's nice.
	often ['ɒfn]	oft; häufig	I **often** get up late on Saturdays.
p. 29	**living room** ['lɪvɪŋ ˌrʊm]	Wohnzimmer	I do my homework in the **living room**.
	opposite ['ɒpəzɪt]	gegenüber	The school is **opposite** the market.

Topic 1

p. 30	**usually** ['ju:ʒli]	normalerweise; gewöhnlich	Luke **usually** plays football on Mondays.
	guinea pig ['gɪni ˌpɪg]	Meerschweinchen	
	to **empty the dishwasher** [ˌemti ðə 'dɪʃwɒʃə]	die Spülmaschine ausräumen	After school I **empty the dishwasher**.
	to **tidy** ['taɪdi]	aufräumen; in Ordnung bringen	I always have to **tidy** my bedroom.
	to **clean** [kli:n]	sauber machen; putzen	My father **cleans** the car. 
	cage [keɪdʒ]	Käfig	
	to **take out** [ˌteɪk‿'aʊt]	*hier:* hinausbringen	I **take out** the rubbish every week.
	before [bɪ'fɔ:]	vor; bevor	**before** ↔ after
	to **load the dishwasher** [ˌləʊd ðə 'dɪʃwɒʃə]	die Spülmaschine einräumen	My mum **loads the dishwasher**.
	cooking ['kʊkɪŋ]	Kochen; Koch-	I love **cooking** with my mum.
	never ['nevə]	nie; niemals	**never** ↔ always
	to **hoover** ['hu:və]	staubsaugen	I usually **hoover** the living room.
	kitchen ['kɪtʃɪn]	Küche	We eat together in the **kitchen**. 
	bathroom ['bɑ:θrʊm]	Bad(ezimmer)	
	to **cook** [kʊk]	kochen	My dad often **cooks** dinner for our family.

Das kenne ich schon

at home

bedroom ['bedrʊm]	Kinderzimmer; Schlafzimmer	bathroom ['bɑ:θrʊm]	Bad(ezimmer)
living room ['lɪvɪŋ ˌrʊm]	Wohnzimmer	balcony ['bælkəni]	Balkon
kitchen ['kɪtʃɪn]	Küche	garden ['gɑ:dn]	Garten

Das kenne ich schon

adverbs of frequency

always ['ɔ:lweɪz]	immer	often ['ɒfn]	oft; häufig
usually ['ju:ʒli]	normalerweise; gewöhnlich	sometimes ['sʌmtaɪmz]	manchmal
		never ['nevə]	nie; niemals

Topic 2

p. 33	**to change** [tʃeɪndʒ]	verändern; ändern; wechseln	Luke **changed** things in his bedroom.
	wardrobe ['wɔ:drəʊb]	Kleiderschrank	Put your clothes in the **wardrobe**. 
	shelf *(sg)* [ʃelf], **shelves** *(pl)* [ʃelvz]	Regal; Regalbrett	
	above [ə'bʌv]	über; oberhalb	The shelf is **above** the bed.
	wall [wɔ:l]	Wand; Mauer	My bedroom **wall** is now yellow.
	desk [desk]	Schreibtisch; Tisch	 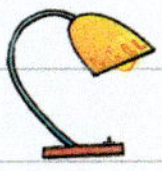
	lamp [læmp]	Lampe	
	poster ['pəʊstə]	Poster	I like your new Arsenal **poster**.
	to think [θɪŋk], **thought** [θɔ:t]	denken; glauben	I **think** your old posters are good too.
	best [best]	am besten; beste; am liebsten	This poster here is **best**. 
	comic ['kɒmɪk]	Comic(heft)	R комикс
	carpet ['kɑ:pɪt]	Teppich	The **carpet** is new too.
	better ['betə]	besser	**better** → good
	sports shop ['spɔ:ts ˌʃɒp]	Sportgeschäft	Let's go to the **sports shop**, I need a ball.

Das kenne ich schon

furniture

wardrobe ['wɔ:drəʊb]	Kleiderschrank	TV [ˌti:'vi:]	Fernseher
shelf *(sg)* [ʃelf], shelves *(pl)* [ʃelvz]	Regal; Regalbrett	lamp [læmp]	Lampe
		carpet ['kɑ:pɪt]	Teppich
desk [desk]	Schreibtisch	bed [bed]	Bett
table ['teɪbl]	Tisch	chair [tʃeə]	Stuhl

Topic 3

p. 36	**trainer** ['treɪnə]	Turnschuh	
	size [saɪz]	Größe	What **size** do you need?
	foot *(sg)* [fʊt], **feet** *(pl)* [fi:t]	Fuß	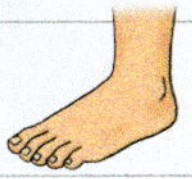
	these [ði:z]	diese	I like **these** trainers here best.
	large [lɑ:dʒ]	groß	**large** = big
	cheap [tʃi:p]	günstig; billig	**cheap** ↔ expensive
	than [ðæn]	als	The red coat is cheaper **than** the blue coat.
	those [ðəʊz]	jene	These are nice, **those** are nicer.
	to try on [ˌtraɪ 'ɒn]	anprobieren	Can I **try** the red trainers **on**, please?
	next [nekst]	als Nächstes	**Next** they went to the bag shop.

	T-shirt ['ti:ʃɜ:t]	T-Shirt	
	pretty ['prɪti]	hübsch	That's a **pretty** T-shirt, Holly. – Thanks.
	short [ʃɔ:t]	kurz	This T-shirt is too **short**.
	worse [wɜ:s]	schlechter; schlimmer	These are bad, but those are **worse**.
p. 37	**UK (United Kingdom)** [ˌju:'keɪ (ju:ˌnaɪtɪd 'kɪŋdəm)]	Vereinigtes Königreich von Großbritannien und Nordirland	

Das kenne ich schon

clothes

scarf *(sg)* [skɑ:f], scarves *(pl)* [skɑ:vz]	Schal; Tuch	pullover ['pʊləʊvə]	Pullover
trainers ['treɪnəz]	Turnschuhe	dress [dres]	Kleid
shoes [ʃu:z]	Schuhe	coat [kəʊt]	Jacke
shirt [ʃɜ:t]	Hemd; Shirt	T-shirt ['ti:ʃɜ:t]	T-Shirt
		jeans *(pl)* [dʒi:nz]	Jeans

I love your style

style [staɪl]	Stil
no matter [nəʊ 'mætə]	egal; ganz gleich
no one would ever guess ['nəʊ wʌn wʊd ˌevə 'ges]	niemand würde es erraten
tank top ['tæŋk ˌtɒp]	ärmelloses T-Shirt
brand [brænd]	Marke
what the logo means [ˌwɒt ðə 'ləʊgəʊ mi:nz]	was das Logo bedeutet
you look just great in everything you wear [ju lʊk dʒʌst 'greɪt ɪn ˌevriθɪŋ ju weə]	du siehst gut aus, egal was du anziehst
if you choose this suit [ɪf ju ˌtʃu:z ðɪs 'su:t]	wenn du diesen Anzug aussuchst
to pick [pɪk]	wählen
if you spend a little more, or a little less [ɪf ju spend‿ə lɪtl 'mɔ:r‿ɔ:r‿ə lɪtl ˌles]	ob du ein bisschen mehr oder ein bisschen weniger ausgibst
it's just important to feel good [ɪts dʒʌst ɪmˌpɔ:tnt tə ˌfi:l 'gʊd]	es ist nur wichtig, sich wohlzufühlen
it's not that high fashion thing [ɪts 'nɒt ðæt ˌhaɪ fæʃn 'θɪŋ]	es geht nicht darum, topmodisch zu sein
bling [blɪŋ]	bling *(schöne, teure Sachen)*
you do your own thing [ju 'du: jɔ:r‿əʊn 'θɪŋ]	du machst dein eigenes Ding
in the spotlight [ɪn ðə 'spɒtlaɪt]	im Rampenlicht
everywhere you go ['evriweə ju ˌgəʊ]	überall wo du hingehst

Text

p. 40	**everyone** ['evriwʌn]	alle; jeder; zusammen	I love **everyone** in my family.
	to have got [hæv 'gɒt]	haben; besitzen	I **have got** two brothers and a sister.
	half past (seven) [ˌhɑ:f 'pɑ:st]	halb (acht)	2:30 = It's **half past** two.

to **wash** [wɒʃ]	(sich) waschen; spülen	I get up and **wash** my face.
work [wɜ:k]	Arbeit	**work** → to work
early ['ɜ:li]	früh	I get up **early** on Sundays. At six o'clock.
past [pɑ:st]	nach *(bei Uhrzeitangaben)*	7:10 = It's ten **past** seven.
quarter to/past ['kwɔ:tə tə/pɑ:st]	Viertel vor/nach	6:45 = It's **quarter to** seven. 7:15 = It's **quarter past** seven.
to **look after** [ˌlʊk‿'ɑ:ftə]	aufpassen auf; hüten; sich kümmern um	I **look after** my brother on Saturdays.
worst [wɜ:st]	schlimmste; schlechteste	The neighbour's cat is the **worst** of all.
to **bark** [bɑ:k]	bellen	The dog **barked**.
to **run away** [ˌrʌn‿ə'weɪ]	weglaufen	Sherlock barks and the cat **runs away**.
to **run** [rʌn], **ran** [ræn]	laufen; rennen; fahren	I **run** with my dog in the park.
p. 41 to **learn** [lɜ:n]	lernen	I **learn** new tricks at dog school.
word [wɜ:d]	Wort	I have to learn lots of English **words**.
to **throw** [θrəʊ], **threw** [θru:]	werfen	Luke **threw** the ball.
to **sleep** [sli:p], **slept** [slept]	schlafen	
a busy day [ə ˌbɪzi 'deɪ]	ein ausgefüllter Tag	After **a busy day** I'm very tired.

Das kenne ich schon

telling the time

half past seven [ˌhɑ:f pɑ:st 'sevn]	halb acht	twenty past eight [ˌtwenti pɑ:st‿'eɪt]	zwanzig nach acht
quarter past three [ˌkwɔ:tə‿pɑ:st 'θri:]	Viertel nach drei	twenty-five past four [ˌtwentifaɪv pɑ:st 'fɔ:]	fünfundzwanzig nach vier
quarter to nine [ˌkwɔ:tə‿tə 'naɪn]	Viertel vor neun	ten to twelve [ˌten tə 'twelv]	zehn vor zwölf
five past six [ˌfaɪv pɑ:st 'sɪks]	fünf nach sechs	twenty to ten [ˌtwenti‿tə‿'ten]	zwanzig vor zehn
ten past two [ˌten pɑ:s‿'tu:]	zehn nach zwei	twenty-five to five [ˌtwentifaɪv tə‿'faɪv]	fünfundzwanzig vor fünf

Film

how to … ['haʊ tə]	wie man …	crazy ['kreɪzi]	verrückt
polite [pə'laɪt]	höflich	escalator ['eskəleɪtə]	Rolltreppe
Excuse me. [ɪk'skju:z mi]	Entschuldigung.	to wake up [ˌweɪk‿'ʌp]	aufwachen
queue [kju:]	Warteschlange	at the end [ˌət ði 'end]	am Ende

Unit 3 London life

p. 48	**life** *(sg)* [laɪf], **lives** *(pl)* [laɪvz]	Leben	My **life** is great.

Intro

	Poland ['pəʊlənd]	Polen	Luke's cousin is from **Poland**.
	sight [saɪt]	Sehenswürdigkeit	Come and see the **sights** of London!
	big wheel [ˌbɪg 'wiːl]	Riesenrad	The London Eye is a **big wheel**.
	German ['dʒɜːmən]	Deutscher; Deutsche; deutsch; aus Deutschland	**Germans** helped with the London Eye.
	to **build** [bɪld], **built** [bɪlt]	bauen	We **built** our house with friends. 
p. 49	**tower** ['taʊə]	Turm	
	clock [klɒk]	Uhr	Big Ben is a famous tower with a **clock**. 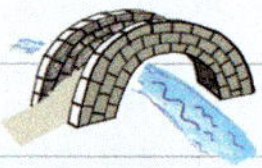
	bridge [brɪdʒ]	Brücke	
	every ['evri]	alle	People clean the clock **every** five years.
	museum [mjuː'ziːəm]	Museum	R музей
	about [ə'baʊt]	ungefähr; circa; etwa	The museum is **about** 180 years old.
	wax [wæks]	Wachs	Madame Tussauds is a **wax** museum.
	figure ['fɪgə]	Figur; Gestalt	There are wax **figures** in the museum.
	king [kɪŋ]	König	 
	queen [kwiːn]	Königin	
	church [tʃɜːtʃ]	Kirche	
	metre ['miːtə]	Meter	Achtung Schreibweise! metre
	high [haɪ]	hoch; groß	

Topic 1

p. 50	**up** [ʌp]	hinauf; oben; hoch	Let's go **up** high on the London Eye.
	height [haɪt]	Höhe	Achtung Schreibweise! height
	fact [fækt]	Fakt; Tatsache	I know lots of **facts** about London.
	diameter [daɪ'æmɪtə]	Durchmesser	The **diameter** of the wheel is 120 metres.
	step [step]	Stufe; Schritt	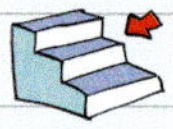 
	lift [lɪft]	Aufzug	
	bell [bel]	Glocke	
	Europe ['jʊərəp]	Europa	Germany and England are in **Europe**.

telephone box ['telɪfəʊn ˌbɒks]	Telefonzelle	
tall [tɔ:l]	hoch; groß	
building ['bɪldɪŋ]	Gebäude; Bauwerk	**buildings**: houses, schools, cinemas, …
floor [flɔ:]	Stockwerk; Etage	The building has 45 **floors**.
city centre [ˌsɪti 'sentə]	Stadtzentrum; Stadtmitte	Let's go to the **city centre**.
tomorrow [tə'mɒrəʊ]	morgen	**Tomorrow** is Saturday! Great, no school!
sure [ʃʊə]	sicher	I'm **sure** it's very interesting.
which [wɪtʃ]	welche; was	**Which** bands do you like?
near [nɪə]	nah	Where is the **nearest** book shop?
map [mæp]	Karte; Plan	Let's look at the **map**.
information [ˌɪnfə'meɪʃn]	Information(en)	I need more **information**.
p. 51 **visitor** ['vɪzɪtə]	Besucher; Besucherin	**visitor** → to visit

Das kenne ich schon

numbers up to 1,000

a/one hundred and thirty-five 135 [ə/wʌn ˌhʌndrəd‿ən θɜ:ti'faɪv]	hundertfünfunddreißig
two hundred 200 [tu: 'hʌndrəd]	zweihundert
three hundred 300 [θri: 'hʌndrəd]	dreihundert
three hundred and ten 310 [θri: ˌhʌndrəd‿ən 'ten]	dreihundertzehn
four hundred 400 [fɔ: 'hʌndrəd]	vierhundert
five hundred 500 [faɪv 'hʌndrəd]	fünfhundert
six hundred 600 [sɪks 'hʌndrəd]	sechshundert
seven hundred 700 [sevn 'hʌndrəd]	siebenhundert
eight hundred 800 [eɪt 'hʌndrəd]	achthundert
nine hundred 900 [naɪn 'hʌndrəd]	neunhundert
a/one thousand 1,000 [ə/wʌn 'θaʊznd]	eintausend

Das kenne ich schon

years

1650 sixteen fifty [ˌsɪksti:n 'fɪfti]	sechzehnhundertfünfzig
1776 seventeen seventy-six [ˌsevnti:n sevnti'sɪks]	siebzehnhundertsechsundsiebzig
1865 eighteen sixty-five [ˌeɪti:n sɪksti'faɪv]	achtzehnhundertfünfundsechzig
1905 nineteen oh five [ˌnaɪnti:n‿əʊ 'faɪv]	neunzehnhundertfünf
1999 nineteen ninety-nine [ˌnaɪnti:n naɪnti'naɪn]	neunzehnhundertneunundneunzig
2012 twenty twelve, two thousand and twelve [ˌtwenti 'twelv, ˌtu: θaʊznd‿ən 'twelv]	zweitausendzwölf

Das kenne ich schon

places in town / sights

tower ['taʊə]	Turm	market ['mɑ:kɪt]	Markt
bridge [brɪdʒ]	Brücke	stadium ['steɪdiəm]	Stadion
museum [mju:'zi:əm]	Museum	park [pɑ:k]	Park
church [tʃɜ:tʃ]	Kirche	city centre [ˌsɪti 'sentə]	Stadtzentrum; Stadtmitte
shopping centre ['ʃɒpɪŋ ˌsentə]	Einkaufszentrum	cinema ['sɪnəmə]	Kino
clock [klɒk]	Uhr		

Topic 2

p. 53	to **stand** [stænd], **stood** [stʊd]	stehen	Luke **stood** in front of the shop.
	queue [kju:]	Warteschlange	
	at the moment [ət ðə 'məʊmənt]	im Moment; momentan	He's in the shop **at the moment**.
	to **wait (for)** [weɪt]	warten (auf)	I **waited** for you. Where were you?
	to [tu:]	um zu; an	He said he was too old **to** work.
	to **read** [ri:d], **read** [red]	lesen; vorlesen	I have to **read** this book for school.
	message ['mesɪdʒ]	Nachricht; SMS	Jay sends Dave a **message**.
	to **drink** [drɪŋk], **drank** [dræŋk]	trinken	The man is **drinking** some juice.
	trumpet ['trʌmpɪt]	Trompete	

Topic 3

p. 57	**treasure hunt** ['treʒə ˌhʌnt]	Schnitzeljagd; Schatzsuche	The **treasure hunt** in London was great.
	into ['ɪntu]	in; in … hinein	He goes **into** the house and sees the dog.
	souvenir [ˌsu:vn'ɪə]	Souvenir; Andenken	I bought a T-shirt as a **souvenir**.
	Excuse me. [ɪk'skju:z mi]	Entschuldigung.	**Excuse me**, where is the city centre?
	on the right [ɒn ðə 'raɪt]	rechts; auf der rechten Seite	Greenwich Park is **on the right**.
	newspaper kiosk ['nju:speɪpə ˌki:ɒsk]	Zeitungsstand	The bus stop is near the **newspaper kiosk**.
	us [ʌs]	uns; wir	Can you tell **us** the way there, please?
	to **turn** [tɜ:n]	abbiegen	**Turn** at the park.
	across [ə'krɒs]	über	Go **across** the street.
	second ['seknd]	zweite	Take the **second** street on the right.

on the left [ɒn ðə 'left]	links; auf der linken Seite	**on the left** ↔ on the right
straight on [streɪt‿'ɒn]	geradeaus	Go **straight on**.
third [θɜ:d]	dritte	first, second, **third**, …

Das kenne ich schon

prepositions

across [ə'krɒs]	über	out of ['aʊt‿əv]	aus … heraus
opposite ['ɒpəzɪt]	gegenüber	next to ['nekst tə]	neben
behind [bɪ'haɪnd]	hinter	in front of [ɪn 'frʌnt‿əv]	vor
on [ɒn]	auf; an; am	past [pɑ:st]	vorbei (an)

Text

p. 60	**wizard** ['wɪzəd]	Zauberer	
	once upon a time [ˌwʌns əpɒn‿ə 'taɪm]	es war einmal	**Once upon a time**, there was a wizard.
	all of ['ɔ:l‿əv]	ganz	We saw **all of** London from the London Eye.
	to **check** [tʃek]	überprüfen; kontrollieren	Let's **check** our poster again.
	to **fly** [flaɪ], **flew** [flu:]	fliegen	Ronnie **flew** from sight to sight.
	top [tɒp]	Spitze; oberer Teil; oberes Ende	He looked from the **top** of Big Ben.
	to **do magic** [ˌdu: 'mædʒɪk]	zaubern	Ronnie wanted to **do magic** and have fun.
	pop [pɒp]	Pop *(Musik)*	I like **pop** music.
	tourist ['tʊərɪst]	Tourist; Touristin	There are lots of **tourists** in London.
	crown jewels *(pl)* [ˌkraʊn 'dʒu:əlz]	Kronjuwelen	
	around [ə'raʊnd]	um … herum	Ronnie flew **around** London.
	neck [nek]	Hals; Nacken	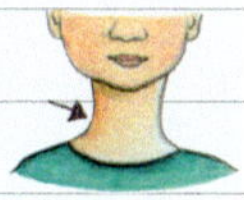
	to **be fun** [bi: 'fʌn]	Spaß machen; witzig sein	It **was fun** in the park on Sunday.
p. 61	**without** [wɪ'ðaʊt]	ohne	**without** ↔ with
	to **correct** [kə'rekt]	richtigstellen; verbessern; korrigieren	Don't worry. I can **correct** everything.
	when [wen]	als; wenn	I was surprised **when** I saw it.

Film

southwest [ˌsaʊθ'west]	Südwesten	See you then. [ˌsi: jə 'ðen]	Bis dann.

Unit 4 The school year

Intro

p. 68	**event** [ɪ'vent]	Veranstaltung; Ereignis	There are many **events** in the school year.
	planner ['plænə]	Kalender; Planer	 
	lantern ['læntən]	Laterne	
	procession [prə'seʃn]	Umzug; Festzug	The best event is the lantern **procession**.
	month [mʌnθ]	Monat	**months**: January, February, March, April, …
	to make [meɪk]	*hier:* basteln	We **made** lanterns at school.
	own [əʊn]	eigene	I like my **own** lantern best.
	school trip [ˌskuːl 'trɪp]	Klassenfahrt; Schulausflug	We went on a **school trip** in April.
	at the end [ˌət ði 'end]	am Ende	Christmas is **at the end** of December.
	hostel ['hɒstl]	Herberge; Hostel	We stayed in a youth **hostel**.
	local ['ləʊkl]	örtlich; lokal; hiesig	We also visited the **local** museum.
p. 69	**fair** [feə]	Fest; Messe; Jahrmarkt	The summer **fair** is in June.
	to raise money [ˌreɪz 'mʌni]	Geld sammeln; Geld aufbringen	We **raise money** at the summer fair.
	charity ['tʃærɪti]	Wohltätigkeitsorganisation; Stiftung; wohltätige Zwecke; Wohltätigkeits-	The money goes to **charities**.
	project ['prɒdʒekt]	Projekt	R проект T proje
	sports day ['spɔːts ˌdeɪ]	Sportfest	**Sports day** is in July. 
	long jump ['lɒŋ ˌdʒʌmp]	Weitsprung	
	that's why ['ðæts waɪ]	deshalb; deswegen	It's cold. **That's why** I need my coat.
	to invite [ɪn'vaɪt]	einladen	We **invite** our families to sports day.
	beginning [bɪ'gɪnɪŋ]	Anfang; Beginn	**beginning** ↔ end
p. 68	**must** [mʌst]	müssen	I **must** go now. I'm late.

Topic 1

p. 70	**bad** [bæd]	schlimm	I saw a **bad** accident.
	cold [kəʊld]	Erkältung; Kälte	I had three **colds** last winter.
	a little (bit) [ə 'lɪtl (bɪt)]	ein (kleines) bisschen; ein (klein) wenig	I'm feeling **a little** bit better now.
	wash [wɒʃ]	Wäsche	I helped with the car **wash** at the fair.
	other ['ʌðə]	andere	There were lots of **other** stalls.
	face painting ['feɪs peɪntɪŋ]	Schminken	

	raffle ['ræfl]	Gewinnspiel; Tombola	There was a **raffle** at the fair too.
	prize [praɪz]	Preis; Gewinn	There were lots of great **prizes**.
	ticket ['tɪkɪt]	Ticket; Eintrittskarte; Fahrschein	
	won [wʌn]	simple past von *to win* (gewinnen)	I **won** = ich gewann/ich habe gewonnen
	sold [səʊld]	simple past von *to sell* (verkaufen)	I **sold** = ich verkaufte/ich habe verkauft
	hot dog ['hɒt ˌdɒg]	Hotdog	T hot dog 
	that [ðæt]	dass	I'm sad **that** I had a bad cold.
	to **miss** [mɪs]	verpassen; vermissen	I **missed** the stalls and the raffle.
p. 73	**hard** [hɑ:d]	hart; schwer; schwierig	The summer fair was **hard** work.

Das kenne ich schon

ordinal numbers

first 1st ['fɜ:st]	erste	twelfth 12th [twelfθ]	zwölfte
second 2nd ['seknd]	zweite	thirteenth 13th [θɜ:'ti:nθ]	dreizehnte
third 3rd [θɜ:d]	dritte	twentieth 20th ['twentiəθ]	zwanzigste
fourth 4th [fɔ:θ]	vierte	twenty-first 21st [ˌtwenti'fɜ:st]	einundzwanzigste
fifth 5th [fɪfθ]	fünfte	twenty-second 22nd [ˌtwenti'seknd]	zweiundzwanzigste
sixth 6th [sɪksθ]	sechste	thirtieth 30th ['θɜ:tiəθ]	dreißigste
seventh 7th ['sevnθ]	siebte	thirty-first 31st [ˌθɜ:ti'fɜ:st]	einunddreißigste
eighth 8th [eɪtθ]	achte		
ninth 9th [naɪnθ]	neunte		
tenth 10th [tenθ]	zehnte		
eleventh 11th [ɪ'levnθ]	elfte		

Topic 2

p. 74	**playing field** ['pleɪɪŋ ˌfi:ld]	Sportplatz	The sports day is at the **playing field**.
	warm-up ['wɔ:mʌp]	Aufwärmtraining; Aufwärmen	The **warm-up** is at 9 o'clock.
	200 metre race ['tu: hʌndrəd mi:tə ˌreɪs]	200-Meter-Lauf	I won the **200 metre race** last year. 
	race [reɪs]	Wettrennen; Rennen; Wettlauf	
	sack race ['sæk ˌreɪs]	Sackhüpfen	My brother loves the **sack race**. 
	medal ['medl]	Medaille	
	to **last** [lɑ:st]	dauern; andauern	The film **lasted** 90 minutes.
	hour [aʊə]	Stunde	1 **hour** = 60 minutes
	to **take part (in)** [ˌteɪk 'pɑ:t]	mitmachen (bei); teilnehmen (an)	Students **take part** in lots of races.

Das kenne ich schon

time

minute ['mɪnɪt]	Minute	week [wi:k]	Woche
hour [aʊə]	Stunde	month [mʌnθ]	Monat
day [deɪ]	Tag	year [jɪə]	Jahr

Text

p. 78	**Come on!** [ˌkʌm‿'ɒn]	Komm(t) jetzt!	**Come on!** Let's go!
	nearly ['nɪəli]	fast; beinahe	It's **nearly** time for dinner.
	transport ['trænspɔ:t]	Verkehr; Transport	We visited the **transport** museum.
	to put on [ˌpʊt‿'ɒn]	anziehen	I have to **put** my shoes **on** first.
	trick [trɪk]	Streich	The boys love **tricks**.
p. 79	**tent** [tent]	Zelt	
	in the middle of [ɪn ðə 'mɪdl‿əv]	mitten in	I heard a noise **in the middle of** the night.
	outside [ˌaʊt'saɪd]	außerhalb; außen; draußen; im Freien	There was an animal **outside** the tent.
	wolf *(sg)* [wʊlf], **wolves** *(pl)* [wʊlvz]	Wolf	We thought it was a **wolf**.
	maybe ['meɪbi]	vielleicht	**Maybe** it was a mouse.
	part [pɑ:t]	Rolle; Teil	I have a **part** in 'Little Red Riding Hood'.
p. 78	**to laugh** [lɑ:f]	lachen	They all **laugh** about their tricks.
	others ['ʌðəz]	anderen	Luke and Jay tell the **others** a scary story.

Das kenne ich schon

part of something

at the beginning of … [ət ðə bɪ'gɪnɪŋ‿əv]	am Anfang von …	at the end of … [ət ði 'end‿əv]	am Ende von …
in the middle of … [ɪn ðə 'mɪdl‿əv]	mitten in …		

Film

to pass [pɑ:s]	herüberreichen; reichen	Help yourselves! [ˌhelp jɔ:'selvz]	Bedient euch!; Bedienen Sie sich!
Korean [kə'ri:n]	koreanisch	delicious [dɪ'lɪʃəs]	lecker; köstlich
snack food ['snæk ˌfu:d]	Snacks *(Pl.)*	of course [əv 'kɔ:s]	natürlich; selbstverständlich

Unit 5 Everyone's a star

Intro

p. 86	**player** ['pleɪə]	Spieler; Spielerin	That's my favourite football **player**.
	stage [steɪdʒ]	Bühne	
	Africa ['æfrɪkə]	Afrika	We raised money for people in **Africa**.
p. 87	**them** [ðem]	ihnen	People gave **them** money for charities.
	wrote [rəʊt]	simple past von *to write* (schreiben)	I **wrote** = ich schrieb/ich habe geschrieben
	mouth [maʊθ]	Mund	
	chimpanzee [ˌtʃɪmpn'ziː]	Schimpanse	Jane Goodall loves **chimpanzees**.
	to fight [faɪt], **fought** [fɔːt]	kämpfen; (sich) streiten	She **fights** for them.
	to stop [stɒp]	beenden; aufhören; anhalten	The teacher **stopped** the argument.
	experiment [ɪk'sperɪmənt]	Versuch; Experiment	Jane wants to stop animal **experiments**.
	all around the world [ɔːl‿əˌraʊnd ðə 'wɜːld]	in aller Welt	Her projects are **all around the world**.
	to save [seɪv]	retten; sparen	We can all help to **save** chimpanzees.
	environment [ɪn'vaɪrnmənt]	Umwelt; Umgebung	We can also help to save the **environment**.

Topic 1

p. 88	**e-mail** ['iːmeɪl]	E-Mail	We stay in contact by **e-mail**.
	to be lucky [biː‿'lʌki]	Glück haben	I'**m lucky** my dad can help me.
	restaurant ['restrɒnt]	Restaurant	
	to watch [wɒtʃ]	zuschauen; zusehen; beobachten	I **watch** my dad in the kitchen. 
	chef [ʃef]	Koch; Köchin; Küchenchef; Küchenchefin	
	to show [ʃəʊ]	zeigen	He **shows** and tells me things.
	quite [kwaɪt]	ziemlich; ganz; völlig	I'm **quite** good at cooking.
	meal [miːl]	Mahlzeit; Essen	**meals**: breakfast, lunch, dinner
	chicken fried rice ['tʃɪkɪn ˌfraɪd 'raɪs]	gebratener Reis mit Hühnerfleisch	I can cook **chicken fried rice** without help.
	nobody ['nəʊbədi]	niemand	**Nobody** can cook it like me.
	fast [fɑːst]	schnell	I'm really **fast** in the kitchen too.
	a cup of [ə 'kʌp‿əv]	eine Tasse …	Would you like **a cup of** tea?

a piece of [ə 'pi:s‿əv]	ein Stück …	I'd like **a piece of** cake, please.
a bottle of [ə 'bɒtl‿əv]	eine Flasche …	
oil [ɔɪl]	Öl	You need a bottle of **oil**.
to **go skating** [ˌgəʊ 'skeɪtɪŋ]	inlineskaten gehen; Schlittschuhlaufen gehen	I **went skating** yesterday.
still [stɪl]	noch; immer noch	I'm **still** learning, but it was fun.
hobby ['hɒbi]	Hobby	R хобби T hobi
to **skate** [skeɪt]	inlineskaten; Schlittschuh laufen	I **skated** for about two hours.
of course [əv 'kɔ:s]	natürlich; selbstverständlich	We all wore helmets **of course**.
quiet [kwaɪət]	leise; ruhig; still	My dad's sleeping so I have to be **quiet**.
this morning [ðɪs 'mɔ:nɪŋ]	heute Morgen	He finished work at 3:00 **this morning**.
her [hɜ:]	sie	Holly is great! I like **her**.
Yours, [jɔ:z]	Dein *(Grußformel in Briefen oder E-Mails)*	So kannst du im Englischen Briefe und E-Mails abschließen: **Yours, …**

Das kenne ich schon

of

a cup of … [ə 'kʌp‿əv]	eine Tasse …	a bag of … [ə 'bæg‿əv]	eine Tüte …
a piece of … [ə 'pi:s‿əv]	ein Stück …	a box of … [ə 'bɒks‿əv]	eine Box; Schachtel …
a bottle of … [ə 'bɒtl‿əv]	eine Flasche …	a kilo of … [ə 'ki:ləʊ əv]	ein Kilo …

Das kenne ich schon

object pronouns

me [mi:]	mich; mir	it [ɪt]	es; ihm
you [ju:]	dich; dir; Sie; Ihnen	us [ʌs]	uns
him [hɪm]	ihn; ihm	you [ju:]	euch; Sie; Ihnen
her [hɜ:]	sie; ihr	them [ðem]	sie *(Pl.)*; ihnen *(Pl.)*

Chinese food

Chinese [tʃaɪ'ni:z]	chinesisch	I smell food in the air [aɪ smel ˌfu:d ɪn ði 'eə]	ich rieche Essen in der Luft
balling ['bɔ:lɪŋ]	Ballspielen	noodle ['nu:dl]	Nudel
to go clubbing [ˌgəʊ 'klʌbɪŋ]	ausgehen	chow mein [ˌtʃaʊ 'meɪn]	Chow Mein *(chinesisches Gericht)*
hugging ['hʌgɪŋ]	umarmen		
grumpy ['grʌmpi]	mürrisch; schlecht gelaunt		

Topic 2

p. 92	**on** [ɒn]	*hier:* mit	Olivia had an accident **on** her bike.
	at the doctor's [ət ðə 'dɒktəz]	beim Arzt	I was **at the doctor's** yesterday.
	to fall off [ˌfɔ:l‿'ɒf]	von etw. stürzen; herunterfallen; hinunterfallen	I **fell off** my bike this morning.
	to hurt [hɜ:t], **hurt** [hɜ:t]	verletzen; wehtun	I **hurt** my face when I fell off.
	tooth *(sg)* [tu:θ], **teeth** *(pl)* [ti:θ]	Zahn	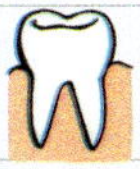
	nose [nəʊz]	Nase	My **nose** also hurts.
	arm [ɑ:m]	Arm	 
	head [hed]	Kopf	
	leg [leg]	Bein	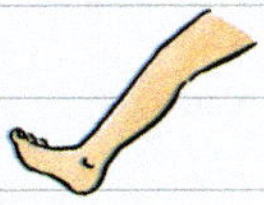
	headache ['hedeɪk]	Kopfweh; Kopfschmerzen	I have a **headache** too.
	nothing ['nʌθɪŋ]	nichts	Do **nothing** today and tomorrow.
	serious ['sɪəriəs]	ernst; schwer	I think it's nothing **serious**.

Das kenne ich schon

parts of the body

foot *(sg)* [fʊt], feet *(pl)* [fi:t]	Fuß	head [hed]	Kopf
tooth *(sg)* [tu:θ], teeth *(pl)* [ti:θ]	Zahn	face [feɪs]	Gesicht
leg [leg]	Bein	eye [aɪ]	Auge
arm [ɑ:m]	Arm	nose [nəʊz]	Nase
hand [hænd]	Hand	mouth [maʊθ]	Mund

Text

p. 96	**teen** [ti:n]	Jugend-; Teenager; Teenagerin; Jugendlicher; Jugendliche	Joe is the best **teen** chef. He won a prize.
	to test [test]	testen; prüfen	I have a dream job, I **test** ice cream.
	roller coaster ['rəʊlə ˌkəʊstə]	Achterbahn	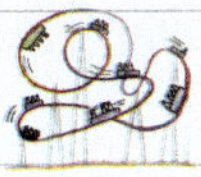
	ride [raɪd]	Fahrt; Fahrgeschäft; Ritt	I like scary **rides**. 
	theme park ['θi:m ˌpɑ:k]	Freizeitpark	
	amazing [ə'meɪzɪŋ]	erstaunlich; unglaublich; toll	Emma is an **amazing** teen.
	young [jʌŋ]	jung	**young** ↔ old
	magician [mə'dʒɪʃn]	Zauberkünstler; Zauberkünstlerin	
	all over [ˌɔ:l‿'əʊvə]	in ganz; überall	She sang **all over** Great Britain.

	Britain ['brɪtn]	Großbritannien	**Britain** is part of the UK.
	a/one thousand ['θaʊznd]	tausend; eintausend	She won **a thousand** pounds.
p. 97	to **climb** [klaɪm]	besteigen; klettern; erklettern; steigen	to **climb** → rock climbing
	mountain ['maʊntɪn]	Berg	
	to **become** [bɪ'kʌm], **became** [bɪ'keɪm]	(zu etw.) werden	I **became** the youngest winner of the race.
	person ['pɜ:sn]	Mensch; Person	one **person** – two people
	Chinese [tʃaɪ'ni:z]	chinesisch; Chinesisch; aus China; Chinese; Chinesin	My family likes **Chinese** food.
	side [saɪd]	Seite	We were on this **side** of the road.
	continent ['kɒntɪnənt]	Kontinent; Erdteil	Europe is a **continent**.
	Antarctica [æn'tɑ:ktɪkə]	Antarktis	There are mountains in **Antarctica**.
	to **spend** [spend], **spent** [spent]	verbringen *(Zeit)*; ausgeben *(Geld)*	Lily **spends** lots of time at the doctor's.
	hospital ['hɒspɪtl]	Krankenhaus	
	to **hold** [həʊld], **held** [held]	halten; festhalten	I **hold** my sister's hand in hospital.
	to **take** [teɪk]	*hier:* hinbringen	I **take** Lily to the skateboard park.

Film

acting workshop ['æktɪŋ ˌwɜ:kʃɒp]	Schauspielworkshop	to believe [bɪ'li:v]	glauben
drama ['drɑ:mə]	Theater-	See you. ['si: ˌju:]	Tschüss.; Bis bald.

Unit 6 Goodbye Greenwich

Intro

p. 105	**captain** ['kæptɪn]	Kapitän; Kapitänin; Mannschaftsführer; Mannschaftsführerin	Luke is **captain** of the football team.
	Guess what? [ges 'wɒt]	Stellt euch vor!; Stell dir vor!	**Guess what?** My dad has a new job!
	engineer [ˌendʒɪ'nɪə]	Ingenieur; Ingenieurin; Techniker; Technikerin	R инженер
	to **leave** [li:v], **left** [left]	verlassen; lassen; abfahren; weggehen	We **leave** Greenwich in August.
	soon [su:n]	bald	We can talk **soon**.
	will [wɪl]	werden	We **will** miss you!
	to **believe** [bɪ'li:v]	glauben	I can't **believe** it.

	so [səʊ]	so; dermaßen	I'm **so** sad. I don't want to go.
	far [fɑː]	weit	Chicago is so **far** away.
	to **be a long way away** [biː ə ˈlɒŋ ˌweɪ əˈweɪ]	weit weg sein	Dave's new home **is a long way away**.
	to **hope (for)** [həʊp]	hoffen (auf)	Luke **hopes** Dave will visit them soon.
	to **agree (with)** [əˈgriː]	zustimmen; einer Meinung sein (mit)	You're right. I **agree** with you.
p. 104	**pier** [pɪə]	Pier	Let's go to the **pier** on Saturday.
	to **move** [muːv]	umziehen	Dave's family **moves** to Chicago.
p. 105	**news** [njuːz]	Neuigkeit(en); Nachricht(en)	I have great **news**!
	excited [ɪkˈsaɪtɪd]	aufgeregt; begeistert	The game is tomorrow. I'm so **excited**!
	answer [ˈɑːnsə]	Antwort	Thank you for your **answer**.
	Congratulations! [kənˌgrætʃəˈleɪʃnz]	Glückwunsch!	**Congratulations!** You're the winner!
	That's too bad. [ˌðæts tuː ˈbæd]	Schade!	Sorry, I can't come. – **That's too bad.**
	Well done! [ˌwel ˈdʌn]	Gut gemacht!	**Well done!** You won first prize.

Topic 1

p. 106	**What's the weather like?** [ˌwɒts ðə ˈweðə laɪk]	Wie ist das Wetter?	**What's the weather like** in your town?
	weather [ˈweðə]	Wetter; Witterung	The **weather** is fine today.
	warm [wɔːm]	warm	**warm** ↔ cold
	sunny [ˈsʌni]	sonnig	The weather here is warm and **sunny**.
	shorts *(pl)* [ʃɔːts]	Shorts; kurze Hose	
	mountain lion [ˈmaʊntɪn ˌlaɪən]	Puma	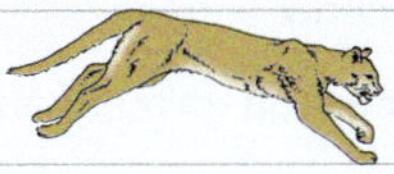
	rainy [ˈreɪni]	regnerisch	**rainy** → to rain 
	snow [snəʊ]	Schnee	
	cloudy [ˈklaʊdi]	bewölkt; wolkig	It's very **cloudy** today.
	season [ˈsiːzn]	Jahreszeit; Saison	**seasons**: winter, summer, …
	hat [hæt]	Mütze; Hut	
	glove [glʌv]	Handschuh	
	bear [beə]	Bär	
	snowy [ˈsnəʊi]	schneereich; verschneit	It is cold and **snowy** in Chicago. 
	sun [sʌn]	Sonne	
	spring [sprɪŋ]	Frühling	**spring**: March, April, May

	autumn ['ɔ:təm]	Herbst	**autumn**: September, October, November
	mild [maɪld]	mild	Achtung Aussprache!
	windy ['wɪndi]	windig	**windy** → wind
	rest [rest]	Rest	Would you like the **rest** of the cake?
	dry [draɪ]	trocken	**dry** ↔ wet
	alligator ['ælɪgeɪtə]	Alligator	R аллигатор T alligator 
	cloud [klaʊd]	Wolke	
p. 109	**United States** [ju:ˌnaɪtɪd'steɪts]	Vereinigte Staaten	

Das kenne ich schon

weather adjectives

sunny ['sʌni]	sonnig	cloudy ['klaʊdi]	bewölkt; wolkig
wet [wet]	nass	snowy ['snəʊi]	schneereich; verschneit
cold [kəʊld]	kalt	dry [draɪ]	trocken
hot [hɒt]	heiß	mild [maɪld]	mild
windy ['wɪndi]	windig	rainy ['reɪni]	regnerisch
warm [wɔ:m]	warm		

Das kenne ich schon

seasons

spring [sprɪŋ]	Frühling	autumn ['ɔ:təm]	Herbst
summer ['sʌmə]	Sommer	winter ['wɪntə]	Winter

Topic 2

p. 110	**leaving** ['li:vɪŋ]	Abschieds-	There's a **leaving** party on Dave's last day.
	American [ə'merɪkən]	amerikanisch; Amerikanisch; aus Amerika; Amerikaner; Amerikanerin	T Amerikali
	muffin ['mʌfɪn]	Muffin	
	Is something wrong? [ɪz 'sʌmθɪŋ rɒŋ]	Stimmt etwas nicht?	**Is something wrong**, Dave?
	Well, … [wel]	Na ja, …; Also …	**Well**, I'm a little bit worried.
	won't (= will not) [wəʊnt]	nicht werden	We **won't** go away. = We will not go away.
	to make friends [ˌmeɪk 'frendz]	Freundschaft(en) schließen	
	silly ['sɪli]	albern	Don't be **silly**! We won't forget you.
	to chat [tʃæt]	chatten; plaudern	We can **chat**.
	online [ˌɒn'laɪn]	online; Online-	We can play a game **online**.

	at the same time [ət ðə seɪm 'taɪm]	gleichzeitig; nebenher	We arrived **at the same time**.
	to **upload** [ʌp'ləʊd]	hochladen	Dave **uploads** photos for his friends.
	to **keep in touch** [ˌki:p ɪn 'tʌtʃ]	in Kontakt bleiben	I hope we'll **keep in touch**.
	to **keep** [ki:p], **kept** [kept]	halten	A coat **keeps** you warm.
p. 113	**See you.** ['si: ˌju:]	Wir sehen uns.; Bis bald.; Tschüss.	**See you** in June.

Text

p. 114	**ago** [ə'gəʊ]	vor	We arrived in Chicago three weeks **ago**.
	to **catch** [kætʃ], **caught** [kɔ:t]	fangen	Sid **caught** two mice yesterday.
	to **ask about** ['ɑ:sk əˌbaʊt]	fragen nach; sich erkundigen nach	Holly **asked about** the shops in Chicago.
	everywhere ['evriweə]	überallhin; überall	People go **everywhere** by car.
	mall [mɔ:l]	Einkaufspassage; Einkaufszentrum	You can buy nearly everything in **malls**.
	kind [kaɪnd]	Art; Sorte	What **kind** of music do you like?
	... as well as ... [əz 'wel‿əz]	sowohl ... als auch ...	I like pop music **as well as** rap music.
	to **travel** ['trævl]	*hier:* fahren; reisen	I **travelled** on the underground yesterday.
	once [wʌns]	einmal; einst	I visited the museum **once**. It was boring.
	to **understand** [ˌʌndə'stænd], **understood** [ˌʌndə'stʊd]	verstehen	Did you **understand** everything?
p. 115	**grade** *(AE)* [greɪd]	Klasse; Jahrgangsstufe; Note	AE: **grade** BE: year; mark
	junior high school [ˌdʒu:niə 'haɪ sku:l]	Junior Highschool *(Mittelschule in den USA, in der Regel Klassenstufe 7–9)*	I'm in 8th grade at **junior high school**.
	square dance ['skweə ˌdɑ:ns]	Squaredance *(amerikanischer Volkstanz)*	My favourite club here is **square dance**.
	wall painting ['wɔ:l peɪntɪŋ]	Wandmalerei	
	to **paint** [peɪnt]	bemalen; malen; streichen	They **paint** walls in the school.
	design [dɪ'zaɪn]	Design; Gestaltung; Entwurf	Your **design** looks great.
	soccer *(AE)* ['sɒkə]	Fußball	AE: **soccer** BE: football
	American football [əˌmerɪkən 'fʊtbɔ:l]	American Football	 
	basketball ['bɑ:skɪtbɔ:l]	Basketball	

All the best, [ɔ:l ðə 'best]	Alles Gute	So kannst du im Englischen Briefe und E-Mails abschließen: **All the best, …**

Film

cave [keɪv]	Höhle
grandad ['grændæd]	Opa
to be called [bi: 'kɔ:ld]	heißen; genannt werden
to tell sb to do sth ['tel sʌmbədi tə ˌdu: sʌmθɪŋ]	jmdm. etw. auftragen
to stay away from [ˌsteɪ ə'weɪ frəm]	sich fernhalten von
I think so too. [aɪ 'θɪŋk səʊ ˌtu:]	Das denke ich auch.
I don't think so. [ˌaɪ dəʊnt 'θɪŋk səʊ]	Das glaube ich nicht.

Dictionary

Die Abkürzungen geben an, wo das Wort zum ersten Mal vorkommt.
Verwendete Abkürzungen und Zeichen:

U = Unit
* = unregelmäßige Verben

I = Band 1
II U4, 70 = Band 2, Unit 4, S. 70
<II U4, 75> = nur zum Nachschlagen, gehört nicht zum Lernwortschatz

A

a [ə] ein; eine I
a little (bit) [ə 'lɪtl (bɪt)] ein (kleines) bisschen; ein (klein) wenig II U4, 70
a lot [ə 'lɒt] viel; sehr I
a lot of [ə 'lɒt‿əv] viel; viele; eine Menge I
a/one hundred ['hʌndrəd] hundert; einhundert I
a/one thousand ['θaʊznd] tausend; eintausend II U5, 96
a.m. [ˌeɪ'em] vormittags *(Uhrzeit)* <II U4, 75>
about [ə'baʊt] über I; ungefähr; circa; etwa II U3, 49; an <II U3, 64>
to hang about [ˌhæŋ‿ə'baʊt] herumhängen I
above [ə'bʌv] über; oberhalb II U2, 33
Abracadabra! [ˌæbrəkə'dæbrə] Abrakadabra! II U3, 60
accident ['æksɪdnt] Unfall I
acrobat ['ækrəbæt] Akrobat; Akrobatin <II U5, 101>
across [ə'krɒs] über II U3, 57
to **act** [ækt] spielen <I>
to act out ['ækt aʊt] aufführen <II U4, 83>
acting workshop ['æktɪŋ ˌwɜ:kʃɒp] Schauspielworkshop <II U5, 99>
activity [æk'tɪvəti] Aktivität I
actor ['æktə] Darsteller; Schauspieler; Schauspielerin <II U3, 62>
to **add** [æd] hinzufügen <I>
address [ə'dres] Adresse <II U6, 116>
adult ['ædʌlt] Erwachsener; Erwachsene <II U3, 62>
adventure [əd'ventʃə] Abenteuer <II U6, 116>
aeroball ['eərəbɔ:l] Aeroball <II U6, 116>
aerobics [eə'rəʊbɪks] Aerobic <II U4, 171>
after ['ɑ:ftə] nach I
after that [ˌɑ:ftə 'ðæt] danach I
afternoon [ˌɑ:ftə'nu:n] Nachmittag I
again [ə'gen] noch einmal; wieder I
ago [ə'gəʊ] vor II U6, 114
to **agree** (with) [ə'gri:] zustimmen; einer Meinung sein (mit) II U6, 105
alarm clock [ə'lɑ:m ˌklɒk] Wecker <II U2, 164>
all [ɔ:l] alle; ganz I
all of ['ɔ:l‿əv] ganz II U3, 60
all over [ˌɔ:l‿'əʊvə] in ganz; überall II U5, 96
all around the world [ɔ:l‿əˌraʊnd ðə 'wɜ:ld] in aller Welt II U5, 87
All the best, [ɔ:l ðə 'best] Alles Gute II U6, 115
allergy ['ælədʒi] Allergie <II U6, 116>
alligator ['ælɪgeɪtə] Alligator II U6, 106
alphabet ['ælfəbet] Alphabet <I>
alphabetical [ˌælfə'betɪkl] alphabetisch <II U5, 96>
also ['ɔ:lsəʊ] auch I
always ['ɔ:lweɪz] immer I
am [æm] bin I
amazing [ə'meɪzɪŋ] unglaublich; erstaunlich; toll II U5, 96
American [ə'merɪkən] amerikanisch; Amerikanisch; aus Amerika; Amerikaner; Amerikanerin II U6, 110
American football [əˌmerɪkən 'fʊtbɔ:l] American Football II U6, 115
an [æn] ein; eine I
and [ænd] und I
And you? [ənd 'ju:] Und du? I
angry ['æŋgri] wütend; zornig; verärgert; böse II U1, 15
animal ['ænɪml] Tier I
animal rescue shelter [ˌænɪml 'reskju: ˌʃeltə] Tierheim I
announcement [ə'naʊnsmənt] Durchsage; Ankündigung <II U4, 75>
another [ə'nʌðə] ein anderer; noch ein <I>
answer ['ɑ:nsə] Antwort II U6, 105
to **answer** ['ɑ:nsə] antworten; beantworten II U1, 20
any ['eni] irgendwelche; irgendeine I
Anything else? [ˌeniθɪŋ 'els] Darf es sonst noch etwas sein? I
apple ['æpl] Apfel I
April ['eɪprl] April I
are [ɑ:] bist; sind I
argument ['ɑ:gjəmənt] Auseinandersetzung; Streit II U1, 15
arm [ɑ:m] Arm II U5, 92
around [ə'raʊnd] um … herum II U3, 60
to walk around [ˌwɔ:k‿ə'raʊnd] umherlaufen; herumlaufen <I>
to **arrive** [ə'raɪv] ankommen I
Art [ɑ:t] Kunst I
as [æz] wie; als II U1, 15
… as well as … [əz 'wel‿əz] sowohl … als auch … II U6, 114
to **ask** [ɑ:sk] fragen I
to ask about ['ɑ:sk əˌbaʊt] fragen nach; sich erkundigen nach II U6, 114
to ask the way [ˌɑ:sk ðə 'weɪ] nach dem Weg fragen <II U3, 59>
assistant [ə'sɪstnt] Verkäufer; Verkäuferin I
at [æt] zu; in; an; auf; um; bei I

at home [ət 'həʊm] zu Hause; daheim I
at school [ət 'sku:l] in der Schule I
at the back (of) [ət ðə 'bæk] hinten (in) <II U3, 166>
at the doctor's [ət ðə 'dɒktəz] beim Arzt II U5, 92
at the end [ˌət ði 'end] am Ende II U4, 68
at the front (of) [ət ðə 'frʌnt] vorne (in) <II U3, 166>
at the moment [ət ðə 'məʊmənt] im Moment; momentan II U3, 53
at the same time [ət ðə seɪm 'taɪm] gleichzeitig; nebenher II U6, 110
at the seaside [ət ðə 'si:saɪd] am Meer I

ate [eɪt] simple past von *to eat* II U1, 10
attic ['ætɪk] Dachboden I
audio guide ['ɔ:diəʊ ˌgaɪd] Audioguide <II U3, 64>
August ['ɔ:gəst] August I
aunt [ɑ:nt] Tante I
autumn ['ɔ:təm] Herbst II U6, 106
away [ə'weɪ] weg; entfernt II U2, 40
to be a long way away [bi: ə 'lɒŋ ˌweɪ ə'weɪ] weit weg sein II U6, 105
to stay away from [ˌsteɪ ə'weɪ frəm] sich fernhalten von <II U6, 117>
awful ['ɔ:fl] schrecklich; furchtbar I

B

baby ['beɪbi] Baby <II U3, 64>
*to **babysit** ['beɪbisɪt] babysitten <II U5, 174>
at the **back** (of) [ət ðə 'bæk] hinten (in) <II U3, 166>
back [bæk] zurück II U1, 8
bacon ['beɪkn] Speck I
bad [bæd] schlecht I; schlimm II U4, 70
That's too bad. [ˌðæts tu: 'bæd] Schade! II U6, 105
badminton ['bædmɪntən] Badminton; Federball <II U4, 80>
bag [bæg] Tasche; Tüte; Sack I
bakery ['beɪkri] Bäckerei <II U4, 169>
balcony ['bælkəni] Balkon I
ball [bɔ:l] Ball I
banana [bə'nɑ:nə] Banane I
band [bænd] Band; Musikgruppe II U1, 10
snack **bar** ['snæk ˌbɑ:] Imbissstube; Café I
barbecue ['bɑ:bɪkju:] Grill; Grillfest I
to **bark** [bɑ:k] bellen II U2, 40
baseball cap ['beɪsbɔ:l ˌkæp] Baseballkappe <II U2, 165>
basketball ['bɑ:skɪtbɔ:l] Basketball II U6, 115
bat [bæt] Fledermaus I
bathroom ['bɑ:θrʊm] Bad(ezimmer) II U2, 30
battery ['bætri] Batterie; Akku <II U1, 23>
*to **be** [bi:] sein I
to be a long way away [bi: ə 'lɒŋ ˌweɪ ə'weɪ] weit weg sein II U6, 105
to be called [bi: 'kɔ:ld] heißen; genannt werden <II U6, 117>
to be fun [bi: 'fʌn] Spaß machen; witzig sein II U3, 60
to be good at [bi: 'gʊd‿ət] gut sein in; gut sein bei I
to be late [bi: 'leɪt] zu spät kommen II U1, 8
to be lucky [bi:‿'lʌki] Glück haben II U5, 88
to be scared [bi: 'skeəd] Angst haben I
to be sick [bi: 'sɪk] sich übergeben I
to be stuck [bi: 'stʌk] feststecken; stecken bleiben I
beach [bi:tʃ] Strand I
bear [beə] Bär II U6, 106
became [bɪ'keɪm] simple past von *to become* II U5, 97
because [bɪ'kɒz] weil; da I
*to **become** [bɪ'kʌm] (zu etw.) werden II U5, 97
bed [bed] Bett I
to go to bed [ˌgəʊ tə 'bed] ins Bett gehen I
bedroom ['bedrʊm] Kinderzimmer; Schlafzimmer II U2, 28
bedside table [ˌbedsaɪd 'teɪbl] Nachttisch <II U2, 42>
before [bɪ'fɔ:] vor; bevor II U2, 30
beginning [bɪ'gɪnɪŋ] Anfang; Beginn II U4, 69
behind [bɪ'haɪnd] hinter I
to **believe** [bɪ'li:v] glauben II U6, 105
bell [bel] Glocke II U3, 50
best [best] am besten; beste; am liebsten II U2, 33
All the best, [ɔ:l ðə 'best] Alles Gute II U6, 115
Best wishes, [ˌbest 'wɪʃɪz] Viele Grüße; Alles Gute I
better ['betə] besser II U2, 33
between [bɪ'twi:n] zwischen <II U6, 115>
big [bɪg] groß I
big wheel [ˌbɪg 'wi:l] Riesenrad II U3, 48
bike [baɪk] Fahrrad I
to go bike riding [ˌgəʊ 'baɪk ˌraɪdɪŋ] Fahrrad fahren II U1, 10
Biology [baɪ'ɒlədʒi] Biologie I
date of **birth** [ˌdeɪt‿əv 'bɜ:θ] Geburtsdatum <II U6, 116>
birthday ['bɜ:θdeɪ] Geburtstag I
bit [bɪt] Teil; Stück <II U3, 62>
black [blæk] schwarz I
blackboard ['blækbɔ:d] Tafel I
blog [blɒg] Blog; Internettagebuch I
blouse [blaʊz] Bluse <II U2, 165>
blue [blu:] blau I
board game ['bɔ:d ˌgeɪm] Brettspiel <II U6, 116>
boccia ['bɒtʃə] Boccia *(italienisches Kugelspiel)* <II U4, 170>
book [bʊk] Buch; Heft I
exercise book ['eksəsaɪz ˌbʊk] Übungsheft I
bored [bɔ:d] gelangweilt <II U6, 116>
boring ['bɔ:rɪŋ] langweilig I
to **borrow** ['bɒrəʊ] (sich) ausleihen II U1, 15
botanical [bə'tænɪkl] botanisch <II U3, 167>
a **bottle** of [ə 'bɒtl‿əv] eine Flasche … II U5, 88
bottle bank ['bɒtl ˌbæŋk] Altglascontainer <II U2, 163>
bought [bɔ:t] simple past von *to buy* I
to **bounce** [baʊns] hüpfen <II U6, 116>
bowling ['bəʊlɪŋ] Bowlen <II U4, 169>
box [bɒks] Box; Kiste; Schachtel I
telephone box ['telɪfəʊn ˌbɒks] Telefonzelle II U3, 50

boy [bɔɪ] Junge; Bub I
bread [bred] Brot I
break [breɪk] Pause I
breakfast ['brekfəst] Frühstück I
to have breakfast [ˌhæv 'brekfəst] frühstücken I
bridge [brɪdʒ] Brücke II U3, 49
brilliant ['brɪliənt] toll <II U1, 161>
*to **bring** [brɪŋ] mitbringen; bringen II U1, 15
brother ['brʌðə] Bruder I
brought [brɔ:t] simple past von *to bring* II U1, 15
brown [braʊn] braun I
*to **build** [bɪld] bauen II U3, 48
building ['bɪldɪŋ] Gebäude; Bauwerk II U3, 50
built [bɪlt] simple past von *to build* II U3, 48
burger ['bɜ:gə] Hamburger I
bus [bʌs] Bus I
on the bus [ˌɒn ðə 'bʌs] im Bus II U1, 20
busy ['bɪzi] beschäftigt I
a busy day [ə ˌbɪzi 'deɪ] ein ausgefüllter Tag II U2, 41
but [bʌt] aber I
butter ['bʌtə] Butter I
*to **buy** [baɪ] kaufen I
by [baɪ] von <II U3, 62>
by (train) [baɪ] mit (dem Zug) I
Bye. [baɪ] Tschüss. I

C

café ['kæfeɪ] Café <II U3, 54>
cafeteria [kæfə'tɪəriə] Cafeteria; Mensa I
cage [keɪdʒ] Käfig II U2, 30
cake [keɪk] Kuchen I
calculator ['kælkjəleɪtə] Taschenrechner I
phone **call** ['fəʊn ˌkɔ:l] Telefonanruf; Anruf I
*to be **called** [bi: 'kɔ:ld] heißen; genannt werden <II U6, 117>
call me ['kɔ:l ˌmi] nenne mich I
caller ['kɔ:lə] Anrufer; Anruferin <II U5, 93>
came [keɪm] simple past von *to come* I
*to go **camping** [ˌgəʊ 'kæmpɪŋ] zelten gehen; campen gehen <II U1, 162>
campsite ['kæmpsaɪt] Campingplatz; Zeltplatz <II U1, 22>
can [kæn] Dose <II U4, 170>
can [kæn] können I
can't [kɑ:nt] nicht können I
canoeing [kə'nu:ɪŋ] Kanufahren I
capital (city) ['kæpɪtl] Hauptstadt I
captain ['kæptɪn] Kapitän; Kapitänin; Mannschaftsführer; Mannschaftsführerin II U6, 105
car [kɑ:] Auto I
card [kɑ:d] Karte <I>
cardigan ['kɑ:dɪgən] Strickjacke <II U2, 165>
carefully ['keəfli] sorgfältig; vorsichtig <II U4, 77>
caretaker ['keəˌteɪkə] Hausmeister; Hausmeisterin I
carnival ['kɑ:nɪvl] Karneval; Fasching I
carpet ['kɑ:pɪt] Teppich II U2, 33
castle ['kɑ:sl] Burg; Schloss <II U3, 167>
cat [kæt] Katze I
*to **catch** [kætʃ] fangen II U6, 114
cathedral [kə'θi:drl] Kathedrale; Dom <II U3, 167>
caught [kɔ:t] simple past von *to catch* II U6, 114
cave [keɪv] Höhle <II U6, 117>
centre ['sentə] Zentrum; Center <II U3, 64>
city centre [ˌsɪti 'sentə] Stadtzentrum; Stadtmitte II U3, 50
shopping centre ['ʃɒpɪŋ ˌsentə] Einkaufszentrum I
sports centre ['spɔ:ts ˌsentə] Sportzentrum I
chair [tʃeə] Stuhl I
champion ['tʃæmpiən] Gewinner; Gewinnerin; Sieger; Siegerin <I>
change [tʃeɪndʒ] Wechselgeld I
Here's your change. [ˌhɪəz jɔ: 'tʃeɪndʒ] Hier ist dein Wechselgeld. I
to **change** [tʃeɪndʒ] verändern; ändern; wechseln II U2, 33
chant [tʃɑ:nt] Sprechgesang <I>
character ['kærəktə] Figur; Charakter <II U3, 67>
charades [ʃə'rɑ:dz] Scharaden <II U3, 56>
charity ['tʃærɪti] Wohltätigkeitsorganisation; Stiftung; wohltätige Zwecke; Wohltätigkeits- II U4, 69
chart [tʃɑ:t] Tabelle; Diagramm <I>
to **chat** [tʃæt] chatten; plaudern II U6, 110
cheap [tʃi:p] günstig; billig II U2, 36
to **check** [tʃek] überprüfen; kontrollieren II U3, 60
checklist ['tʃeklɪst] Checkliste <I>
checkout ['tʃekaʊt] Kontrolle <I>
cheese [tʃi:z] Käse I
chef [ʃef] Koch; Köchin; Küchenchef; **Küchenchefin** II U5, 88
chess [tʃes] Schach <II U5, 174>
chest of drawers [ˌtʃest‿əv 'drɔ:z] Kommode <II U2, 42>
chicken ['tʃɪkɪn] Hähnchen; Huhn I
chicken fried rice ['tʃɪkɪn ˌfraɪd 'raɪs] gebratener Reis mit Hühnerfleisch II U5, 88
child *(sg)* [tʃaɪld] Kind <II U3, 62>
children *(pl)* ['tʃɪldrən] Kinder I
chimpanzee [ˌtʃɪmpn'zi:] Schimpanse II U5, 87
Chinese [tʃaɪ'ni:z] chinesisch; Chinesisch; aus China; Chinese; Chinesin II U5, 97
chips *(pl)* [tʃɪps] Pommes frites I
chocolate ['tʃɒklət] Schokolade I
choir [kwaɪə] Chor <II U5, 174>
*to **choose** [tʃu:z] wählen; auswählen <I>
chorus ['kɔ:rəs] Refrain <I>
Christmas ['krɪsməs] Weihnachten I
Merry Christmas! [ˌmeri 'krɪsməs] Frohe Weihnachten! I
church [tʃɜ:tʃ] Kirche II U3, 49
cinema ['sɪnəmə] Kino I
city ['sɪti] Stadt; Großstadt I
city centre [ˌsɪti 'sentə] Stadtzentrum; Stadtmitte II U3, 50
class [klɑ:s] Klasse I
classmate ['klɑ:smeɪt] Klassenkamerad; Klassenkameradin; Mitschüler; Mitschülerin <II U1, 22>

to clean [kli:n] sauber machen; putzen II U2, 30
to clear the table [ˌklɪə ðə 'teɪbl] den Tisch abräumen <II U2, 163>
That was very **clear.** [ðæt wɒz veri 'klɪə] Das war sehr klar. <I>
to climb [klaɪm] besteigen; klettern; erklettern; steigen II U5, 97
clock [klɒk] Uhr II U3, 49
o'clock [ə'klɒk] Uhr *(Zeitangabe bei vollen Stunden)* I
to close [kləʊz] zumachen; schließen I
closed [kləʊzd] geschlossen I
clothes *(pl only)* [kləʊðz] Kleider; Kleidung I
cloud [klaʊd] Wolke II U6, 106
cloudy ['klaʊdi] bewölkt; wolkig II U6, 106
club [klʌb] Klub; Treff; Schul-AG I
clue [klu:] Hinweis; Spur I
coast [kəʊst] Küste <II U5, 98>
coat [kəʊt] Jacke I
cola ['kəʊlə] Cola I
cold [kəʊld] kalt I; Erkältung; Kälte II U4, 70
collar ['kɒlə] Halsband I
to collect [kə'lekt] sammeln <I>
colour ['kʌlə] Farbe I
*__to come__ [kʌm] kommen I
Come on! [ˌkʌm_'ɒn] Komm(t) jetzt! II U4, 78
comic ['kɒmɪk] Comic(heft) II U2, 33
company ['kʌmpəni] Unternehmen; Firma; Gesellschaft II U1, 20
to compare [kəm'peə] vergleichen <I>
competition [ˌkɒmpə'tɪʃn] Wettbewerb <II U3, 67>
to complete [kəm'pli:t] vervollständigen <I>
computer [ˌkəm'pju:tə] Computer I
concert ['kɒnsət] Konzert I
conclusion [kən'klu:ʒn] Schluss; Schlussfolgerung <II U5, 100>
Congratulations! [kənˌgrætʃə'leɪʃnz] Glückwunsch! II U6, 105
contact ['kɒntækt] Kontakt I
continent ['kɒntɪnənt] Kontinent; Erdteil II U5, 97
to cook [kʊk] kochen II U2, 30
cooking ['kʊkɪŋ] Kochen; Koch- II U2, 30
cool [ku:l] cool; super I
to correct [kə'rekt] verbessern; richtigstellen; korrigieren II U3, 61
correct [kə'rekt] richtig; korrekt <I>
costume ['kɒstju:m] Kostüm I
country ['kʌntri] Land; ländliche Gegend I
of course [əv 'kɔ:s] natürlich; selbstverständlich II U5, 88
cousin ['kʌzn] Cousin; Cousine II U1, 10
crazy ['kreɪzi] verrückt <II U2, 43>
creative [kri'eɪtɪv] kreativ <II U4, 80>
cricket ['krɪkɪt] Kricket II U1, 10
crown jewels *(pl)* [ˌkraʊn 'dʒu:əlz] Kronjuwelen II U3, 60
culture ['kʌltʃə] Kultur <I>
a **cup** of [ə 'kʌp_əv] eine Tasse … II U5, 88
customer ['kʌstəmə] Kunde; Kundin I
*__to cut out__ ['kʌt_aʊt] ausschneiden <II U6, 118>

D

dad [dæd] Papa; Vati I
dance [dɑ:ns] Tanz <II U4, 80>
square dance ['skweə ˌdɑ:ns] Squaredance *(amerikanischer Volkstanz)* II U6, 115
to dance [dɑ:ns] tanzen I
dancer ['dɑ:nsə] Tänzer; Tänzerin I
dark [dɑ:k] dunkel I
date [deɪt] Datum; Zeitpunkt <II U4, 71>
date of birth [ˌdeɪt_əv 'bɜ:θ] Geburtsdatum <II U6, 116>
daughter ['dɔ:tə] Tochter I
day [deɪ] Tag I
a busy day [ə ˌbɪzi 'deɪ] ein ausgefüllter Tag II U2, 41
lucky day [ˌlʌki 'deɪ] Glückstag II U1, 20
one day ['wʌn deɪ] eines Tages I
open day ['əʊpn ˌdeɪ] Tag der offenen Tür <II U4, 80>
sports day ['spɔ:ts ˌdeɪ] Sportfest II U4, 69
Dear …, [dɪə] Liebe(r) …, *(Anrede in Briefen)* I
December [dɪ'sembə] Dezember I
delicious [dɪ'lɪʃəs] lecker; köstlich <II U4, 81>
design [dɪ'zaɪn] Design; Gestaltung; Entwurf II U6, 115
DT (Design Technology) [ˌdi:'ti: (dɪˌzaɪn tek'nɒlədʒi)] Technik I
to design [dɪ'zaɪn] gestalten; entwerfen <II U4, 170>
desk [desk] Schreibtisch; Tisch II U2, 33
detective [dɪ'tektɪv] Detektiv; Detektivin I
dialogue ['daɪəlɒg] Dialog; Gespräch II U1, 18
diameter [daɪ'æmɪtə] Durchmesser II U3, 50
diamond ['daɪəmənd] Diamant <II U6, 108>
diary ['daɪəri] Tagebuch I
dictionary ['dɪkʃnri] Wörterbuch <II U5, 95>
did [dɪd] simple past von *to do* I
different ['dɪfrnt] verschieden; unterschiedlich; anders I
dinner ['dɪnə] Mittagessen; Abendessen I
giving **directions** [ˌgɪvɪŋ dɪ'rekʃnz] eine Wegbeschreibung geben; Anweisungen geben <II U3, 59>
director [dɪ'rektə] Leiter; Leiterin <II U5, 98>
dirty ['dɜ:ti] dreckig; schmutzig I
to empty the **dishwasher** [ˌemti ðə 'dɪʃwɒʃə] die Spülmaschine ausräumen II U2, 30
to load the **dishwasher** [ˌləʊd ðə 'dɪʃwɒʃə] die Spülmaschine einräumen II U2, 30
*__to do__ [du:] machen; tun I
to do homework [ˌdu: 'həʊmwɜ:k] Hausaufgabe(n) machen I
to do magic [ˌdu: 'mædʒɪk] zaubern II U3, 60
to do the washing up [ˌdu: ðə 'wɒʃɪŋ_ʌp] abspülen <II U2, 163>
doctor ['dɒktə] Arzt; Ärztin II U5, 92
at the doctor's [ət ðə 'dɒktəz] beim Arzt II U5, 92
dog [dɒg] Hund I
door [dɔ:] Tür II U1, 20

doorbell ['dɔ:bel] Türklingel I
double-decker bus [ˌdʌbldekə 'bʌs] Doppeldeckerbus <II U3, 166>
down [daʊn] hinunter; herunter <II U6, 116>
draft [drɑ:ft] Entwurf <II U6, 109>
drama ['drɑ:mə] Theater- <II U5, 99>
drank [dræŋk] simple past von *to drink* II U3, 53
*to **draw** [drɔ:] zeichnen <I>
dream [dri:m] Traum I
dress [dres] Kleid I
fancy dress [ˌfænsi 'dres] Kostüm; Verkleidung I
drink [drɪŋk] Getränk I
*to **drink** [drɪŋk] trinken II U3, 53
dry [draɪ] trocken II U6, 106
DT (Design Technology) [ˌdi:'ti: (dɪˌzaɪn tek'nɒlədʒi)] Technik I
DVD [ˌdi:vi:'di:] DVD I

E

e.g. (= for example) [ˌi:'dʒi:] z. B. (= zum Beispiel) <II U1, 13>
e-mail ['i:meɪl] E-Mail II U5, 88
each [i:tʃ] jede <I>
early ['ɜ:li] früh II U2, 40
east [i:st] Ost- <II U5, 98>
Easter bonnet [ˌi:stə 'bɒnɪt] Osterhut <II U3, 67>
easy ['i:zi] einfach; leicht I
*to **eat** [i:t] essen I
special **effect** [ˌspeʃl ɪ'fekt] Spezialeffekt <II U3, 62>
egg [eg] Ei I
Eid [i:d] *muslimisches Fest* I
eight [eɪt] acht I
eighteen [ˌeɪ'ti:n] achtzehn I
eighty ['eɪti] achtzig I
elephant ['elɪfənt] Elefant <II U3, 64>
eleven [ɪ'levn] elf I
to **empty** the dishwasher [ˌemti ðə 'dɪʃwɒʃə] die Spülmaschine ausräumen II U2, 30
end [end] Ende; Schluss II U4, 68
at the end [ˌət ði 'end] am Ende II U4, 68
end-of-term [ˌend‿əv 'tɜ:m] Schuljahresabschluss <I>
to **end** [end] enden; beenden <II U1, 24>
engineer [ˌendʒɪ'nɪə] Ingenieur; Ingenieurin; Techniker; Technikerin II U6, 105
English ['ɪŋglɪʃ] Englisch I
to **enjoy** [ɪn'dʒɔɪ] genießen <II U6, 116>
entry ['entri] Eintrag; Eintritt <II U6, 106>
environment [ɪn'vaɪrnmənt] Umwelt; Umgebung II U5, 87
escalator ['eskəleɪtə] Rolltreppe <II U2, 43>
evening ['i:vnɪŋ] Abend I
in the evening [ɪn ði‿'i:vnɪŋ] abends I
event [ɪ'vent] Veranstaltung; Ereignis II U4, 68
every ['evri] jede I; alle II U3, 49
everyday ['evrideɪ] täglich; alltäglich; Alltags- <II U2, 44>
everyone ['evriwʌn] alle; jeder; zusammen II U2, 40
everything ['evriθɪŋ] alles II U1, 20
everywhere ['evriweə] überallhin; überall II U6, 114
example [ɪg'zɑ:mpl] Beispiel <II U4, 82>
excited [ɪk'saɪtɪd] aufgeregt; begeistert II U6, 105
exciting [ɪk'saɪtɪŋ] spannend; aufregend I
Excuse me. [ɪk'skju:z mi] Entschuldigung. II U3, 57
exercise ['eksəsaɪz] Übung I
exercise book ['eksəsaɪz ˌbʊk] Übungsheft I
to get some exercise [get sʌm 'eksəsaɪz] sich etwas Bewegung verschaffen <II U4, 80>
expensive [ɪk'spensɪv] teuer I
experiment [ɪk'sperɪmənt] Versuch; Experiment II U5, 87
to **explain** [ɪk'spleɪn] erklären <II U1, 23>
to **explore** [ɪk'splɔ:] erkunden; erforschen <II U6, 116>
extra ['ekstrə] extra; besonders <II U2, 165>
eye [aɪ] Auge I

F

face [feɪs] Gesicht I
face painting ['feɪs peɪntɪŋ] Schminken II U4, 70
fact [fækt] Fakt; Tatsache II U3, 50
fair [feə] Fest; Messe; Jahrmarkt II U4, 69
*to **fall** [fɔ:l] fallen; hinfallen I
to fall off [ˌfɔ:l‿'ɒf] von etw. stürzen; herunterfallen; hinunterfallen II U5, 92
family ['fæmli] Familie I
family tree [ˌfæmli 'tri:] Familienstammbaum <I>
famous ['feɪməs] berühmt I
fan [fæn] Fan I
fancy dress [ˌfænsi 'dres] Kostüm; Verkleidung I
fantastic [fæn'tæstɪk] fantastisch; großartig II U1, 9
far [fɑ:] weit II U6, 105
farewell [ˌfeə'wel] Abschieds-; Abschied <II U6, 175>
farm [fɑ:m] Bauernhof I
farmer ['fɑ:mə] Bauer; Bäuerin; Landwirt; Landwirtin I
fast [fɑ:st] schnell II U5, 88
father ['fɑ:ðə] Vater I
favourite ['feɪvrɪt] Lieblings- I
February ['februri] Februar I
fed [fed] simple past von *to feed* I
*to **feed** [fi:d] füttern I
feedback ['fi:dbæk] Rückmeldung; Feedback <I>
*to **feel** [fi:l] (sich) fühlen II U1, 10
feeling ['fi:lɪŋ] Gefühl <II U1, 16>
fell [fel] simple past von *to fall* I
felt [felt] simple past von *to feel* II U1, 10
festival ['festɪvl] Fest; Festival <II U4, 169>
science **fiction** [ˌsaɪəns 'fɪkʃn] Science-Fiction I
playing **field** ['pleɪɪŋ ˌfi:ld] Sportplatz II U4, 74
fifteen [ˌfɪf'ti:n] fünfzehn I
fifty ['fɪfti] fünfzig I
*to **fight** [faɪt] kämpfen; (sich) streiten II U5, 87
figure ['fɪgə] Figur; Gestalt II U3, 49
to **fill** [fɪl] füllen <II U4, 70>

to fill in [ˌfɪl‿ˈɪn] eintragen; ausfüllen <II U6, 109>
film [fɪlm] Film I
to film [fɪlm] filmen <II U4, 83>
*to **find** [faɪnd] finden; herausfinden I; entdecken <II U4, 80>
to find out [ˌfaɪnd‿ˈaʊt] herausfinden; erkundigen <I>
fine [faɪn] gut; in Ordnung; schön I
I'm fine. [ˌaɪm ˈfaɪn] Mir geht es gut. I
to **finish** [ˈfɪnɪʃ] fertigstellen; vervollständigen I; beenden; fertig machen; erledigen; enden; aufhören II U1, 20
fire brigade [ˈfaɪə brɪˌgeɪd] Feuerwehr <II U4, 169>
first [ˈfɜ:st] erste I; zuerst; als Erstes II U1, 20
the first time [ðə fɜ:st ˈtaɪm] das erste Mal I
fish *(sg)* [fɪʃ], **fish** *(pl)* [fɪʃ] Fisch I
five [faɪv] fünf I
flag [flæg] Flagge; Fahne <II U6, 118>
flat [flæt] Wohnung I
flea [fli:] Floh I
flea market [ˈfli: ˌmɑ:kɪt] Flohmarkt I
flew [flu:] simple past von *to fly* II U3, 60
floor [flɔ:] Fußboden <II U2, 163>; Stockwerk; Etage II U3, 50
*to **fly** [flaɪ] fliegen II U3, 60
to **follow** [ˈfɒləʊ] folgen <II U5, 98>
food [fu:d] Essen; Lebensmittel I
foot *(sg)* [fʊt], **feet** *(pl)* [fi:t] Fuß II U2, 36
on foot [ɒn ˈfʊt] zu Fuß I
football [ˈfʊtbɔ:l] Fußball I
American football [əˌmerɪkən ˈfʊtbɔ:l] American Football II U6, 115
football boot [ˈfʊtbɔ:l bu:t] Fußballschuh <II U2, 163>
footbridge [ˈfʊtbrɪdʒ] Fußgängerbrücke <II U3, 167>
for [fɔ:] für I
*to **forget** [fəˈget] vergessen II U1, 20
forgot [fəˈgɒt] simple past von *to forget* II U1, 20
form [fɔ:m] Form <I>
forty [ˈfɔ:ti] vierzig I
fought [fɔ:t] simple past von *to fight* II U5, 87
found [faʊnd] simple past von *to find* II U1, 15
fountain [ˈfaʊntɪn] Brunnen <II U3, 167>
four [fɔ:] vier I
fourteen [ˌfɔ:ˈti:n] vierzehn I
free [fri:] frei; kostenlos <II U4, 80>
free time [ˌfri: ˈtaɪm] Freizeit I
free-time [ˌfri:ˈtaɪm] Freizeit- <I>
freeze frame [ˈfri:z ˌfreɪm] Standbild <II U3, 61>
Friday [ˈfraɪdeɪ] Freitag I
fridge [frɪdʒ] Kühlschrank <II U6, 175>
chicken **fried** rice [ˈtʃɪkɪn ˌfraɪd ˈraɪs] gebratener Reis mit Hühnerfleisch II U5, 88
friend [frend] Freund; Freundin I
to make friends [ˌmeɪk ˈfrendz] Freundschaft(en) schließen II U6, 110
frisbee [ˈfrɪzbi] Frisbee; Frisbeescheibe I
from [frɒm] aus; von I
Where are you from? [ˌweər‿ə ju ˈfrɒm] Woher kommst du? I
at the **front** (of) [ət ðə ˈfrʌnt] vorne (in) <II U3, 166>
in **front** [ɪn ˈfrʌnt] vorn II U1, 10
in **front of** [ɪn ˈfrʌnt‿əv] vor; davor I
fruit [fru:t] Obst; Frucht I
fun [fʌn] Spaß; Freude I; spaßig; amüsant <II U6, 116>
to be fun [bi: ˈfʌn] Spaß machen; witzig sein II U3, 60
funny [ˈfʌni] merkwürdig; komisch; lustig I

G

gallery walk [ˈgæləri ˌwɔ:k] Galerierundgang <II U6, 119>
game [geɪm] Spiel I
gap [gæp] Lücke; Spalt <II U4, 70>
garden [ˈgɑ:dn] Garten I
gate [geɪt] Tor <II U3, 167>
gave [geɪv] simple past von *to give* I
German [ˈdʒɜ:mən] Deutsch I; Deutscher; Deutsche; deutsch; aus Deutschland II U3, 48
*to **get** [get] bekommen; werden; kommen I
to get into [ˌget‿ˈɪntə] bilden <I>
to get off [ˌget‿ˈɒf] aussteigen II U1, 20
to get some exercise [get sʌm ˈeksəsaɪz] sich etwas Bewegung verschaffen <II U4, 80>
to get up [ˌget‿ˈʌp] aufstehen I
ghost [gəʊst] Geist <II U6, 117>
girl [gɜ:l] Mädchen I
*to **give** [gɪv] geben; schenken I
giving directions [ˌgɪvɪŋ dɪˈrekʃnz] eine Wegbeschreibung geben; Anweisungen geben <II U3, 59>
glove [glʌv] Handschuh II U6, 106
*to **go** [gəʊ] gehen; fahren I
to go bike riding [ˌgəʊ ˈbaɪk ˌraɪdɪŋ] Fahrrad fahren II U1, 10
to go camping [ˌgəʊ ˈkæmpɪŋ] zelten gehen; campen gehen <II U1, 162>
to go skateboarding [ˌgəʊ ˈskeɪtbɔ:dɪŋ] Skateboard fahren <II U5, 174>
to go skating [ˌgəʊ ˈskeɪtɪŋ] inlineskaten gehen; Schlittschuhlaufen gehen II U5, 88
to go swimming [ˌgəʊ ˈswɪmɪŋ] schwimmen gehen I
to go tandem bike riding [ˌgəʊ ˈtændəm ˌbaɪk raɪdɪŋ] Tandem fahren II U1, 10
to go to bed [ˌgəʊ tə ˈbed] ins Bett gehen I
goal [gəʊl] Treffer; Tor; Ziel <II U6, 116>
good [gʊd] gut I
to be good at [bi: ˈgʊd‿ət] gut sein in; gut sein bei I
Good luck! [ˌgʊd ˈlʌk] Alles Gute! <II U6, 175>
Goodbye. [gʊdˈbaɪ] Auf Wiedersehen. I
gorilla [gəˈrɪlə] Gorilla <II U3, 64>
got [gɒt] simple past von *to get* I
to have got [hæv ˈgɒt] haben; besitzen II U2, 40
to have (got) to [ˈhæv (gɒt) tə] müssen II U1, 15
GPS (Global Positioning System) [ˌdʒi:pi:ˈes] GPS *(ein satelliten-*

gestütztes System zur weltweiten Positionsbestimmung) I
grade *(AE)* [ɡreɪd] Klasse; Jahrgangsstufe; Note II U6, 115
grammar ['ɡræmə] Grammatik <I>
grandad ['ɡrændæd] Opa <II U6, 117>
grandfather ['ɡrænˌfɑ:ðə] Großvater II U1, 10
grandma ['ɡrænmɑ:] Oma I
grandparents *(pl)* ['ɡrænˌpeərnts] Großeltern II U1, 9
graph [ɡrɑ:f] Diagramm; Schaubild <II U2, 45>
great [ɡreɪt] großartig; toll I
great-great-grandad [ˌɡreɪtɡreɪt 'ɡrændæd] Ururopa I
green [ɡri:n] grün I
greeting ['ɡri:tɪŋ] Gruß <II U1, 22>
grey [ɡreɪ] grau I
group [ɡru:p] Gruppe <I>
to **guess** [ɡes] überlegen; raten; erraten I
Guess what? [ɡes 'wɒt] Stellt euch vor!; Stell dir vor! II U6, 105
to **guide** [ɡaɪd] führen <II U3, 62>
guinea pig ['ɡɪni ˌpɪɡ] Meerschweinchen II U2, 30
gym [dʒɪm] Turnhalle <II U4, 171>

H

had [hæd] simple past von *to have* I
half past (seven) [ˌhɑ:f 'pɑ:st] halb (acht) II U2, 40
hall [hɔ:l] Halle <II U4, 171>
main hall [ˌmeɪn 'hɔ:l] Aula <II U4, 80>
Halloween [ˌhæləʊ'i:n] Halloween I
hamster ['hæmstə] Hamster I
hand [hænd] Hand II U1, 20
handball ['hændbɔ:l] Handball <II U5, 174>
handwriting ['hændˌraɪtɪŋ] Handschrift <II U6, 119>
*to **hang** about [ˌhæŋ‿ə'baʊt] herumhängen I
to **happen** ['hæpn] passieren; geschehen II U1, 15
That's what happened. [ˌðæts wɒt 'hæpnd] Das ist passiert. II U1, 15
happy ['hæpi] glücklich I; zufrieden <II U6, 119>
hard [hɑ:d] hart; schwer; schwierig II U4, 73
hat [hæt] Mütze; Hut II U6, 106
to **hate** [heɪt] hassen; nicht mögen I
*to **have** [hæv] haben; besitzen; essen; trinken I
to have a party [ˌhæv‿ə 'pɑ:ti] eine Party feiern I
to have breakfast [ˌhæv 'brekfəst] frühstücken I
to have got [hæv 'ɡɒt] haben; besitzen II U2, 40
to have (got) to ['hæv (ɡɒt) tə] müssen II U1, 15
Have a safe trip! [ˌhæv‿ə 'seɪf trɪp] Gute Fahrt! <II U6, 175>
he [hi:] er I
head [hed] Kopf II U5, 92
headache ['hedeɪk] Kopfweh; Kopfschmerzen II U5, 92
heading ['hedɪŋ] Überschrift <I>
*to **hear** [hɪə] hören II U1, 10
heard [hɜ:d] simple past von *to hear* II U1, 20
hearing ['hɪərɪŋ] Gehör II U1, 20
heated ['hi:tɪd] beheizt <II U6, 116>
height [haɪt] Höhe II U3, 50
held [held] simple past von *to hold* II U5, 97
Hello. [hə'ləʊ] Hallo. I
helmet ['helmət] Helm I
help [help] Hilfe I
to **help** [help] helfen I
Help yourselves! [ˌhelp jɔ:'selvz] Bedient euch!; Bedienen Sie sich! <II U4, 81>
How can I help you? [ˌhaʊ kæn aɪ 'help‿ju:] Was kann ich für euch/dich tun? I
her [hɜ:] ihr I; sie II U5, 88
here [hɪə] hier I
Here's your change. [ˌhɪəz jɔ: 'tʃeɪndʒ] Hier ist dein Wechselgeld. I
Here you are. [ˌhɪə ju‿'ɑ:] Bitte schön. I
Hi. [haɪ] Hi.; Hallo. I
high [haɪ] hoch; groß II U3, 49
high ropes course [haɪ 'rəʊps ˌkɔ:s] Hochseilgarten <II U4, 172>
junior high school [ˌdʒu:niə 'haɪ sku:l] Junior Highschool *(Mittelschule in den USA, in der Regel Klassenstufe 7–9)* II U6, 115
hiking ['haɪkɪŋ] Wandern <II U1, 162>
him [hɪm] ihm; ihn II U1, 14
hip-hop ['hɪphɒp] Hip-Hop *(Musik)* <II U4, 171>
his [hɪz] sein I
history ['hɪstri] Geschichte <II U3, 62>
hobby ['hɒbi] Hobby II U5, 88
*to **hold** [həʊld] halten; festhalten II U5, 97
hole [həʊl] Loch I
holiday ['hɒlədeɪ] Ferien; Urlaub II U1, 9
home [həʊm] Zuhause; Heim; nach Hause I
at home [ət 'həʊm] zu Hause; daheim I
homework ['həʊmwɜ:k] Hausaufgabe(n) I
to do homework [ˌdu: 'həʊmwɜ:k] Hausaufgabe(n) machen I
hoodie ['hʊdi] Kapuzenpullover <II U2, 165>
to **hoover** ['hu:və] staubsaugen II U2, 30
to **hope** (for) [həʊp] hoffen (auf) II U6, 105
horse [hɔ:s] Pferd I
horse riding ['hɔ:s ˌraɪdɪŋ] Reiten I
hospital ['hɒspɪtl] Krankenhaus II U5, 97
hostel ['hɒstl] Herberge; Hostel II U4, 68
hot [hɒt] heiß I
hot dog ['hɒt ˌdɒɡ] Hotdog II U4, 70
hotel [həʊ'tel] Hotel <II U1, 162>
hour [aʊə] Stunde II U4, 74
house [haʊs] Haus I
how [haʊ] wie I
How are you? [ˌhaʊ‿'ɑ: jə] Wie geht es dir? I
How can I help you? [ˌhaʊ kæn aɪ 'help‿ju:] Was kann ich für euch/dich tun? I
How much (is/are) …? [ˌhaʊ 'mʌtʃ‿ɪz/ɑ:] Wie viel (kostet/kosten) …? I
How old are you? [haʊ‿'əʊld‿ə ˌju:] Wie alt bist du? I

how to … ['haʊ tə] wie man … <II U2, 43>
huge [hju:dʒ] riesig; riesengroß <II U1, 22>
a/one **hundred** ['hʌndrəd] hundert; einhundert I
hungry ['hʌŋgri] hungrig I
treasure **hunt** ['treʒə ˌhʌnt] Schnitzeljagd; Schatzsuche II U3, 57
*to **hurt** [hɜ:t] verletzen; wehtun II U5, 92
hurt [hɜ:t] simple past von *to hurt* II U5, 92

I

I [aɪ] ich I
I can't find … [aɪ kɑ:nt 'faɪnd] ich kann … nicht finden I
I don't know. [ˌaɪ dəʊnt 'nəʊ] Ich weiß (es) nicht! I
I won't be long. [aɪ ˌwəʊnt bi 'lɒŋ] Ich werde nicht lange weg sein. <II U6, 175>
I wouldn't like (to) … [aɪ 'wʊdnt laɪk] ich möchte nicht …; ich würde nicht gerne … I
I'd (= I would) [aɪd] ich würde; ich hätte gern I
I'd like (to) … (= I would like to) [aɪd 'laɪk] ich möchte …; ich würde gerne … I
I'm fine. [ˌaɪm 'faɪn] Mir geht es gut. I
I'm sorry. [aɪm 'sɒri] Es tut mir leid.; Entschuldigung. II U1, 15
ice cream [ˌaɪs 'kri:m] Eis; Eiscreme II U1, 10
ice skating ['aɪs ˌskeɪtɪŋ] Schlittschuhlaufen <II U4, 169>
idea [aɪ'dɪə] Idee I
if [ɪf] wenn; falls <II U2, 32>
to **imagine** [ɪ'mædʒɪn] sich vorstellen <II U6, 115>
important [ɪm'pɔ:tnt] wichtig <II U3, 65>
in [ɪn] im; in; auf; am I; an <II U2, 44>
in front [ɪn 'frʌnt] vorn II U1, 10
in the middle of [ɪn ðə 'mɪdl‿əv] mitten in II U4, 79
in a park [ɪn‿ə 'pɑ:k] im Park I
in front of [ɪn 'frʌnt‿əv] vor; davor I
in the evening [ɪn ði‿'i:vnɪŋ] abends I
information [ˌɪnfə'meɪʃn] Information(en) II U3, 50
inside cover [ˌɪnsaɪd 'kʌvə] Umschlaginnenseite <II U6, 106>
institute ['ɪnstɪtʃu:t] Institut; Einrichtung <II U5, 98>
instrument ['ɪnstrəmənt] Instrument <II U4, 82>
interest ['ɪntrəst] Interesse <II U4, 80>
interesting ['ɪntrəstɪŋ] interessant I
internet ['ɪntənet] Internet I
interview ['ɪntəvju:] Interview; Befragung <I>
to **interview** ['ɪntəvju:] befragen; interviewen <II U6, 111>
into ['ɪntu] in; in … hinein II U3, 57
intro ['ɪntrəʊ] Auftakt; Einführung <I>
introduction [ˌɪntrə'dʌkʃn] Einleitung; Einführung <II U5, 100>
invitation [ˌɪnvɪ'teɪʃn] Einladung I
to **invite** [ɪn'vaɪt] einladen II U4, 69
is [ɪz] ist I
Is something wrong? [ɪz 'sʌmθɪŋ rɒŋ] Stimmt etwas nicht? II U6, 110
it [ɪt] es; er; sie I; ihn; ihm II U1, 10
it's (= it is) [ɪts] es ist I
It's ten pounds. [ɪts ˌten 'paʊndz] Es kostet zehn Pfund. I
its [ɪts] sein; ihr I

J

jacket ['dʒækɪt] Jacke <II U2, 165>
January ['dʒænjuri] Januar I
jeans *(pl)* [dʒi:nz] Jeans I
crown **jewels** *(pl)* [ˌkraʊn 'dʒu:əlz] Kronjuwelen II U3, 60
jewellery ['dʒu:əlri] Schmuck <II U4, 170>
job [dʒɒb] Job I; Aufgabe; Tätigkeit <II U2, 30>
jogging ['dʒɒgɪŋ] Joggen <II U5, 174>
to **join** [dʒɔɪn] beitreten; sich anschließen <II U4, 80>
judge [dʒʌdʒ] Juror; Jurorin <II U5, 98>
judo ['dʒu:dəʊ] Judo <II U5, 174>
juice [dʒu:s] Saft I
July [dʒʊ'laɪ] Juli I
long **jump** ['lɒŋ ˌdʒʌmp] Weitsprung II U4, 69
June [dʒu:n] Juni I
junior high school [ˌdʒu:niə 'haɪ sku:l] Junior Highschool *(Mittelschule in den USA, in der Regel Klassenstufe 7–9)* II U6, 115
just [dʒʌst] einfach <II U6, 116>
just for fun [ˌdʒʌst fə 'fʌn] nur (so) zum Spaß <I>

K

karaoke [ˌkæri'əʊki] Karaoke <II U4, 170>
*to **keep** [ki:p] halten II U6, 110
to keep + -ing [ˌki:p '…ɪŋ] … immer weiter; … immer wieder <II U6, 119>
to keep in touch [ˌki:p ɪn 'tʌtʃ] in Kontakt bleiben II U6, 110
kept [kept] simple past von *to keep* II U6, 110
keyword ['ki:wɜ:d] Stichwort <II U5, 101>
kid [kɪd] Kind I
kilo (kg, kilogram) ['kɪləʊ] Kilo (kg, Kilogramm) I
kind [kaɪnd] Art; Sorte II U6, 114
king [kɪŋ] König II U3, 49
newspaper **kiosk** ['nju:speɪpə ˌki:ɒsk] Zeitungsstand II U3, 57
kitchen ['kɪtʃɪn] Küche II U2, 30
to **knock down** [ˌnɒk 'daʊn] umwerfen <II U4, 170>
*to **know** [nəʊ] wissen; kennen I
I don't know. [ˌaɪ dəʊnt 'nəʊ] Ich weiß (es) nicht! I
Korean [kə'ri:n] koreanisch <II U4, 81>

L

to **label** ['leɪbl] beschriften <II U2, 35>
ladder ['lædə] Leiter I
lake [leɪk] See <II U4, 172>
lamp [læmp] Lampe II U2, 33
language ['læŋgwɪdʒ] Grammatik; Sprache <I>
lantern ['læntən] Laterne II U4, 68
laptop ['læptɒp] Laptop I
large [lɑ:dʒ] groß II U2, 36
to **last** [lɑ:st] dauern; andauern II U4, 74
last [lɑ:st] letzte I
late [leɪt] (zu) spät II U1, 8

to be late [bi: 'leɪt] zu spät kommen II U1, 8
later ['leɪtə] später I
See you later. [ˌsi: jə 'leɪtə] Bis später.; Bis dann. <II U6, 175>
to **laugh** [lɑ:f] lachen II U4, 78
to mow the **lawn** [ˌməʊ ðə 'lɔ:n] den Rasen mähen <II U2, 163>
*to **lay** the table [ˌleɪ ðə 'teɪbl] den Tisch decken <II U2, 163>
to **learn** [lɜ:n] lernen II U2, 41
*to **leave** [li:v] verlassen; lassen; abfahren; weggehen II U6, 105
leaving ['li:vɪŋ] Abschieds- II U6, 110
left [left] simple past von *to leave* II U6, 105
left [left] links II U3, 57
on the left [ɒn ðə 'left] links; auf der linken Seite II U3, 57
leg [leg] Bein II U5, 92
lemon ['lemən] Zitrone <II U1, 23>
lesson ['lesn] Schulstunde; Unterricht I
Let me see. [ˌlet mi 'si:] Lass mich mal schauen. I
let's (= let us) [lets] lass(t) uns I
library ['laɪbri] Bibliothek; Bücherei <II U4, 169>
life *(sg)* [laɪf], **lives** *(pl)* [laɪvz] Leben II U3, 48
lift [lɪft] Aufzug II U3, 50
to **like** [laɪk] mögen; gernhaben I
like + -ing [ˌlaɪk '…ɪŋ] … gerne I
like [laɪk] wie I
like this [laɪk 'ðɪs] so; auf diese Weise <I>
line [laɪn] Zeile <II U1, 25>
mountain **lion** ['maʊntɪn ˌlaɪən] Puma II U6, 106
list [lɪst] Liste <I>
shopping list ['ʃɒpɪŋ ˌlɪst] Einkaufszettel I
to **listen** (to) ['lɪsn] anhören; hören; zuhören I
listening ['lɪsnɪŋ] Hörverstehen <I>
listening skills ['lɪsnɪŋ ˌskɪlz] Fertigkeit Hören <I>
little ['lɪtl] klein I
a little (bit) [ə 'lɪtl (bɪt)] ein (kleines) bisschen; ein (klein) wenig II U4, 70

to **live** [lɪv] wohnen; leben I
live [laɪv] Live- <II U4, 82>
living room ['lɪvɪŋ ˌrʊm] Wohnzimmer II U2, 29
to **load** the dishwasher [ˌləʊd ðə 'dɪʃwɒʃə] die Spülmaschine einräumen II U2, 30
local ['ləʊkl] örtlich; lokal; hiesig II U4, 68
locked [lɒkt] abgeschlossen I
*to be a **long** way away [bi: ə 'lɒŋ ˌweɪ ə'weɪ] weit weg sein II U6, 105
long jump ['lɒŋ ˌdʒʌmp] Weitsprung II U4, 69
longer ['lɒŋgə] länger I
to **look** [lʊk] schauen; aussehen; sehen; nachschauen I
to look after [ˌlʊk_'ɑ:ftə] aufpassen auf; hüten; sich kümmern um II U2, 40
to look at ['lʊk_ət] anschauen I
Look. [lʊk] Schau mal. I
*to **lose** [lu:z] verlieren II U1, 15
lost [lɒst] simple past von *to lose* II U1, 15
a **lot** [ə 'lɒt] viel; sehr I
a **lot** of [ə 'lɒt_əv] viel; viele; eine Menge I
lots of ['lɒts_əv] jede Menge; viel; viele I
loud [laʊd] laut I
Love, [lʌv] Liebe Grüße; Herzliche Grüße I
to **love** [lʌv] lieben; gern mögen I
Good **luck**! [ˌgʊd 'lʌk] Alles Gute! <II U6, 175>
lucky ['lʌki] glücklich; Glück bringend II U1, 20
to be lucky [bi:_'lʌki] Glück haben II U5, 88
lucky day [ˌlʌki 'deɪ] Glückstag II U1, 20
lunch [lʌnʃ] Mittagessen I
lunchtime ['lʌnʃtaɪm] Mittagspause; Mittagszeit I

M

made [meɪd] simple past von *to make* II U1, 10
magazine [ˌmægə'zi:n] Zeitschrift <I>

*to do **magic** [ˌdu: 'mædʒɪk] zaubern II U3, 60
magician [mə'dʒɪʃn] Zauberkünstler; Zauberkünstlerin II U5, 96
main hall [ˌmeɪn 'hɔ:l] Aula <II U4, 80>
*to **make** [meɪk] erstellen; basteln II U4, 68; machen; tun I; bilden <II U1, 10>; ausmachen <II U5, 86>
to make friends [ˌmeɪk 'frendz] Freundschaft(en) schließen II U6, 110
to make sb smile [meɪk sʌmbədi 'smaɪl] jmdn. zum Lächeln bringen <II U5, 173>
mall [mɔ:l] Einkaufspassage; Einkaufszentrum II U6, 114
man *(sg)* [mæn], **men** *(pl)* [men] Mann I
many ['meni] viele I
map [mæp] Karte; Plan II U3, 50
March [mɑ:tʃ] März I
market ['mɑ:kɪt] Markt I
flea market ['fli: ˌmɑ:kɪt] Flohmarkt I
match [mætʃ] Spiel; Match I
to **match** [mætʃ] zuordnen <I>
Maths [mæθs] Mathe I
It doesn't **matter.** [ɪt ˌdʌznt 'mætə] Es ist egal. <II U1, 161>
May [meɪ] Mai I
maybe ['meɪbi] vielleicht II U4, 79
me [mi:] ich; mich; mir I
call me ['kɔ:l ˌmi] nenne mich I
meal [mi:l] Essen; Mahlzeit II U5, 88
*to **mean** [mi:n] meinen <II U1, 161>
medal ['medl] Medaille II U4, 74
media ['mi:diə] Medien <II U6, 111>
mediation [ˌmi:di'eɪʃn] Sprachmittlung <I>
mediation skills [ˌmi:di'eɪʃn ˌskɪlz] Fertigkeit Sprachmittlung <I>
medical condition [ˌmedɪkl kən'dɪʃn] Erkrankung; Krankheit <II U6, 116>
medium ['mi:diəm] mittel <II U2, 165>
*to **meet** [mi:t] kennenlernen; treffen I; (sich) treffen II U1, 10
Merry Christmas! [ˌmeri 'krɪsməs] Frohe Weihnachten! I
mess [mes] Durcheinander; Unordnung I

message [ˈmesɪdʒ] Nachricht; SMS II U3, 53
met [met] simple past von *to meet* II U1, 10
metre [ˈmiːtə] Meter II U3, 49
200 **metre** race [ˈtuː hʌndrəd miːtə ˌreɪs] 200-Meter-Lauf II U4, 74
microphone [ˈmaɪkrəfəʊn] Mikrofon <II U3, 65>
in the **middle** of [ɪn ðə ˈmɪdl‿əv] mitten in II U4, 79
mild [maɪld] mild II U6, 106
million [ˈmɪljən] Million I
mind map [ˈmaɪnd ˌmæp] Wörternetz <I>
Never **mind**. [ˌnevə ˈmaɪnd] Macht nichts.; Schon gut.; Mach dir nichts draus. II U1, 15
minute [ˈmɪnɪt] Minute I
to **miss** [mɪs] verpassen; vermissen II U4, 70
model [ˈmɒdl] Vorlage; Muster <I>
modern [ˈmɒdn] modern I
at the **moment** [ət ðə ˈməʊmənt] im Moment; momentan II U3, 53
Monday [ˈmʌndeɪ] Montag I
money [ˈmʌni] Geld I
to raise **money** [ˌreɪz ˈmʌni] Geld sammeln; Geld aufbringen II U4, 69
month [mʌnθ] Monat II U4, 68
monument [ˈmɒnjəmənt] Denkmal <II U3, 167>
more [mɔː] mehr; weitere II U1, 10
morning [ˈmɔːnɪŋ] Morgen; Vormittag I
this **morning** [ðɪs ˈmɔːnɪŋ] heute Morgen II U5, 88
mosque [mɒsk] Moschee <II U3, 167>
mother [ˈmʌðə] Mutter I
mountain [ˈmaʊntɪn] Berg II U5, 97
mountain lion [ˈmaʊntɪn ˌlaɪən] Puma II U6, 106
mouse *(sg)* [maʊs], **mice** *(pl)* [maɪs] Maus I
mouth [maʊθ] Mund II U5, 87
to **move** [muːv] umziehen II U6, 104
to **mow** the lawn [ˌməʊ ðə ˈlɔːn] den Rasen mähen <II U2, 163>
Mr [ˈmɪstə] Herr *(Anrede)* I
Mrs [ˈmɪsɪz] Frau *(Anrede)* I
Ms [mɪz] Frau *(Anrede)* <II U1, 22>
much [mʌtʃ] viel I
How **much** (is/are) …? [ˌhaʊ ˈmʌtʃ‿ɪz/ɑː] Wie viel (kostet/kosten) …? I
mud [mʌd] Schlamm; Matsch I
muffin [ˈmʌfɪn] Muffin II U6, 110
mum [mʌm] Mama; Mutti I
museum [mjuːˈziːəm] Museum II U3, 49
music [ˈmjuːzɪk] Musik I
Muslim [ˈmʊzlɪm] Muslim; Muslimin I
must [mʌst] müssen II U4, 68
my [maɪ] mein I
My name is … [maɪ ˈneɪm‿ɪz] Ich heiße … I

N

nail [neɪl] Nagel <II U1, 23>
name [neɪm] Name I
to **name** [neɪm] benennen <I>
narrator [nəˈreɪtə] Erzähler; Erzählerin I
near [nɪə] in der Nähe von I; nah II U3, 50
nearly [ˈnɪəli] fast; beinahe II U4, 78
neck [nek] Hals; Nacken II U3, 60
to **need** [niːd] brauchen I
neighbour [ˈneɪbə] Nachbar; Nachbarin I
netball [ˈnetbɔːl] Korbball I
never [ˈnevə] nie; niemals II U2, 30
Never mind. [ˌnevə ˈmaɪnd] Macht nichts.; Schon gut.; Mach dir nichts draus. II U1, 15
new [njuː] neu I
news [njuːz] Neuigkeit(en); Nachricht(en) II U6, 105
newspaper kiosk [ˈnjuːspeɪpə ˌkiːɒsk] Zeitungsstand II U3, 57
next [nekst] nächste I; als Nächstes II U2, 36
next to [ˈnekst tə] neben I
nice [naɪs] schön; nett I
Nice to meet you. [ˌnaɪs tə ˈmiːt juː] Schön, dich kennenzulernen. I
night [naɪt] Nacht I
nine [naɪn] neun I
nineteen [ˌnaɪnˈtiːn] neunzehn I
ninety [ˈnaɪnti] neunzig I
no [nəʊ] kein; keine; nein I
no one [ˈnəʊ wʌn] niemand I
nobody [ˈnəʊbədi] niemand II U5, 88
noise [nɔɪz] Geräusch I
nose [nəʊz] Nase II U5, 92
not [nɒt] nicht I
note [nəʊt] Zettel; Nachricht; Notiz <II U6, 175>
notes *(pl)* [nəʊts] Notizen <I>
to take **notes** [ˌteɪk ˈnəʊts] sich Notizen machen <I>
nothing [ˈnʌθɪŋ] nichts II U5, 92
notice board [ˈnəʊtɪs bɔːd] Pinnwand <II U2, 164>
November [nəˈvembə] November I
now [naʊ] jetzt; nun I
Now over to David. [ˈnaʊ əʊvə tuː ˌdeɪvɪd] Jetzt zu David. <II U4, 83>
number [ˈnʌmbə] Zahl; Nummer I
number of [ˈnʌmbər‿əv] Anzahl von <II U2, 44>
nut [nʌt] Nuss <II U6, 116>

O

o'clock [əˈklɒk] Uhr *(Zeitangabe bei vollen Stunden)* I
October [ɒkˈtəʊbə] Oktober I
odd one out [ˌɒd wʌn‿ˈaʊt] das Wort, das nicht in die Gruppe passt <I>
of [ɒv] von I
of course [əv ˈkɔːs] natürlich; selbstverständlich II U5, 88
police officer [pəˈliːs‿ɒfɪsə] Polizeibeamter; Polizeibeamtin I
often [ˈɒfn] oft; häufig II U2, 28
oil [ɔɪl] Öl II U5, 88
OK (okay) [əʊˈkeɪ] okay I
old [əʊld] alt I
How **old** are you? [haʊ‿ˈəʊld‿ə ˌjuː] Wie alt bist du? I
on [ɒn] auf; an; am I; mit II U5, 92; bei <II U6, 116>; über <II U6, 119>
on foot [ɒn ˈfʊt] zu Fuß I
on Saturdays [ɒn ˈsætədeɪz] samstags I
on the bus [ˌɒn ðə ˈbʌs] im Bus II U1, 20
on the left [ɒn ðə ˈleft] links; auf der linken Seite II U3, 57
on the right [ɒn ðə ˈraɪt] rechts; auf der rechten Seite II U3, 57

on TV [ɒn ˌtiːˈviː] im Fernsehen <II U5, 98>
to put on [ˌpʊt‿ˈɒn] anziehen II U4, 78
to try on [ˌtraɪ ˈɒn] anprobieren II U2, 36
once [wʌns] einmal; einst II U6, 114
once upon a time [ˌwʌns əpɒn‿ə ˈtaɪm] es war einmal II U3, 60
one [wʌn] eins; ein I
a/one hundred [ˈhʌndrəd] hundert; einhundert I
a/one thousand [ˈθaʊznd] tausend; eintausend II U5, 96
no one [ˈnəʊ wʌn] niemand I
one day [ˈwʌn deɪ] eines Tages I
online [ˌɒnˈlaɪn] online; Online- II U6, 110
only [ˈəʊnli] nur I
to **open** [ˈəʊpn] öffnen; aufmachen I
open [ˈəʊpn] geöffnet I
open day [ˈəʊpn ˌdeɪ] Tag der offenen Tür <II U4, 80>
opposite [ˈɒpəzɪt] Gegenteil <I>; gegenüber II U2, 29
or [ɔː] oder I
orange [ˈɒrɪndʒ] orange; Orange I
order [ˈɔːdə] Reihenfolge <I>
word order [ˈwɜːd‿ˌɔːdə] Wortstellung; Satzstellung <II U4, 76>
to **organize** [ˈɔːgənaɪz] organisieren I
orienteering [ˌɔːriənˈtɪərɪŋ] Orientierungslauf <II U6, 116>
other [ˈʌðə] andere II U4, 70
others [ˈʌðəz] anderen II U4, 78
our [aʊə] unser I
out of ... [ˈaʊt‿əv] aus ... heraus I
outside [ˌaʊtˈsaɪd] außerhalb; außen; draußen; im Freien II U4, 79
over [ˈəʊvə] vorbei <II U1, 13>
all over [ˌɔːl‿ˈəʊvə] in ganz; überall II U5, 96
own [əʊn] eigene II U4, 68

P

p.m. [ˌpiːˈem] nachmittags *(Uhrzeit)* <II U4, 75>
page [peɪdʒ] Seite <I>
to **paint** [peɪnt] bemalen; malen; streichen II U6, 115
face **painting** [ˈfeɪs peɪntɪŋ] Schminken II U4, 70
wall **painting** [ˈwɔːl peɪntɪŋ] Wandmalerei II U6, 115
pair [peə] Paar <II U2, 37>
parents *(pl)* [ˈpeərnts] Eltern I
park [pɑːk] Park I
theme park [ˈθiːm ˌpɑːk] Freizeitpark II U5, 96
part [pɑːt] Teil; Rolle II U4, 79
to take part (in) [ˌteɪk ˈpɑːt] mitmachen (bei); teilnehmen (an) II U4, 74
partner [ˈpɑːtnə] Partner; Partnerin I
party [ˈpɑːti] Party; Feier I
to have a party [ˌhæv‿ə ˈpɑːti] eine Party feiern I
to **pass** [pɑːs] herüberreichen; reichen <II U4, 81>
past [pɑːst] Vergangenheit <II U1, 13>
past [pɑːst] vorbei (an) I; nach *(bei Uhrzeitangaben)* II U2, 40
half past (seven) [ˌhɑːf ˈpɑːst] halb (acht) II U2, 40
quarter to/past [ˈkwɔːtə tə/pɑːst] Viertel vor/nach II U2, 40
PE (Physical Education) [ˌpiːˈiː (ˌfɪzɪkl edʒʊˈkeɪʃn)] Sportunterricht I
pen [pen] Stift; Füller I
pencil [ˈpensl] Bleistift I
penny *(sg)* [ˈpeni], **pence** *(pl)* [pens] Penny *(brit. Währungseinheit)* <II U1, 23>
people *(pl only)* [ˈpiːpl] Leute; Menschen I
per [pɜː] pro <II U3, 67>
to **perform** [pəˈfɔːm] aufführen <II U4, 172>
person [ˈpɜːsn] Mensch; Person II U5, 97
pet [pet] Haustier I
phone [fəʊn] Telefon I
phone call [ˈfəʊn ˌkɔːl] Telefonanruf; Anruf I
to **phone** [fəʊn] anrufen; telefonieren II U1, 20
photo [ˈfəʊtəʊ] Foto I
to take photos (of) [ˌteɪk ˈfəʊtəʊz] Fotos machen; fotografieren II U1, 10
phrase [freɪz] Satz; Satzteil; Redewendung <II U1, 25>
picnic [ˈpɪknɪk] Picknick I
picture [ˈpɪktʃə] Bild I
a **piece** of [ə ˈpiːs‿əv] ein Stück ... II U5, 88
pier [pɪə] Pier II U6, 104
pink [pɪŋk] pink; rosa I
pizza [ˈpiːtsə] Pizza I
place [pleɪs] Platz; Stelle; Ort I
plan [plæn] Plan <II U3, 58>
to **plan** [plæn] planen <II U4, 77>
planner [ˈplænə] Kalender; Planer II U4, 68
play [pleɪ] Theaterstück <I>
to **play** [pleɪ] spielen I
player [ˈpleɪə] Spieler; Spielerin II U5, 86
playground [ˈpleɪgraʊnd] Schulhof; Pausenhof; Spielplatz I
playing field [ˈpleɪɪŋ ˌfiːld] Sportplatz II U4, 74
please [pliːz] bitte I
plum [plʌm] Pflaume I
poem [ˈpəʊɪm] Gedicht <II U6, 108>
to **point** [pɔɪnt] zeigen <I>
police officer [pəˈliːs‿ɒfɪsə] Polizeibeamter; Polizeibeamtin I
polite [pəˈlaɪt] höflich <II U2, 43>
pony [ˈpəʊni] Pony <II U3, 64>
swimming **pool** [ˈswɪmɪŋ ˌpuːl] Schwimmbad I
pop [pɒp] Pop *(Musik)* II U3, 60
postcard [ˈpəʊstkɑːd] Postkarte I
poster [ˈpəʊstə] Poster II U2, 33
potato and spoon race [pəˌteɪtəʊ ən ˈspuːn ˌreɪs] Kartoffellauf <II U4, 170>
pound (£) [paʊnd] Pfund *(brit. Währungseinheit)* I
practice [ˈpræktɪs] Training; Übung I
to **practise** [ˈpræktɪs] üben; trainieren <II U6, 115>
to **prepare** [prɪˈpeə] vorbereiten <II U5, 98>
present [ˈpreznt] Geschenk I
present progressive [ˌpreznt prəˈgresɪv] Verlaufsform der Gegenwart <II U3, 54>
to **present** [prɪˈzent] präsentieren <I>

presentation [ˌprezn'teɪʃn] Präsentation; Vortrag <II U5, 100>
pretty ['prɪti] hübsch II U2, 36
price [praɪs] Preis I
walk-up price ['wɔ:kʌp ˌpraɪs] Schalterpreis <II U3, 62>
prize [praɪz] Preis; Gewinn II U4, 70
problem ['prɒbləm] Problem I
procession [prə'seʃn] Umzug; Festzug II U4, 68
professional [prə'feʃnl] professionell <II U3, 62>
programme ['prəʊgræm] Sendung; Programm <II U4, 82>
present **progressive** [ˌpreznt prə'gresɪv] Verlaufsform der Gegenwart <II U3, 54>
project ['prɒdʒekt] Projekt II U4, 69
to **pull** [pʊl] ziehen I
pullover ['pʊləʊvə] Pullover I
to **push** [pʊʃ] schieben I
*to **put** [pʊt] setzen; legen; stellen I; bringen <II U1, 13>; stecken II U1, 20
to put in [ˌpʊt‿'ɪn] einsetzen <I>
to put on [ˌpʊt‿'ɒn] anziehen II U4, 78
put [pʊt] simple past von *to put* I

Q

quality ['kwɒləti] Eigenschaft <II U5, 173>
quarter to/past ['kwɔ:tə tə/pɑ:st] Viertel vor/nach II U2, 40
queen [kwi:n] Königin II U3, 49
question ['kwestʃən] Frage I
queue [kju:] Warteschlange II U3, 53
quiet [kwaɪət] leise; ruhig; still II U5, 88
quite [kwaɪt] ziemlich; ganz; völlig II U5, 88
quiz [kwɪz] Rätsel <I>; Quiz; Ratespiel <II U4, 170>

R

rabbit ['ræbɪt] Kaninchen I
raccoon [rə'ku:n] Waschbär I
race [reɪs] Wettrennen; Rennen; Wettlauf II U4, 74
200 metre race ['tu: hʌndrəd mi:tə ˌreɪs] 200-Meter-Lauf II U4, 74
sack race ['sæk ˌreɪs] Sackhüpfen II U4, 74
raffle ['ræfl] Gewinnspiel; Tombola II U4, 70
raft building ['rɑ:ft bɪldɪŋ] Floßbau <II U6, 116>
to **rain** [reɪn] regnen I
raindrop ['reɪndrɒp] Regentropfen <II U6, 119>
rainy ['reɪni] regnerisch II U6, 106
to **raise** money [ˌreɪz 'mʌni] Geld sammeln; Geld aufbringen II U4, 69
ran [ræn] simple past von *to run* II U2, 40
rang [ræŋ] simple past von *to ring* II U1, 20
rap [ræp] Rap I
*to **read** [ri:d] lesen; vorlesen II U3, 53
read [red] simple past von *to read* II U3, 53
reading ['ri:dɪŋ] Lesen <I>
reading skills ['ri:dɪŋ ˌskɪlz] Fertigkeit Lesen <I>
ready ['redi] bereit; fertig I
real [rɪəl] echt; richtig; wirklich <II U3, 62>
really ['rɪəli] wirklich; eigentlich I
recipe ['resɪpi] Rezept <II U3, 66>
to **record** [rɪ'kɔ:d] aufnehmen; aufzeichnen <I>
red [red] rot I
registration [ˌredʒɪ'streɪʃn] Überprüfung der Anwesenheit I
registration form [redʒɪ'streɪʃn ˌfɔ:m] Anmeldeformular <II U6, 116>
to **relax** [rɪ'læks] entspannen; ausruhen <II U6, 116>
relay race ['ri:leɪ ˌreɪs] Staffellauf <II U4, 171>
to **remember** [rɪ'membə] sich erinnern (an); sich merken <II U1, 12>
to **repeat** [rɪ'pi:t] wiederholen <I>
report [rɪ'pɔ:t] Bericht <II U1, 11>
animal **rescue** shelter [ˌænɪml 'reskju: ˌʃeltə] Tierheim I
rest [rest] Rest II U6, 106
restaurant ['restrɒnt] Restaurant II U5, 88
result [rɪ'zʌlt] Ergebnis <I>
rice [raɪs] Reis II U5, 88
chicken fried rice ['tʃɪkɪn ˌfraɪd 'raɪs] gebratener Reis mit Hühnerfleisch II U5, 88
ride [raɪd] Fahrt; Fahrgeschäft; Ritt II U5, 96; Tour <II U4, 172>
*to **ride** [raɪd] fahren; reiten I
horse **riding** ['hɔ:s ˌraɪdɪŋ] Reiten I
right [raɪt] richtig; korrekt I; rechts; rechte II U3, 57
on the right [ɒn ðə 'raɪt] rechts; auf der rechten Seite II U3, 57
You're right. [jɔ:‿'raɪt] Du hast recht. I
*to **ring** [rɪŋ] klingeln; läuten I
river ['rɪvə] Fluss I
road [rəʊd] Straße I
rock climbing ['rɒk ˌklaɪmɪŋ] Klettern I
role [rəʊl] Rolle <II U1, 24>
role play ['rəʊl ˌpleɪ] Rollenspiel <I>
roller coaster ['rəʊlə ˌkəʊstə] Achterbahn II U5, 96
room [ru:m] Zimmer; Raum I
rubber ['rʌbə] Radiergummi I
rubbish ['rʌbɪʃ] Müll; Abfall I
rule [ru:l] Regel <I>
ruler ['ru:lə] Lineal I
*to **run** [rʌn] laufen; rennen; fahren II U2, 40
to run away [ˌrʌn‿ə'weɪ] weglaufen II U2, 40

S

sack race ['sæk ˌreɪs] Sackhüpfen II U4, 74
sad [sæd] traurig I
said [sed] simple past von *to say* I
salad ['sæləd] Salat I
sale [seɪl] Verkauf <II U4, 170>
the **same** [ðə 'seɪm] der gleiche; derselbe; gleich; genauso II U1, 15
at the same time [ət ðə seɪm 'taɪm] gleichzeitig; nebenher II U6, 110
sandwich ['sænwɪdʒ] Sandwich; belegtes Brot I
sang [sæŋ] simple past von *to sing* II U1, 10
Saturday ['sætədeɪ] Samstag I
on Saturdays [ɒn 'sætədeɪz] samstags I
to **save** [seɪv] retten; sparen II U5, 87

saw [sɔ:] simple past von *to see* I
saxophone ['sæksəfəʊn] Saxofon I
*to **say** [seɪ] nennen; sagen; nachsprechen; sprechen I
to **scare** [skeə] erschrecken <II U6, 117>
*to be **scared** [bi: 'skeəd] Angst haben I
scarf *(sg)* [skɑ:f], **scarves** *(pl)* [skɑ:vz] Schal; Tuch II U1, 9
scary ['skeəri] unheimlich; gruselig; beängstigend I
scene [si:n] Szene <II U1, 21>
school [sku:l] Schule I
at school [ət 'sku:l] in der Schule I
junior high school [ˌdʒu:niə 'haɪ sku:l] Junior Highschool *(Mittelschule in den USA, in der Regel Klassenstufe 7–9)* II U6, 115
school trip [ˌsku:l 'trɪp] Klassenfahrt; Schulausflug II U4, 68
science fiction [ˌsaɪəns 'fɪkʃn] Science-Fiction I
to **score** [skɔ:] erzielen <II U6, 116>
sea [si:] Meer I
at the **seaside** [ət ðə 'si:saɪd] am Meer I
season ['si:zn] Jahreszeit; Saison II U6, 106
second ['seknd] Sekunde <I>; zweite II U3, 57
second-hand [seknd 'hænd] gebraucht; secondhand; aus zweiter Hand I
*to **see** [si:] sehen I
See you. ['si: ju:] Tschüss.; Bis bald.; Wir sehen uns. II U6, 113
See you later. [ˌsi: jə 'leɪtə] Bis später.; Bis dann. <II U6, 175>
See you soon. [ˌsi: ju: 'su:n] Bis bald. I
See you then. [ˌsi: jə 'ðen] Bis dann. <II U3, 63>
Let me see. [ˌlet mi 'si:] Lass mich mal schauen. I
*to **sell** [sel] verkaufen I
*to **send** [send] schicken; senden I
sent [sent] simple past von *to send* I
sentence ['sentəns] Satz <I>
September [sep'tembə] September I

serious ['sɪəriəs] ernst; schwer II U5, 92
seven ['sevn] sieben I
seventeen [ˌsevn'ti:n] siebzehn I
seventy ['sevnti] siebzig I
shark [ʃɑ:k] Hai I
she [ʃi:] sie I
sheep *(sg)* [ʃi:p], **sheep** *(pl)* [ʃi:p] Schaf I
shelf *(sg)* [ʃelf], **shelves** *(pl)* [ʃelvz] Regal; Regalbrett II U2, 33
animal rescue **shelter** [ˌænɪml 'reskju: ˌʃeltə] Tierheim I
ship [ʃɪp] Schiff I
shirt [ʃɜ:t] Hemd; Shirt I
T-shirt ['ti:ʃɜ:t] T-Shirt II U2, 36
shoe [ʃu:] Schuh I
shop [ʃɒp] Geschäft; Laden I
sports shop ['spɔ:ts ˌʃɒp] Sportgeschäft II U2, 33
shopping ['ʃɒpɪŋ] Einkaufen I
shopping centre ['ʃɒpɪŋ ˌsentə] Einkaufszentrum I
shopping list ['ʃɒpɪŋ ˌlɪst] Einkaufszettel I
short [ʃɔ:t] kurz II U2, 36
shorts *(pl)* [ʃɔ:ts] Shorts; kurze Hose II U6, 106
to **shout** [ʃaʊt] rufen; schreien I
show [ʃəʊ] Show; Aufführung I
*to **show** [ʃəʊ] zeigen II U5, 88
*to be **sick** [bi: 'sɪk] sich übergeben I
side [saɪd] Seite II U5, 97
sight [saɪt] Sehenswürdigkeit II U3, 48
silly ['sɪli] albern II U6, 110
simple past [ˌsɪmpl 'pɑ:st] einfache Vergangenheit <II U1, 12>
simple present [ˌsɪmpl 'preznt] einfache Gegenwart; Präsens <II U3, 54>
*to **sing** [sɪŋ] singen I
singer ['sɪŋə] Sänger; Sängerin I
sister ['sɪstə] Schwester I
*to **sit** (down) [ˌsɪt 'daʊn] sich setzen; sich hinsetzen I
situation [ˌsɪtju'eɪʃn] Situation <II U1, 16>
six [sɪks] sechs I
sixteen [ˌsɪk'sti:n] sechzehn I
sixty ['sɪksti] sechzig I
size [saɪz] Größe II U2, 36

to **skate** [skeɪt] inlineskaten; Schlittschuh laufen II U5, 88
skateboard ['skeɪtbɔ:d] Skateboard I
*to go **skateboarding** [ˌgəʊ 'skeɪtbɔ:dɪŋ] Skateboard fahren <II U5, 174>
skater ['skeɪtə] Skater; Skaterin I
*to go **skating** [ˌgəʊ 'skeɪtɪŋ] inlineskaten gehen; Schlittschuhlaufen gehen II U5, 88
ice **skating** ['aɪs ˌskeɪtɪŋ] Schlittschuhlaufen <II U4, 169>
sketch [sketʃ] Sketch <II U4, 172>
skiing ['ski:ɪŋ] Skifahren; Ski- <II U1, 162>
skill [skɪl] Fertigkeit; Geschick <II U5, 98>
mediation skills [ˌmi:di'eɪʃn ˌskɪlz] Fertigkeit Sprachmittlung <I>
skirt [skɜ:t] Rock <II U2, 165>
*to **sleep** [sli:p] schlafen II U2, 41
slept [slept] simple past von *to sleep* II U2, 41
small [smɔ:l] klein I
*to **smell** [smel] riechen <II U3, 62>
*to make sb **smile** [meɪk sʌmbədi 'smaɪl] jmdn. zum Lächeln bringen <II U5, 173>
smurf [smɜ:f] Schlumpf I
snack [snæk] Snack; Imbiss <II U3, 64>
snack bar ['snæk ˌbɑ:] Imbissstube; Café I
snack food ['snæk ˌfu:d] Snacks *(Pl.)* <II U4, 81>
snow [snəʊ] Schnee II U6, 106
snowboard ['snəʊbɔ:d] Snowboard I
snowboarding ['snəʊbɔ:dɪŋ] Snowboarden <II U1, 162>
snowy ['snəʊi] schneereich; verschneit II U6, 106
so [səʊ] also; deshalb I; so; dermaßen II U6, 105
soap opera ['səʊp ˌɒprə] Seifenoper <II U5, 98>
soccer *(AE)* ['sɒkə] Fußball II U6, 115
sock [sɒk] Socke <II U2, 165>
sold [səʊld] simple past von *to sell* II U4, 70
some [sʌm] etwas; einige; ein paar I
somebody ['sʌmbədi] jemand I
something ['sʌmθɪŋ] etwas I

Is something wrong? [ɪz ˈsʌmθɪŋ rɒŋ] Stimmt etwas nicht? II U6, 110
sometimes [ˈsʌmtaɪmz] manchmal I
song [sɒŋ] Lied I
soon [su:n] bald II U6, 105
See you soon. [ˌsi: ˌju: ˈsu:n] Bis bald. I
Sorry. [ˈsɒri] Tut mir leid.; Entschuldigung. I
I'm sorry. [aɪm ˈsɒri] Es tut mir leid.; Entschuldigung. II U1, 15
sound [saʊnd] Laut; Geräusch; Ton <I>
southwest [ˌsaʊθˈwest] Südwesten <II U3, 63>
souvenir [ˌsu:vnˈɪə] Souvenir; Andenken II U3, 57
*to **speak** [spi:k] sprechen I
speaking [ˈspi:kɪŋ] Sprechen <I>
speaking skills [ˈspi:kɪŋ ˌskɪlz] Fertigkeit Sprechen <I>
special [ˈspeʃl] besonders; speziell I
special effect [ˌspeʃl ɪˈfekt] Spezialeffekt <II U3, 62>
spelling [ˈspelɪŋ] Rechtschreibung I
*to **spend** [spend] verbringen *(Zeit)*; ausgeben *(Geld)* II U5, 97
spent [spent] simple past von *to spend* II U5, 97
sports *(pl only)* [spɔ:ts] Sportarten I
sports centre [ˈspɔ:ts ˌsentə] Sportzentrum I
sports day [ˈspɔ:ts ˌdeɪ] Sportfest II U4, 69
sports shop [ˈspɔ:ts ˌʃɒp] Sportgeschäft II U2, 33
spring [sprɪŋ] Frühling II U6, 106
to **spy** [spaɪ] sehen I
square dance [ˈskweə ˌdɑ:ns] Squaredance *(amerikanischer Volkstanz)* II U6, 115
stadium [ˈsteɪdiəm] Stadion I
stage [steɪdʒ] Bühne II U5, 86
stall [stɔ:l] Stand; Bude I
*to **stand** [stænd] stehen II U3, 53
star [stɑ:] Star I
start [stɑ:t] Anfang; Beginn; Start <I>
to **start** [stɑ:t] anfangen; beginnen; starten I
state [steɪt] Staat; Bundesstaat <II U6, 118>
station [ˈsteɪʃn] Station; Bahnhof <II U3, 166>
to **stay** [steɪ] bleiben; übernachten I
to stay away from [ˌsteɪ əˈweɪ frəm] sich fernhalten von <II U6, 117>
step [step] Schritt; Stufe II U3, 50
still [stɪl] noch; immer noch II U5, 88
stood [stʊd] simple past von *to stand* II U3, 53
stop [stɒp] Haltestelle; Halt II U1, 20
to **stop** [stɒp] beenden; aufhören; anhalten II U5, 87
to stop sb from doing sth [ˈstɒp frəm ˌdu:ɪŋ] jmdn. davon abhalten, etw. zu tun <II U6, 116>
Stop it! [ˈstɒp‿ɪt] Hör(t) auf! <II U1, 25>
storm [stɔ:m] Sturm I
story [ˈstɔ:ri] Geschichte I
storytelling [ˈstɔ:riˌtelɪŋ] Geschichtenerzählen <II U3, 62>
straight on [streɪt‿ˈɒn] geradeaus II U3, 57
strawberry [ˈstrɔ:bri] Erdbeere I
street [stri:t] Straße I
student [ˈstju:dnt] Schüler; Schülerin I
studio [ˈstju:diəʊ] Studio <II U5, 98>
study skills [ˌstʌdi ˈskɪlz] Fertigkeit Lern- und Arbeitstechniken <I>
subject [ˈsʌbdʒɪkt] Schulfach I
suddenly [ˈsʌdnli] plötzlich; auf einmal I
sugar [ˈʃʊgə] Zucker <II U3, 66>
summer [ˈsʌmə] Sommer II U1, 10
sun [sʌn] Sonne II U6, 106
Sunday [ˈsʌndeɪ] Sonntag I
sunny [ˈsʌni] sonnig II U6, 106
supermarket [ˈsu:pəˌmɑ:kɪt] Supermarkt I
sure [ʃʊə] sicher II U3, 50
surprised [səˈpraɪzd] überrascht II U1, 15
survey [ˈsɜ:veɪ] Umfrage <II U2, 44>
swam [swæm] simple past von *to swim* <II U1, 22>
*to **sweep** [swi:p] fegen <II U2, 163>
sweet [swi:t] Süßigkeit; Bonbon I
*to **swim** [swɪm] schwimmen I
*to go **swimming** [ˌgəʊ ˈswɪmɪŋ] schwimmen gehen I
swimming gala [ˈswɪmɪŋ ˌgɑ:lə] Schwimmfest; Schwimmgala <II U4, 169>
swimming pool [ˈswɪmɪŋ ˌpu:l] Schwimmbad I
synagogue [ˈsɪnəgɒg] Synagoge <II U3, 167>

T

T-shirt [ˈti:ʃɜ:t] T-Shirt II U2, 36
table [ˈteɪbl] Tisch; Tabelle <I>
to clear the table [ˌklɪə ðə ˈteɪbl] den Tisch abräumen <II U2, 163>
to lay the table [ˌleɪ ðə ˈteɪbl] den Tisch decken <II U2, 163>
tail [teɪl] Schwanz I
*to **take** [teɪk] mitnehmen; nehmen I; hinbringen II U5, 97
to take notes [ˌteɪk ˈnəʊts] sich Notizen machen <I>
to take out [ˌteɪk‿ˈaʊt] hinausbringen II U2, 30
to take part (in) [ˌteɪk ˈpɑ:t] mitmachen (bei); teilnehmen (an) II U4, 74
to take photos (of) [ˌteɪk ˈfəʊtəʊz] Fotos machen; fotografieren II U1, 10
to take the dog for a walk [ˌteɪk ðə dɒg fɔ:r‿ə ˈwɔ:k] den Hund ausführen I
to take turns [ˌteɪk ˈtɜ:nz] sich abwechseln <I>
talent [ˈtælənt] Talent; Begabung I
to **talk** (to) [tɔ:k] reden (mit); sprechen (mit) I
tall [tɔ:l] hoch; groß II U3, 50
tandem [ˈtændəm] Tandem II U1, 10
task [tɑ:sk] Aufgabe; Auftrag <I>
taxi [ˈtæksi] Taxi <II U3, 166>
tea [ti:] Tee; Abendessen I
teacher [ˈti:tʃə] Lehrer; Lehrerin I
team [ti:m] Mannschaft; Team; Gruppe I
DT (**Design Technology**) [ˌdi:ˈti: (dɪˌzaɪn tekˈnɒlədʒi)] Technik I
teddy [ˈtedi] Teddybär I
teen [ti:n] Jugend-; Teenager; Teenagerin; Jugendlicher; Jugendliche II U5, 96

p pen • b bed • t ten • d dad • k cat • g grey • tʃ chair • dʒ job • f fan • v very • θ three • ð the

teenage ['ti:neɪdʒ] jugendlich <II U5, 98>
telephone box ['telɪfəʊn ˌbɒks] Telefonzelle II U3, 50
*to **tell** [tel] erzählen; sagen I
to tell sb to do sth ['tel tə ˌdu:] jmdm. etw. auftragen <II U6, 117>
ten [ten] zehn I
tennis ['tenɪs] Tennis I
tent [tent] Zelt II U4, 79
terrible ['terəbl] schrecklich; furchtbar <II U1, 22>
to **test** [test] testen; prüfen II U5, 96
text [tekst] Text <I>
text message ['tekst ˌmesɪdʒ] Textnachricht (SMS) <II U6, 175>
than [ðæn] als II U2, 36
Thank you. ['θæŋk ju] Danke. I
Thanks. [θæŋks] Danke. I
that [ðæt] das; dieses; jene I; die; der <II U3, 52>; dass II U4, 70
after that [ˌɑ:ftə 'ðæt] danach I
that's why ['ðæts waɪ] deshalb; deswegen II U4, 69
That isn't fair! [ˌðæt ˌɪznt 'feə] Das ist ungerecht! <II U1, 25>
that's £3.50 [ðæts ˌθri: paʊndz 'fɪfti] das macht 3 Pfund und 50 Pence I
That's too bad. [ˌðæts tu: 'bæd] Schade! II U6, 105
the [ðə] die; der; das I
theatre ['θɪətə] Theater <II U4, 169>
their [ðeə] ihr I
them [ðem] sie *(Pl.)* I; ihnen II U5, 87
theme [θi:m] Thema; Motto <I>
theme park ['θi:m ˌpɑ:k] Freizeitpark II U5, 96
then [ðen] dann; danach I
See you then. [ˌsi: ˌjə 'ðen] Bis dann. <II U3, 63>
there [ðeə] da; dort; dorthin; dahin I
there are [ðeər‿'ɑ:] da sind; es gibt I
there's (= there is) [ðeəz] da ist; dort ist; es gibt I
these [ði:z] diese II U2, 36
they [ðeɪ] sie *(Pl.)* I
thing [θɪŋ] Sache; Ding I
*to **think** [θɪŋk] denken; glauben II U2, 33; finden <II U1, 25>
to think about sth [ˌθɪŋk‿ə'baʊt ˌsʌmθɪŋ] sich etw. überlegen; an etw. denken <II U1, 16>
to think of ['θɪŋk‿əv] denken an/über; sich einfallen lassen; sich ausdenken <II U3, 52>
I don't think so. [ˌaɪ dəʊnt 'θɪŋk səʊ] Das glaube ich nicht. <II U6, 117>
I think so too. [aɪ 'θɪŋk səʊ ˌtu:] Das denke ich auch. <II U6, 117>
third [θɜ:d] dritte II U3, 57
thirteen [θɜ:'ti:n] dreizehn I
thirty ['θɜ:ti] dreißig I
this [ðɪs] das; dies I
this morning [ðɪs 'mɔ:nɪŋ] heute Morgen II U5, 88
like this [laɪk 'ðɪs] so; auf diese Weise <I>
those [ðəʊz] jene II U2, 36
thought [θɔ:t] simple past von *to think* II U2, 33
a/one **thousand** ['θaʊznd] tausend; eintausend II U5, 96
three [θri:] drei I
threw [θru:] simple past von *to throw* II U2, 41
through [θru:] durch <II U1, 22>
*to **throw** [θrəʊ] werfen II U2, 41
Thursday ['θɜ:zdeɪ] Donnerstag I
ticket ['tɪkɪt] Eintrittskarte; Fahrschein; Ticket II U4, 70
to **tidy** ['taɪdi] aufräumen; in Ordnung bringen II U2, 30
tidy ['taɪdi] ordentlich <II U2, 34>
tie [taɪ] Krawatte; Schlips <II U2, 165>
tiger ['taɪgə] Tiger <II U3, 64>
time [taɪm] Zeit; Uhrzeit; Mal I
at the same time [ət ðə seɪm 'taɪm] gleichzeitig; nebenher II U6, 110
free time [ˌfri: 'taɪm] Freizeit I
once upon a time [ˌwʌns əpɒn‿ə 'taɪm] es war einmal II U3, 60
the first time [ðə fɜ:st 'taɪm] das erste Mal I
timetable ['taɪmˌteɪbl] Stundenplan I
tip [tɪp] Tipp; Ratschlag <I>
tired ['taɪəd] müde I
title ['taɪtl] Titel; Überschrift <I>
to [tu:] zu; nach; in I; an; um zu II U3, 53; auf <II U3, 58>; für <II U5, 101>
quarter to/past ['kwɔ:tə tə/pɑ:st] Viertel vor/nach II U2, 40
today [tə'deɪ] heute I
together [tə'geðə] zusammen I
told [təʊld] simple past von *to tell* I
tomato *(sg)* [tə'mɑ:təʊ], **tomatoes** *(pl)* [tə'mɑ:təʊz] Tomate I
tomorrow [tə'mɒrəʊ] morgen II U3, 50
too [tu:] auch; zu I
took [tʊk] simple past von *to take* II U1, 10
tooth *(sg)* [tu:θ], **teeth** *(pl)* [ti:θ] Zahn II U5, 92
top [tɒp] Oberteil; Top <II U2, 165>; Spitze; oberer Teil; oberes Ende II U3, 60
topic ['tɒpɪk] Thema <I>
torch [tɔ:tʃ] Taschenlampe I
*to keep in **touch** [ˌki:p ɪn 'tʌtʃ] in Kontakt bleiben II U6, 110
to **touch** [tʌtʃ] berühren; anfassen <II U3, 62>
tour [tʊə] Tour; Reise <II U1, 25>
tourist ['tʊərɪst] Tourist; Touristin II U3, 60
tower ['taʊə] Turm II U3, 49
town [taʊn] Stadt I
town hall [ˌtaʊn 'hɔ:l] Rathaus <II U1, 22>
train [treɪn] Zug I
trainer ['treɪnə] Turnschuh II U2, 36
tram [træm] Straßenbahn I
trampolining ['træmpli:nɪŋ] Trampolinspringen <II U6, 116>
transparency [træn'spærnsi] Folie <II U5, 101>
transport ['trænspɔ:t] Verkehr; Transport II U4, 78
to **travel** ['trævl] fahren; reisen II U6, 114
treasure hunt ['treʒə ˌhʌnt] Schnitzeljagd; Schatzsuche II U3, 57
tree [tri:] Baum I
trick [trɪk] Kunststück; Trick I; Streich II U4, 78
trip [trɪp] Ausflug; Fahrt; Reise I
school trip [ˌsku:l 'trɪp] Klassenfahrt; Schulausflug II U4, 68

trousers *(pl)* ['traʊzəz] Hose <II U2, 165>
true [tru:] wahr <II U1, 25>
trumpet ['trʌmpɪt] Trompete II U3, 53
to **try** (to) [traɪ] versuchen; probieren <II U3, 52>
to try on [ˌtraɪ 'ɒn] anprobieren II U2, 36
Tuesday ['tju:zdeɪ] Dienstag I
tug of war [ˌtʌg əv 'wɔ:] Tauziehen <II U4, 171>
It's Holly's **turn.** [ɪts 'hɒliz ˌtɜ:n] Holly ist dran. II U1, 10
to **turn** [tɜ:n] abbiegen II U3, 57
Turn the music down. [ˌtɜ:n ðə mju:zɪk 'daʊn] Mach die Musik leiser. I
*to take **turns** [ˌteɪk 'tɜ:nz] sich abwechseln <I>
TV [ˌti:'vi:] Fernseher I
on TV [ɒn ˌti:'vi:] im Fernsehen <II U5, 98>
to watch TV [ˌwɒtʃ ti:'vi:] fernsehen I
twelve [twelv] zwölf I
twenty ['twenti] zwanzig I
twenty-one [ˌtwenti'wʌn] einundzwanzig I
two [tu:] zwei I
typical ['tɪpɪkl] typisch; charakteristisch <I>

U

uncle ['ʌŋkl] Onkel I
under ['ʌndə] unter I
underground ['ʌndəgraʊnd] U-Bahn I; unterirdisch <II U3, 62>
*to **understand** [ˌʌndə'stænd] verstehen II U6, 114
understood [ˌʌndə'stʊd] simple past von *to understand* II U6, 114
unhappy [ʌn'hæpi] unglücklich; traurig II U1, 15
uniform ['ju:nɪfɔ:m] Uniform I
unit ['ju:nɪt] Lektion; Kapitel <I>
up [ʌp] hinauf; oben; hoch II U3, 50
to **upload** [ʌp'ləʊd] hochladen II U6, 110
us [ʌs] uns; wir II U3, 57
to **use** [ju:z] benutzen; verwenden <I>
usually ['ju:ʒli] normalerweise; gewöhnlich II U2, 30

V

vegetarian [ˌvedʒɪ'teəriən] Vegetarier; Vegetarierin I
verb [vɜ:b] Verb <II U1, 12>
very ['veri] sehr I
video clip ['vɪdiəʊ ˌklɪp] Videoclip <II U5, 100>
viewing ['vju:ɪŋ] Hör-/Sehverstehen <I>
viewing skills ['vju:ɪŋ ˌskɪlz] Fertigkeit Hör-/Sehverstehen <I>
village ['vɪlɪdʒ] Dorf I
visit ['vɪzɪt] Besuch <II U6, 116>
to **visit** ['vɪzɪt] besuchen I
visitor ['vɪzɪtə] Besucher; Besucherin II U3, 51
volleyball ['vɒlibɔ:l] Volleyball <II U6, 116>

W

to **wait** (for) [weɪt] warten (auf) II U3, 53
*to **wake** up [ˌweɪk‿'ʌp] aufwachen <II U2, 43>
walk [wɔ:k] Wanderung; Spaziergang I
to **walk** around [ˌwɔ:k‿ə'raʊnd] umherlaufen; herumlaufen <I>
walk-up price ['wɔ:kʌp ˌpraɪs] Schalterpreis <II U3, 62>
walking ['wɔ:kɪŋ] Wandern <II U1, 22>
wall [wɔ:l] Wand; Mauer II U2, 33
wall painting ['wɔ:l peɪntɪŋ] Wandmalerei II U6, 115
to **want** (to) ['wɒnt] wollen; mögen I
wardrobe ['wɔ:drəʊb] Kleiderschrank II U2, 33
warm [wɔ:m] warm II U6, 106
warm-up ['wɔ:mʌp] Aufwärmtraining; Aufwärmen II U4, 74
was [wɒz] simple past von *to be* I
wash [wɒʃ] Wäsche II U4, 70
to **wash** [wɒʃ] (sich) waschen; spülen II U2, 40
*to do the **washing** up [ˌdu: ðə 'wɒʃɪŋ‿ʌp] abspülen <II U2, 163>
to **watch** [wɒtʃ] anschauen; ansehen I; zuschauen; zusehen; beobachten II U5, 88
to watch TV [ˌwɒtʃ ti:'vi:] fernsehen I
water ['wɔ:tə] Wasser I
wax [wæks] Wachs II U3, 49
way [weɪ] Weg I
to ask the way [ˌɑ:sk ðə 'weɪ] nach dem Weg fragen <II U3, 59>
to be a long way away [bi: ə 'lɒŋ ˌweɪ ə'weɪ] weit weg sein II U6, 105
Way to go! ['weɪ tə ˌgəʊ] Super! <II U4, 83>
we [wi:] wir I
*to **wear** [weə] tragen; anhaben I
weather ['weðə] Wetter; Witterung II U6, 106
website ['websaɪt] Website <I>
Wednesday ['wenzdeɪ] Mittwoch I
week [wi:k] Woche I
weekend ['wi:kend] Wochenende I
welcome (to) ['welkəm] willkommen (bei/in) I
well [wel] gut II U1, 10
... as well as ... [əz 'wel‿əz] sowohl ... als auch ... II U6, 114
Well, ... [wel] Na ja, ...; Also ... II U6, 110
Well done! [ˌwel 'dʌn] Gut gemacht! II U6, 105
went [went] simple past von *to go* I
were [wɜ:] simple past von *to be* I
wet [wet] nass I
what [wɒt] was; welche I
What about ...? [ˌwɒt‿ə'baʊt] Und ...?; Was ist mit ...? II U1, 10
What colour is ...? [ˌwɒt 'kʌlər‿ɪz] Welche Farbe hat ...? I
What time is it? [ˌwɒt 'taɪm‿ɪz‿ɪt] Wie viel Uhr ist es?; Wie spät ist es? I
What's the weather like? [ˌwɒts ðə 'weðə laɪk] Wie ist das Wetter? II U6, 106
What's wrong? [ˌwɒts 'rɒŋ] Was ist los? <II U1, 161>
What's your name? [ˌwɒts jə 'neɪm] Wie heißt du? I
wheel [wi:l] Rad II U3, 48

big wheel [ˌbɪg ˈwiːl] Riesenrad II U3, 48
wheelchair [ˈwiːltʃeə] Rollstuhl I
when [wen] wann I; wenn; als II U3, 61
where [weə] wo; wohin; woher I
Where are you from? [ˌweər‿ə ju ˈfrɒm] Woher kommst du? I
which [wɪtʃ] welche; was II U3, 50
white [waɪt] weiß I
who [huː] wer I; das; der; die <II U5, 98>
why [waɪ] warum I
that's why [ˈðæts waɪ] deshalb; deswegen II U4, 69
wild [waɪld] freie Wildbahn; Wildnis <II U5, 98>
will [wɪl] werden II U6, 105
*to **win** [wɪn] siegen; gewinnen I
wind [wɪnd] Wind I
window [ˈwɪndəʊ] Fenster I
windsurfing [ˈwɪndsɜːfɪŋ] Windsurfen <II U1, 162>
windy [ˈwɪndi] windig II U6, 106
winner [ˈwɪnə] Sieger; Siegerin; Gewinner; Gewinnerin I
winter [ˈwɪntə] Winter I
wire [waɪə] Draht; Kabel <II U1, 23>
Best **wishes**, [ˌbest ˈwɪʃɪz] Viele Grüße; Alles Gute I
with [wɪð] mit I; bei II U1, 19
without [wɪˈðaʊt] ohne II U3, 61
wizard [ˈwɪzəd] Zauberer II U3, 60
wolf *(sg)* [wʊlf], **wolves** *(pl)* [wʊlvz] Wolf II U4, 79
woman *(sg)* [ˈwʊmən], **women** *(pl)* [ˈwɪmɪn] Frau I
won [wʌn] simple past von ***to win*** II U4, 70
won't (= will not) [wəʊnt] nicht werden II U6, 110
wood [wʊd] Holz I
woof [wʊf] wau I
wool [wʊl] Wolle I
word [wɜːd] Wort II U2, 41
word order [ˈwɜːd‿ɔːdə] Wortstellung; Satzstellung <II U4, 76>
wore [wɔː] simple past von ***to wear*** I
work [wɜːk] Arbeit II U2, 40
to **work** [wɜːk] arbeiten I; funktionieren <II U3, 62>
acting **workshop** [ˈæktɪŋ ˌwɜːkʃɒp] Schauspielworkshop <II U5, 99>
world [wɜːld] Welt I
all around the world [ɔːl‿əˌraʊnd ðə ˈwɜːld] in aller Welt II U5, 87
worried [ˈwʌrid] beunruhigt; besorgt II U1, 15
to **worry** [ˈwʌri] sich Sorgen machen I
Don't worry. [ˌdəʊnt ˈwʌri] Mach dir keine Sorgen. I
worse [wɜːs] schlechter; schlimmer II U2, 36
worst [wɜːst] schlimmste; schlechteste II U2, 40
Would you like (to) …? [ˌwʊd jə ˈlaɪk] Möchtest du …?; Würdest du gern …? I
I wouldn't like (to) … [aɪ ˈwʊdnt laɪk] ich möchte nicht …; ich würde nicht gerne … I
I'd (= I would) [aɪd] ich würde; ich hätte gern I
*to **write** [raɪt] schreiben I
writing [ˈraɪtɪŋ] Schreiben <I>
writing skills [ˈraɪtɪŋ ˌskɪlz] Fertigkeit Schreiben <II U5, 91>
wrong [rɒŋ] falsch I
Is something wrong? [ɪz ˈsʌmθɪŋ rɒŋ] Stimmt etwas nicht? II U6, 110
wrote [rəʊt] simple past von ***to write*** II U5, 87

Y

year [jɪə] Klasse; Jahrgangsstufe; Jahr I
yellow [ˈjeləʊ] gelb I
yes [jes] ja I
yesterday [ˈjestədeɪ] gestern I
you [juː] du; Sie; ihr; dich; euch; dir; Ihnen I
young [jʌŋ] jung II U5, 96
your [jɔː] dein; euer; Ihr I
Yours, [jɔːz] Dein *(Grußformel in Briefen oder E-Mails)* II U5, 88
yourself [jɔːˈself] dich selbst <I>
Help **yourselves**! [ˌhelp jɔːˈselvz] Bedient euch!; Bedienen Sie sich! <II U4, 81>
youth [juːθ] Jugend- I
yummy [ˈjʌmi] lecker II U2, 41

Z

zero [ˈzɪərəʊ] null I
zoo [zuː] Tierpark; Zoo <II U3, 64>
to **zoom** in [ˈzuːm‿ɪn] heranzoomen <I>

Boys' names

Amir [ɑːˈmiːr] II U5, 91
Andy [ˈændi] <II U1, 22>
Brad [bræd] II U5, 89
Hamid [ˈhæmɪd] II U5, 91
Hector [ˈhektə] II U3, 60
Jack [dʒæk] II U2, 40
Jamie [ˈdʒeɪmi] II U1, 14
Jinsoo [ˈdʒɪnsuː] <II U1, 23>
Joe [dʒəʊ] II U5, 88
Jordan [ˈdʒɔːdn] II U5, 97
Marc [mɑːk] <II U4, 82>
Marley [ˈmɑːli] <II U1, 23>
Nick [nɪk] II U6, 114
Pablo [ˈpɑbləʊ] II U6, 106
Rick [rɪk] II U3, 58
Ronnie [ˈrɒni] II U3, 60
Simon [ˈsaɪmən] II U5, 89
Terry [ˈteri] II U5, 91

Girls' names

Alice [ˈælɪs] <II U5, 98>
Alicia [əˈlɪʃə] <II U6, 117>
Amber [ˈæmbə] II U1, 11
Anna [ˈænə] II U2, 40
Belinda [bəˈlɪndə] <II U1, 22>
Emily [ˈemɪli] II U5, 87
Emma [ˈemə] II U4, 74
Grace [greɪs] II U5, 87
Gwen [gwen] II U1, 10
Irina [ɪˈriːnə] II U2, 40
Isabel [ˈɪzəbel] <II U6, 116>
Jane [dʒeɪn] II U5, 91
Kimi [ˈkɪmi] II U6, 106
Laura [ˈlɔːrə] <II U2, 43>
Lily [ˈlɪli] II U5, 97
Linda [ˈlɪndə] II U6, 106
Mina [ˈmiːnə] <II U3, 63>
Nicola [ˈnɪklə] II U5, 89
Polly [ˈpɒli] <II U5, 99>
Rosie [ˈrəʊzi] <II U1, 22>
Sally [ˈsæli] II U5, 97
Stella [ˈstelə] II U5, 88

Surnames

Bennett ['benɪt] <II U6, 116>
Berry ['beri] II U2, 29
Brooks [brʊks] II U4, 74
Cussons ['kʌsnz] <II U5, 98>
Dawson ['dɔ:sn] <II U1, 22>
Hardy ['hɑ:di] II U5, 92
McCane [mə'keɪn] <II U5, 99>
Moore [mɔ:] II U5, 96
Nair [neə] <II U5, 99>
Romero [rə'meərəʊ] II U5, 97
Ross [rɒs] <II U4, 83>
Thompson ['tɒmsn] <II U4, 81>
Williams ['wɪljəmz] <II U1, 22>

Place names

Africa ['æfrɪkə] Afrika II U5, 86
Alaska [ə'læskə] *Bundesstaat in den USA* II U6, 106
Anchorage ['æŋkrɪdʒ] *Stadt in den USA* II U6, 106
Antarctica [æn'tɑ:ktɪkə] Antarktis II U5, 97
Arizona [ˌærɪ'zəʊnə] *Bundesstaat in den USA* II U6, 106
Australia [ɒs'treɪliə] Australien I
Belfast [bel'fɑ:st] *Hauptstadt von Nordirland* II U5, 87
Britain ['brɪtn] Großbritannien II U5, 96
Canada ['kænədə] Kanada I
Chicago [ʃɪ'kɑ:gəʊ] *Großstadt in den USA* II U6, 104
Devon ['devn] *Grafschaft in Südwestengland* I
England ['ɪŋglənd] England I
Europe ['jʊərəp] Europa II U3, 50
Exeter ['eksɪtə] *Stadt in Südwestengland* <II U1, 22>
Florida ['flɒrɪdə] *Bundesstaat in den USA* II U6, 106
Germany ['dʒɜ:məni] Deutschland I
Great Britain [ˌgreɪt 'brɪtn] Großbritannien I
Greenwich ['grenɪdʒ] *Stadtteil im Südosten Londons* I
Hampshire ['hæmpʃə] *Grafschaft in Südengland* II U5, 96
India ['ɪndiə] Indien I
Istanbul [ˌɪstæn'bʊl] *Großstadt in der Türkei* I
Jamaica [dʒə'meɪkə] Jamaika II U1, 9
London ['lʌndən] *Hauptstadt von England* I
Manchester ['mæntʃɪstə] *Stadt in Nordengland* II U1, 10
Margate ['mɑ:geɪt] *Ausflugsort in England* I
Miami [maɪ'æmi] *Stadt in den USA* II U6, 106
Moscow ['mɒskəʊ] Moskau I
Munich ['mju:nɪk] München <II U1, 22>
Phoenix ['fi:nɪks] *Großstadt in den USA* II U6, 106
Poland ['pəʊlənd] Polen II U3, 48
Russia ['rʌʃə] Russland I
Salt Lake City [ˌsɔ:lt ˌleɪk 'sɪti] *Stadt in den USA* II U5, 97
Scotland ['skɒtlənd] Schottland I
South Africa [ˌsaʊθ_'æfrɪkə] Südafrika <II U5, 98>
South Devon [ˌsaʊθ 'devn] *Region in Südwestengland* <II U6, 116>
Staffordshire ['stæfədʃə] *Grafschaft in Mittelengland* <II U1, 22>
Stoke-on-Trent [ˌstəʊkɒn'trent] *Stadt in Mittelengland* <II U1, 22>
Taunton ['tɔ:ntən] *Ort in Südwestengland* <II U3, 63>
Thailand ['taɪlænd] Thailand I
Turkey ['tɜ:ki] Türkei I
UK (United Kingdom) [ˌju:'keɪ (ju:ˌnaɪtɪd 'kɪŋdəm)] Vereinigtes Königreich von Großbritannien und Nordirland II U2, 37
United States [ju:ˌnaɪtɪd'steɪts] Vereinigte Staaten II U6, 109
USA (United States of America) [ˌju:es'eɪ (ju:ˌnaɪtɪd ˌsteɪts_əv ə'merɪkə)] USA (Vereinigte Staaten von Amerika) I
Utah ['ju:tɑ:] *Bundesstaat in den USA* II U5, 97
Vancouver [væn'ku:və] *Großstadt in Kanada* I

Other names

Albion St ['ælbiən ˌstri:t] *Straßenname* <II U1, 22>
Alps [ælps] Alpen <II U1, 22>
Arsenal ['ɑ:snl] *Name einer Fußballmannschaft* II U2, 33
Barton Hall [ˌbɑ:tn 'hɔ:l] *Name eines Abenteuerzentrums* <II U6, 116>
BBC1 [ˌbi: bi: 'si: wʌn] *brit. Fernsehsender* <II U5, 98>
BBC2 [ˌbi: bi: 'si: tu:] *brit. Fernsehsender* <II U5, 98>
Big Ben [ˌbɪg 'ben] *Sehenswürdigkeit in London* II U3, 49
The **Bishopsgate Tower** [ðə 'bɪʃəpsgeɪt ˌtaʊə] *Wolkenkratzer in London* II U3, 52
Bold Street ['bəʊld ˌstri:t] *Straßenname* II U3, 59
Bond Street ['bɒnd ˌstri:t] *Londoner Straßenname* II U3, 57
The **BT Tower** [ðə ˌbi:'ti: 'taʊə] *Fernsehturm in London* II U3, 52
Buckingham Palace [ˌbʌkɪŋəm 'pælɪs] Buckingham-Palast <II U3, 166>
Camden Market [ˌkæmdən 'mɑ:kɪt] *Markt im Londoner Stadtteil Camden* <II U3, 63>
Channel 4 ['tʃænl ˌfɔ:] *brit. Fernsehsender* <II U5, 98>
Channel 5 ['tʃænl ˌfaɪv] *brit. Fernsehsender* <II U5, 98>
Chimp Eden [ˌtʃɪmp 'i:dn] *Name einer Schutzstation für Schimpansen* <II U5, 98>
Church Street ['tʃɜ:tʃ ˌstri:t] *Straßenname* II U3, 59
Duke Street ['dju:k ˌstri:t] *Straßenname* II U3, 59
Elizabeth Tower [ɪˌlɪzəbəθ 'taʊə] *Sehenswürdigkeit in London* II U3, 49
Escape to Chimp Eden [ɪ'skeɪp tə ˌtʃɪmp 'i:dn] *Name einer Fernsehsendung* <II U5, 98>
Fantasia III [fæn'teɪziə θri:] *Name eines Computerspiels* II U3, 53
The **Gherkin** [ðə 'gɜ:kɪn] *Wolkenkratzer in London* II U3, 52
Jane Goodall [dʒeɪn 'gʊdɔ:l] *Schimpansenforscherin* II U5, 87
Greenwich Park ['grenɪdʒ ˌpɑ:k] *Park in Greenwich* II U2, 41

Greenwich Shopping Park [ˌgrenɪdʒ ˈʃɒpɪŋ pɑːk] *Einkaufszentrum in Greenwich* II U2, 36

Hartshill Rd [ˌhɑːtshɪl ˈrəʊd] *Straßenname* <II U1, 22>

Help! My dad is an alien. [ˈhelp maɪ ˈdæd ɪz‿ən ˈeɪliən] *Name einer Fernsehsendung* <II U5, 98>

Home and Away [ˈhəʊm‿ən əˌweɪ] *Name einer Fernsehsendung* <II U5, 98>

Hyde Park [ˌhaɪd ˈpɑːk] *Park in London* II U3, 61

Incey [ˈɪnsi] *Tiername* <II U2, 45>

Kidbrooke Gardens [ˌkɪdbrʊk ˈgɑːdnz] *Straßenname* II U2, 28

Little Red Riding Hood [lɪtl red ˈraɪdɪŋ ˌhʊd] Rotkäppchen II U4, 79

The **London Dungeon** [ðə ˌlʌndən ˈdʌndʒn] *Gruselkabinett in London* II U3, 50

The **London Eye** [ðə ˌlʌndən‿ˈaɪ] *Riesenrad in London* II U3, 48

Madame Tussauds [ˌmædəm tʊˈsɔːdz] *Wachsfigurenmuseum in London* II U3, 49

Manchester United [ˌmæntʃɪstə juːˈnaɪtɪd] *Name einer Fußballmannschaft* II U2, 33

Mount Everest [ˌmaʊnt ˈevrest] *höchster Berg der Welt* II U5, 97

The **O2** [ði ˈəʊˌtuː] *Konzertarena in London* <II U3, 166>

Oaklands Drive [ˈəʊkləndz ˌdraɪv] *Straßenname* <II U6, 116>

One Canada Square [wʌn ˈkænədə ˌskweə] *Wolkenkratzer in London* II U3, 52

Oxford Street [ˈɒksfəd ˌstriːt] *Einkaufsstraße in London* II U3, 57

Piccadilly Circus [ˌpɪkədɪli ˈsɜːkəs] *Sehenswürdigkeit in London* <II U3, 166>

Red Nose Day [red ˈnəʊz deɪ] *Spendenmarathon* II U5, 87

Ross [rɒs] *Tiername* II U2, 40

William **Shakespeare** [ˌwɪljəm ˈʃeɪkspɪə] *englischer Schriftsteller* <II U5, 99>

The **Shard** [ðə ˈʃɑːd] *Wolkenkratzer in London* II U3, 50

St Paul's [sənt ˈpɔːlz] *Kirche in London* II U3, 49

Stanley Street [ˈstænli ˌstriːt] *Straßenname* II U3, 59

Teens in the kitchen [ˌtiːnz ɪn ðə ˈkɪtʃɪn] *Name einer Fernsehkochshow* <II U5, 98>

Tom Sawyer [ˌtɒm ˈsɔːjə] *Kurztitel eines Romans von Mark Twain* II U6, 111

Tower Bridge [ˌtaʊə ˈbrɪdʒ] *Brücke in London* II U3, 48

The **Tower of London** [ðə ˌtaʊər‿əv ˈlʌndən] *Sehenswürdigkeit in London* II U3, 60

Victoria Street [vɪkˈtɔːriə ˌstriːt] *Straßenname* II U3, 59

Wembley [ˈwembli] *Name eines Fußballstadions in London* <II U3, 166>

Westminster Abbey [ˌwestmɪnstər‿ˈæbi] *Abtei im Londoner Stadtteil Westminster* <II U3, 166>

Westminster Bridge [ˈwestmɪnstə ˌbrɪdʒ] *Brücke in London* II U3, 49

Windmill Hill [ˌwɪnmɪl ˈhɪl] *Name eines Schullandheims* II U4, 78

Wood Street [ˈwʊd ˌstriːt] *Straßenname* II U3, 59

A

abbiegen to turn II U3, 57
Abend evening I
Abendessen dinner; tea I
abends in the evening I
aber but I
abfahren to leave II U6, 105
Abfall rubbish I
abgeschlossen locked I
Abrakadabra! Abracadabra! II U3, 60
Abschieds- leaving II U6, 110
acht eight I
Achterbahn roller coaster II U5, 96
achtzehn eighteen I
achtzig eighty I
Aktivität activity I
albern silly II U6, 110
alle all I; everyone II U2, 40; every II U3, 49
alles everything II U1, 20
Alles Gute Best wishes, I; All the best, II U6, 115
Alligator alligator II U6, 106
als as II U1, 15; than II U2, 36; when II U3, 61
als Nächstes next II U2, 36
also so I
Also … Well, … II U6, 110
alt old I
am in; on I
am Ende at the end II U4, 68
Amerikaner American II U6, 110
Amerikanerin American II U6, 110
Amerikanisch American II U6, 110
amerikanisch American II U6, 110
American Football American football II U6, 115
an on; at I; to II U3, 53
andauern to last II U4, 74
Andenken souvenir II U3, 57
andere other II U4, 70
anderen others II U4, 78
ändern to change II U2, 33
anders different I
Anfang beginning II U4, 69
anfangen to start I
Angst haben to be scared I
anhaben to wear I
anhalten to stop II U5, 87
anhören to listen (to) I
ankommen to arrive I
anprobieren to try on II U2, 36
Anruf phone call I
anrufen to phone II U1, 20
anschauen to look at; to watch I
ansehen to watch I
Antwort answer II U6, 105
antworten to answer II U1, 20
anziehen to put on II U4, 78
Apfel apple I
April April I
Arbeit work II U2, 40
arbeiten to work I
Arm arm II U5, 92
Art kind II U6, 114
Arzt doctor II U5, 92
Ärztin doctor II U5, 92
auch too; also I
auf in; on; at I
auf der linken Seite on the left II U3, 57
auf der rechten Seite on the right II U3, 57
auf einmal suddenly I
Auf Wiedersehen. Goodbye. I
Geld **aufbringen** to raise money II U4, 69
Aufführung show I
aufgeregt excited II U6, 105
aufhören to finish II U1, 20; to stop II U5, 87
aufmachen to open I
aufpassen auf to look after II U2, 40
aufräumen to tidy II U2, 30
aufregend exciting I
aufstehen to get up I
Aufwärmen warm-up II U4, 74
Aufwärmtraining warm-up II U4, 74
Aufzug lift II U3, 50
Auge eye I
August August I
aus from I
Auseinandersetzung argument II U1, 15
Ausflug trip I
den Hund **ausführen** to take the dog for a walk I
ausgeben *(Geld)* to spend II U5, 97
ein **ausgefüllter** Tag a busy day II U2, 41
(sich) **ausleihen** to borrow II U1, 15
die Spülmaschine **ausräumen** to empty the dishwasher II U2, 30
aussehen to look I
außen outside II U4, 79
außerhalb outside II U4, 79
aussteigen to get off II U1, 20
Auto car I

B

Bad(ezimmer) bathroom II U2, 30
bald soon II U6, 105
Balkon balcony I
Ball ball I
Banane banana I
Band band II U1, 10
Bär bear II U6, 106
Basketball basketball II U6, 115
basteln to make II U4, 68
bauen to build II U3, 48
Bauer farmer I
Bäuerin farmer I
Bauernhof farm I
Baum tree I
Bauwerk building II U3, 50
beängstigend scary I
beantworten to answer II U1, 20
beenden to finish II U1, 20; to stop II U5, 87
Begabung talent I
begeistert excited II U6, 105
Beginn beginning II U4, 69
beginnen to start I
bei at I; with II U1, 19
Bein leg II U5, 92
beinahe nearly II U4, 78
bekommen to get I
bellen to bark II U2, 40
bemalen to paint II U6, 115
beobachten to watch II U5, 88
bereit ready I
Berg mountain II U5, 97
berühmt famous I
beschäftigt busy I
besitzen to have I; to have got II U2, 40
besonders special I
besorgt worried II U1, 15
besser better II U2, 33
beste best II U2, 33
am besten best II U2, 33
besteigen to climb II U5, 97

besuchen to visit I
Besucher visitor II U3, 51
Besucherin visitor II U3, 51
Bett bed I
ins Bett gehen to go to bed I
beunruhigt worried II U1, 15
bevor before II U2, 30
bewölkt cloudy II U6, 106
Bild picture I
billig cheap II U2, 36
Biologie Biology I
Bis bald. See you soon. I; See you. II U6, 113
ein (kleines) bisschen a little (bit) II U4, 70
bitte please I
Bitte schön. Here you are. I
blau blue I
bleiben to stay I
Bleistift pencil I
Blog blog I
Bonbon sweet I
böse angry II U1, 15
Box box I
brauchen to need I
braun brown I
bringen to bring II U1, 15
Brot bread I
belegtes Brot sandwich I
Brücke bridge II U3, 49
Bruder brother I
Bub boy I
Buch book I
Bude stall I
Bühne stage II U5, 86
Bus bus I
Butter butter I

C

Café snack bar I
Cafeteria cafeteria I
chatten to chat II U6, 110
Chinese Chinese II U5, 97
Chinesin Chinese II U5, 97
Chinesisch Chinese II U5, 97
chinesisch Chinese II U5, 97
circa about II U3, 49
Cola cola I
Comic(heft) comic II U2, 33
Computer computer I
cool cool I
Cousin cousin II U1, 10
Cousine cousin II U1, 10

D

da there; because I
Dachboden attic I
daheim at home I
dahin there I
danach then; after that I
Danke. Thanks.; Thank you. I
dann then I
das the; this; that I
dass that II U4, 70
dauern to last II U4, 74
davor in front of I
dein your I
Dein *(Grußformel in Briefen oder E-Mails)* Yours, II U5, 88
denken to think II U2, 33
der the I
dermaßen so II U6, 105
derselbe the same II U1, 15
deshalb so I
Design design II U6, 115
Detektiv detective I
Detektivin detective I
Deutsch German I
deutsch German II U3, 48
Deutsche German II U3, 48
Deutscher German II U3, 48
Dezember December I
Dialog dialogue II U1, 18
dich you I
die the I
Dienstag Tuesday I
dies this I
diese these II U2, 36
dieses that I
Ding thing I
dir you I
Donnerstag Thursday I
Dorf village I
dort there I
dorthin there I
draußen outside II U4, 79
dreckig dirty I
drei three I
dreißig thirty I
dreizehn thirteen I
dritte third II U3, 57
du you I
dunkel dark I
Durcheinander mess I
Durchmesser diameter II U3, 50

E

E-Mail e-mail II U5, 88
Ei egg I
eigene own II U4, 68
eigentlich really I
ein one; a; an I
eine a; an I
einfach easy I
einhundert a/one hundred I
einige some I
Einkaufen shopping I
Einkaufspassage mall II U6, 114
Einkaufszentrum shopping centre I; mall II U6, 114
Einkaufszettel shopping list I
einladen to invite II U4, 69
Einladung invitation I
einmal once II U6, 114
die Spülmaschine einräumen to load the dishwasher II U2, 30
eins one I
einst once II U6, 114
eintausend a/one thousand II U5, 96
Eintrittskarte ticket II U4, 70
einundzwanzig twenty-one I
Eis ice cream II U1, 10
Eiscreme ice cream II U1, 10
elf eleven I
Eltern parents *(pl)* I
Ende end II U4, 68
am Ende at the end II U4, 68
oberes Ende top II U3, 60
enden to finish II U1, 20
Englisch English I
entfernt away II U2, 40
Entschuldigung. Sorry. I; I'm sorry. II U1, 15; Excuse me. II U3, 57
Entwurf design II U6, 115
er it; he I
Erdbeere strawberry I
Erdteil continent II U5, 97
Ereignis event II U4, 68
Erkältung cold II U4, 70
erklettern to climb II U5, 97
sich erkundigen nach to ask about II U6, 114
erledigen to finish II U1, 20

ernst serious II U5, 92
erraten to guess I
erstaunlich amazing II U5, 96
erste first I
das erste Mal the first time I
als **Erstes** first II U1, 20
erzählen to tell I
Erzähler narrator I
Erzählerin narrator I
es it I
Es tut mir leid. I'm sorry. II U1, 15
es war einmal once upon a time II U3, 60
Essen food I; meal II U5, 88
essen to eat; to have I
Etage floor II U3, 50
etwa about II U3, 49
etwas something; some I
Stimmt etwas nicht? Is something wrong? II U6, 110
euch you I
euer your I
Experiment experiment II U5, 87

F

fahren to go; to ride I; to run II U2, 40; to travel II U6, 114
Fahrrad fahren to go bike riding II U1, 10
Tandem fahren to go tandem bike riding II U1, 10
Fahrgeschäft ride II U5, 96
Fahrrad bike I
Fahrrad fahren to go bike riding II U1, 10
Fahrschein ticket II U4, 70
Fahrt trip I; ride II U5, 96
Fakt fact II U3, 50
fallen to fall I
falsch wrong I
Familie family I
Fan fan I
fangen to catch II U6, 114
fantastisch fantastic II U1, 9
Farbe colour I
Fasching carnival I
fast nearly II U4, 78
Februar February I
Feier party I
eine Party **feiern** to have a party I
Fenster window I
Ferien holiday II U1, 9
fernsehen to watch TV I
Fernseher TV I
fertig ready I
fertig machen to finish II U1, 20
fertigstellen to finish I
Fest fair II U4, 69
festhalten to hold II U5, 97
feststecken to be stuck I
Festzug procession II U4, 68
Figur figure II U3, 49
Film film I
finden to find I
Firma company II U1, 20
Fisch fish I
eine **Flasche** … a bottle of II U5, 88
Fledermaus bat I
fliegen to fly II U3, 60
Floh flea I
Flohmarkt flea market I
Fluss river I
American **Football** American football II U6, 115
Foto photo I
Fotos machen to take photos (of) II U1, 10
fotografieren to take photos (of) II U1, 10
Frage question I
fragen to ask I
fragen nach to ask about II U6, 114
Frau woman I
Frau *(Anrede)* Mrs I
im **Freien** outside II U4, 79
Freitag Friday I
Freizeit free time I
Freizeitpark theme park II U5, 96
Freude fun I
Freund friend I
Freundin friend I
Freundschaft(en) schließen to make friends II U6, 110
Frisbee frisbee I
Frisbeescheibe frisbee I
Frohe Weihnachten! Merry Christmas! I
Frucht fruit I
früh early II U2, 40
Frühling spring II U6, 106
Frühstück breakfast I
frühstücken to have breakfast I
(sich) **fühlen** to feel II U1, 10
Füller pen I
fünf five I
fünfzehn fifteen I
fünfzig fifty I
für for I
furchtbar awful I
Fuß foot II U2, 36
zu Fuß on foot I
Fußball football I; soccer *(AE)* II U6, 115
füttern to feed I

G

ganz all I; all of II U3, 60; quite II U5, 88
in ganz all over II U5, 96
Garten garden I
Gebäude building II U3, 50
geben to give I
gebratener Reis mit Hühnerfleisch chicken fried rice II U5, 88
gebraucht second-hand I
Geburtstag birthday I
gegenüber opposite II U2, 29
gehen to go I
inlineskaten gehen to go skating II U5, 88
ins Bett gehen to go to bed I
Schlittschuhlaufen gehen to go skating II U5, 88
Gehör hearing II U1, 20
gelb yellow I
Geld money I
Geld aufbringen to raise money II U4, 69
Geld sammeln to raise money II U4, 69
genauso the same II U1, 15
geöffnet open I
geradeaus straight on II U3, 57
Geräusch noise I
… **gerne** like + -ing I
gernhaben to like I
Geschäft shop I
geschehen to happen II U1, 15
Geschenk present I
Geschichte story I
geschlossen closed I
Gesellschaft company II U1, 20
Gesicht face I

H

I

in der Schule at school I
in ganz all over II U5, 96
in Ordnung fine I
Information(en) information II U3, 50
Ingenieur engineer II U6, 105
Ingenieurin engineer II U6, 105
inlineskaten to skate II U5, 88
inlineskaten gehen to go skating II U5, 88
interessant interesting I
Internettagebuch blog I
irgendeine any I
irgendwelche any I

J

ja yes I
Jacke coat I
Jahr year I
Jahreszeit season II U6, 106
Jahrgangsstufe year I; grade *(AE)* II U6, 115
Jahrmarkt fair II U4, 69
Januar January I
jede every I
jeder everyone II U2, 40
jemand somebody I
jene that I; those II U2, 36
jetzt now I
Job job I
Jugend- youth I; teen II U5, 96
Jugendliche teen II U5, 96
Jugendlicher teen II U5, 96
Juli July I
jung young II U5, 96
Junge boy I
Juni June I

K

Käfig cage II U2, 30
Kalender planner II U4, 68
kalt cold I
Kälte cold II U4, 70
kämpfen to fight II U5, 87
Kaninchen rabbit I
Kanufahren canoeing I
Kapitän captain II U6, 105
Kapitänin captain II U6, 105
Karneval carnival I
Karte map II U3, 50
Käse cheese I
Katze cat I
kaufen to buy I
kein no I
keine no I
kennen to know I
kennenlernen to meet I
Kilo (kg, Kilogramm) kilo (kg, kilogram) I
Kind kid I
Kinder children *(pl)* I
Kinderzimmer bedroom II U2, 28
Kino cinema I
Kirche church II U3, 49
Kiste box I
Klasse year; class I; grade *(AE)* II U6, 115
Klassenfahrt school trip II U4, 68
Klassenzimmer classroom I
Kleid dress I
Kleider clothes *(pl only)* I
Kleiderschrank wardrobe II U2, 33
Kleidung clothes *(pl only)* I
klein little; small I
Klettern rock climbing I
klettern to climb II U5, 97
klingeln to ring I
Klub club I
Koch chef II U5, 88
Köchin chef II U5, 88
Koch- cooking II U2, 30
Kochen cooking II U2, 30
kochen to cook II U2, 30
komisch funny I
kommen to come; to get I
zu spät kommen to be late II U1, 8
König king II U3, 49
Königin queen II U3, 49
können can I
nicht können can't I
Kontakt contact I
in Kontakt bleiben to keep in touch II U6, 110
Kontinent continent II U5, 97
kontrollieren to check II U3, 60
Konzert concert I
Kopf head II U5, 92
Kopfschmerzen headache II U5, 92
Kopfweh headache II U5, 92
Korbball netball I
korrekt right I
korrigieren to correct II U3, 61
Es **kostet** zehn Pfund. It's ten pounds. I
Kostüm costume; fancy dress I
Krankenhaus hospital II U5, 97
Kricket cricket II U1, 10
Kronjuwelen crown jewels *(pl)* II U3, 60
Küche kitchen II U2, 30
Kuchen cake I
Küchenchef chef II U5, 88
Küchenchefin chef II U5, 88
sich **kümmern** um to look after II U2, 40
Kunde customer I
Kundin customer I
Kunst Art I
Kunststück trick I
kurz short II U2, 36
kurze Hose shorts *(pl)* II U6, 106

L

lachen to laugh II U4, 78
Laden shop I
Lampe lamp II U2, 33
Land country I
ländliche Gegend country I
Landwirt farmer I
Landwirtin farmer I
länger longer I
langweilig boring I
Laptop laptop I
lassen to leave II U6, 105
lass(t) uns let's (= let us) I
Laterne lantern II U4, 68
laufen to run II U2, 40
Schlittschuh laufen to skate II U5, 88
laut loud I
läuten to ring I
Leben life II U3, 48
leben to live I
Lebensmittel food I
legen to put I
Lehrer teacher I
Lehrerin teacher I
leicht easy I
Es tut mir **leid**. I'm sorry. II U1, 15
Tut mir **leid**. Sorry. I
leise quiet II U5, 88
Leiter ladder I
lernen to learn II U2, 41

Liebe(r) ..., *(Anrede in Briefen)* Dear ..., I
Liebe Grüße Love, I
lieben to love I
Lieblings- favourite I
am **liebsten** best II U2, 33
Lied song I
Lineal ruler I
links left; on the left II U3, 57
Loch hole I
lokal local II U4, 68
lustig funny I

M

machen to do; to make I
Fotos machen to take photos (of) II U1, 10
Hausaufgabe(n) machen to do homework I
Mach die Musik leiser. Turn the music down. I
Mach dir keine Sorgen. Don't worry. I
Mach dir nichts draus. Never mind. II U1, 15
Macht nichts. Never mind. II U1, 15
Mädchen girl I
Mahlzeit meal II U5, 88
Mai May I
Mal time I
das erste Mal the first time I
malen to paint II U6, 115
Mama mum I
manchmal sometimes I
Mann man I
Mannschaft team I
Mannschaftsführer captain II U6, 105
Mannschaftsführerin captain II U6, 105
Markt market I
März March I
Match match I
Mathe Maths I
Matsch mud I
Mauer wall II U2, 33
Maus mouse I
Medaille medal II U4, 74
Meer sea I
am Meer at the seaside I
Meerschweinchen guinea pig II U2, 30
mehr more II U1, 10
mein my I
einer **Meinung** sein (mit) to agree (with) II U6, 105
eine **Menge** a lot of I
Mensa cafeteria I
Mensch person II U5, 97
Menschen people *(pl only)* I
merkwürdig funny I
Messe fair II U4, 69
Meter metre II U3, 49
200-Meter-Lauf 200 metre race II U4, 74
mich me I
mild mild II U6, 106
Million million I
Minute minute I
mir me I
mit with I; on II U5, 92
mit (dem Zug) by (train) I
mitbringen to bring II U1, 15
mitmachen (bei) to take part (in) II U4, 74
mitnehmen to take I
Mittagessen lunch; dinner I
Mittagspause lunchtime I
Mittagszeit lunchtime I
mitten in in the middle of II U4, 79
Mittwoch Wednesday I
modern modern I
mögen to like; to want (to) I
gern mögen to love I
nicht mögen to hate I
ich möchte ... I'd like (to) ... (= I would like to) I
ich möchte nicht ... I wouldn't like (to) ... I
Möchtest du ...? Would you like (to) ...? I
im **Moment** at the moment II U3, 53
momentan at the moment II U3, 53
Monat month II U4, 68
Montag Monday I
Morgen morning I
heute Morgen this morning II U5, 88
morgen tomorrow II U3, 50
müde tired I
Muffin muffin II U6, 110
Müll rubbish I
Mund mouth II U5, 87
Museum museum II U3, 49
Musik music I
Musikgruppe band II U1, 10
Muslim Muslim I
Muslimin Muslim I
müssen to have (got) to II U1, 15; must II U4, 68
Mutter mother I
Mutti mum I
Mütze hat II U6, 106

N

Na ja, ... Well, ... II U6, 110
nach to; after I
nach *(bei Uhrzeitangaben)* past II U2, 40
nach Hause home I
Nachbar neighbour I
Nachbarin neighbour I
Nachmittag afternoon I
Nachricht message II U3, 53
Nachricht(en) news II U6, 105
nachschauen to look I
nächste next I
als Nächstes next II U2, 36
Nacht night I
Nacken neck II U3, 60
nah near II U3, 50
in der **Nähe** von near I
Name name I
Nase nose II U5, 92
nass wet I
natürlich of course II U5, 88
neben next to I
nebenher at the same time II U6, 110
nehmen to take I
nein no I
nenne mich call me I
nett nice I
neu new I
Neuigkeit(en) news II U6, 105
neun nine I
neunzehn nineteen I
neunzig ninety I
nicht not I
nicht können can't I
nicht mögen to hate I
nichts nothing II U5, 92
nie never II U2, 30
niemals never II U2, 30
niemand no one I; nobody II U5, 88

noch still II U5, 88
immer noch still II U5, 88
noch einmal again I
normalerweise usually II U2, 30
Note grade *(AE)* II U6, 115
November November I
null zero I
Nummer number I
nun now I
nur only I

O

oben up II U3, 50
oberer Teil top II U3, 60
oberes Ende top II U3, 60
oberhalb above II U2, 33
Obst fruit I
oder or I
öffnen to open I
oft often II U2, 28
ohne without II U3, 61
okay OK (okay) I
Oktober October I
Öl oil II U5, 88
Oma grandma I
Onkel uncle I
online online II U6, 110
Online- online II U6, 110
Orange orange I
orange orange I
in **Ordnung** fine I
in Ordnung bringen to tidy II U2, 30
organisieren to organize I
Ort place I
örtlich local II U4, 68

P

ein **paar** some I
Papa dad I
Park park I
Partner partner I
Partnerin partner I
Party party I
eine Party feiern to have a party I
passieren to happen II U1, 15
Das ist passiert. That's what happened. II U1, 15
Pause break I
Pausenhof playground I
Person person II U5, 97
Pferd horse I
Pflaume plum I
Pfund *(brit. Währungseinheit)* pound (£) I
Picknick picnic I
Pier pier II U6, 104
pink pink I
Pizza pizza I
Plan map II U3, 50
Planer planner II U4, 68
Platz place I
plaudern to chat II U6, 110
plötzlich suddenly I
Polizeibeamter police officer I
Polizeibeamtin police officer I
Pommes frites chips *(pl)* I
Pop *(Musik)* pop II U3, 60
Poster poster II U2, 33
Postkarte postcard I
Preis price I; prize II U4, 70
Problem problem I
Projekt project II U4, 69
prüfen to test II U5, 96
Pullover pullover I
Puma mountain lion II U6, 106
putzen to clean II U2, 30

R

Rad wheel II U3, 48
Radiergummi rubber I
Rap rap I
raten to guess I
Raum room I
Du hast **recht**. You're right. I
rechte right II U3, 57
rechts right; on the right II U3, 57
Rechtschreibung spelling I
reden (mit) to talk (to) I
Regal shelf II U2, 33
Regalbrett shelf II U2, 33
regnen to rain I
regnerisch rainy II U6, 106
Reis rice II U5, 88
gebratener Reis mit Hühnerfleisch chicken fried rice II U5, 88
Reise trip I
reisen to travel II U6, 114
Reiten horse riding I
reiten to ride I
Rennen race II U4, 74
rennen to run II U2, 40
Rest rest II U6, 106
Restaurant restaurant II U5, 88
retten to save II U5, 87
richtig right I
richtigstellen to correct II U3, 61
Riesenrad big wheel II U3, 48
Ritt ride II U5, 96
Rolle part II U4, 79
Rollstuhl wheelchair I
rosa pink I
rot red I
rufen to shout I
ruhig quiet II U5, 88

S

Sache thing I
Sack bag I
Sackhüpfen sack race II U4, 74
Saft juice I
sagen to say; to tell I
Saison season II U6, 106
Salat salad I
Geld **sammeln** to raise money II U4, 69
Samstag Saturday I
samstags on Saturdays I
Sandwich sandwich I
Sänger singer I
Sängerin singer I
sauber machen to clean II U2, 30
Saxofon saxophone I
Schachtel box I
Schade! That's too bad. II U6, 105
Schaf sheep I
Schal scarf II U1, 9
Schatzsuche treasure hunt II U3, 57
Schau mal. Look. I
schauen to look I
Lass mich mal schauen. Let me see. I
schenken to give I
schicken to send I
schieben to push I
Schiff ship I
Schimpanse chimpanzee II U5, 87
schlafen to sleep II U2, 41
Schlafzimmer bedroom II U2, 28
Schlamm mud I
schlecht bad I
schlechter worse II U2, 36
schlechteste worst II U2, 40
schließen to close I

streichen to paint II U6, 115
Streit argument II U1, 15
(sich) **streiten** to fight II U5, 87
ein **Stück** ... a piece of II U5, 88
Stufe step II U3, 50
Stuhl chair I
Stunde hour II U4, 74
Stundenplan timetable I
Sturm storm I
von etw. **stürzen** to fall off II U5, 92
super cool I
Supermarkt supermarket I
Süßigkeit sweet I

T

Tafel blackboard I
Tag day I
ein ausgefüllter Tag a busy day II U2, 41
eines Tages one day I
Tagebuch diary I
Talent talent I
Talentwettbewerb talent show I
Tandem tandem II U1, 10
Tandem fahren to go tandem bike riding II U1, 10
Tante aunt I
tanzen to dance I
Tänzer dancer I
Tänzerin dancer I
Tasche bag I
Taschenlampe torch I
Taschenrechner calculator I
eine **Tasse** ... a cup of II U5, 88
Tatsache fact II U3, 50
tausend a/one thousand II U5, 96
Team team I
Technik DT (Design Technology) I
Techniker engineer II U6, 105
Technikerin engineer II U6, 105
Teddybär teddy I
Tee tea I
Teenager teen II U5, 96
Teenagerin teen II U5, 96
Teil part II U4, 79
oberer Teil top II U3, 60
teilnehmen (an) to take part (in) II U4, 74
Telefon phone I
Telefonanruf phone call I
telefonieren to phone II U1, 20
Telefonzelle telephone box II U3, 50
Tennis tennis I
Teppich carpet II U2, 33
testen to test II U5, 96
teuer expensive I
Ticket ticket II U4, 70
Tier animal I
Tierheim animal rescue shelter I
Tisch table I; desk II U2, 33
Tochter daughter I
toll great I; amazing II U5, 96
Tomate tomato I
Tombola raffle II U4, 70
Tourist tourist II U3, 60
Touristin tourist II U3, 60
tragen to wear I
Training practice I
Transport transport II U4, 78
Traum dream I
traurig sad I; unhappy II U1, 15
Treff club I
treffen to meet I
(sich) treffen to meet II U1, 10
Trick trick I
trinken to have I; to drink II U3, 53
trocken dry II U6, 106
Trompete trumpet II U3, 53
Tschüss. Bye. I; See you. II U6, 113
T-Shirt T-shirt II U2, 36
Tuch scarf II U1, 9
tun to do; to make I
Tut mir leid. Sorry. I
Tür door II U1, 20
Türklingel doorbell I
Turm tower II U3, 49
Turnschuh trainer II U2, 36
Tüte bag I

U

U-Bahn underground I
über about I; above II U2, 33; across II U3, 57
überall all over II U5, 96; everywhere II U6, 114
überallhin everywhere II U6, 114
sich **übergeben** to be sick I
überlegen to guess I
übernachten to stay I
überprüfen to check II U3, 60
überrascht surprised II U1, 15
Übung exercise; practice I
Übungsheft exercise book I
Uhr clock II U3, 49
Wie viel Uhr ist es? What time is it? I
Uhr *(Zeitangabe bei vollen Stunden)* o'clock I
Uhrzeit time I
um at I
um zu to II U3, 53
um ... herum around II U3, 60
Umgebung environment II U5, 87
Umwelt environment II U5, 87
umziehen to move II U6, 104
Umzug procession II U4, 68
und and I
Und ...? What about ...? II U1, 10
Unfall accident I
ungefähr about II U3, 49
unglaublich amazing II U5, 96
unglücklich unhappy II U1, 15
unheimlich scary I
Uniform uniform I
Unordnung mess I
uns us II U3, 57
unser our I
unter under I
Unternehmen company II U1, 20
Unterricht lesson I
unterschiedlich different I
Urlaub holiday II U1, 9
Ururopa great-great-grandad I

V

Vater father I
Vati dad I
Vegetarier vegetarian I
Vegetarierin vegetarian I
verändern to change II U2, 33
Veranstaltung event II U4, 68
verärgert angry II U1, 15
verbessern to correct II U3, 61
verbringen *(Zeit)* to spend II U5, 97
vergessen to forget II U1, 20
verkaufen to sell I
Verkäufer assistant I
Verkäuferin assistant I
Verkehr transport II U4, 78
Verkleidung fancy dress I
verlassen to leave II U6, 105
verletzen to hurt II U5, 92
verlieren to lose II U1, 15

W

Z

zuhören to listen (to) I
zumachen to close I
zurück back II U1, 8
zusammen together I; everyone II U2, 40
zuschauen to watch II U5, 88
zusehen to watch II U5, 88
zustimmen to agree (with) II U6, 105
zwanzig twenty I
wohltätige **Zwecke** charity II U4, 69
zwei two I
zweite second II U3, 57
  aus zweiter Hand second-hand I
zwölf twelve I

Instructions

Arbeitsanweisungen mit Operatoren

Act the dialogue with your partner.	**Spiele** den Dialog mit deinem Partner / deiner Partnerin.
Answer the questions.	**Beantworte** die Fragen.
Ask questions.	**Stelle Fragen.**
Ask your partner.	**Frage** deinen Partner / deine Partnerin.
Ask for feedback.	**Bitte um** Rückmeldung.
Check the sentences.	**Überprüfe** die Sätze.
Choose one of the tasks • the right answers.	**Wähle** eine der Aufgaben • die richtigen Antworten **aus.**
Collect ideas • pictures.	**Sammle** Ideen • Bilder.
Complete the sentences • the dialogue.	**Vervollständige** die Sätze • den Dialog.
Correct the wrong sentences.	**Verbessere** die falschen Sätze.
Draw a picture.	**Zeichne** ein Bild.
Find the names • the words • the answers.	**Finde** die Namen • die Wörter • die Antworten.
Find out about the country.	**Finde** etwas über das Land **heraus.**
Finish the sentences.	**Vervollständige** die Sätze.
Give feedback.	**Gib Rückmeldung.**
Guess.	**Überlege.**
Listen and **point**.	**Höre zu** und **zeige darauf**.
Listen, **read** and **say**.	**Höre zu, lies mit** und **sprich nach**.
Look at the photos • the pictures (again).	**Schau** dir die Fotos • die Bilder (noch einmal) **an.**
Make sentences • questions.	**Bilde** Sätze • Fragen.
Make a dialogue with your partner.	**Erstelle** einen Dialog mit deinem Partner / deiner Partnerin.
Make a poster • a mind map • a chart.	**Erstelle** ein Poster • ein Wörternetz • eine Tabelle.
Match the words • the sentences.	**Ordne** die Wörter • die Sätze **zu.**
Match the sentences with the pictures.	**Ordne** die Sätze den Bildern **zu.**
Put in the right word • the right form.	**Setze** das richtige Wort • die richtige Form **ein.**
Put the pictures • the words • the sentences **in the right order**.	**Bringe** die Bilder • die Wörter • die Sätze **in die richtige Reihenfolge.**
Read the story • the dialogue • the text.	**Lies** die Geschichte • den Dialog • den Text.
Read your sentences • your text to your class.	**Lies** deine Sätze • deinen Text deiner Klasse **vor.**
Are the sentences **right or wrong**?	Sind die Sätze **richtig oder falsch**?
Say the names • the numbers.	**Nenne** die Namen • die Zahlen.
Show your leaflet • your report to your group.	**Zeige** deiner Gruppe deine Broschüre • deinen Bericht.
Take notes.	**Mache dir Notizen.**
Talk about your friends • your free time.	**Sprich über** deine Freunde • deine Freizeit.
Talk to your partner.	**Sprich mit** deinem Partner / deiner Partnerin.
Tell your partner **about** your family • your weekend.	**Erzähle** deinem Partner / deiner Partnerin **von** deiner Familie • deinem Wochenende.
Watch the film.	**Schau** den Film **an.**
What are the words?	**Wie** heißen die Wörter?
What (else) can you see in the photo?	**Was** kannst du **(noch)** auf dem Foto sehen?
Where are the things?	**Wo** sind die Dinge?
Who is • says it?	**Wer** ist • sagt das?
Why (not)?	**Warum** (nicht)?
Write sentences • the words • a text.	**Schreibe** Sätze • die Wörter • einen Text.

Classroom phrases

Before or after the lesson

Good morning, Mr/Mrs/Miss ...	Guten Morgen, Herr/Frau ...
I'm sorry I'm late.	Tut mir leid, dass ich mich verspätet habe.
I'm sorry I don't have my exercise book / my homework with me.	Tut mir leid, ich habe mein Heft / meine Hausaufgaben nicht dabei.
What's for homework?	Was haben wir als Hausaufgabe auf?

Asking for help

What page are we on?	Auf welcher Seite sind wir?
Can you help me, please?	Können Sie / Kannst du mir bitte helfen?
What does ... mean?	Was heißt ... ?
Can you say that again, please?	Können Sie / Kannst du das bitte wiederholen?
Can you write that on the board?	Können Sie das an die Tafel schreiben?
Can I go to the toilet, please?	Kann ich bitte auf die Toilette gehen?
Mr/Mrs/Miss ..., I don't feel well.	Herr/Frau ..., mir geht es nicht gut.

Asking for information

What page is it, please?	Auf welcher Seite ist das?
What's the German/English word for ... ?	Was ist das deutsche/englische Wort für ... ?
How do you spell ... ?	Wie schreibt man ... ?
What does that mean?	Was heißt/bedeutet das?
Sorry, I don't understand.	Tut mir leid, ich verstehe das nicht.

Working together

Can we work in pairs/groups?	Können wir zu zweit / in Gruppen arbeiten?
Do you want to work with me/us?	Willst du / Wollt ihr mit mir/uns arbeiten?
Let's make/draw a ...	Lass(t) uns ein ... machen/zeichnen.
Whose turn is it?	Wer ist dran?
It's my/your turn.	Ich bin dran. / Du bist dran.

Your teacher can say ...

Listen, please.	Hört bitte zu.
Open your books at page	Öffnet eure Bücher auf Seite ....
Turn to page	Schlagt Seite ... auf.
Look at line	Schaue in Zeile ....
Take out your pens.	Holt eure Stifte raus.
Do exercise	Macht Aufgabe ....
Look at the board.	Schaut an die Tafel.
Who can do number ... ?	Wer kann Nummer ... machen?
Put your hands up, please.	Meldet euch, bitte.
Try again.	Versuche es noch einmal.
Sit down, please, and be quiet.	Setz dich bitte und sei ruhig. / Setzt euch bitte und seid ruhig.
Talk to your partner.	Sprecht mit eurem Partner / eurer Partnerin.
Please speak up.	Bitte sprich lauter.

Bildquellennachweis

Cover.1 February Films (Andrew Kemp), London; **Cover.2** Alamy stock photo (Andriy Kravchenko), Abingdon, Oxon; **Vorsatz.1, Vorsatz.2, Vorsatz.3, Vorsatz.4, Vorsatz.5** February Films (Andrew Kemp), London; **8.1, 9.1, 10.1, 11.1** February Films (Andrew Kemp), London; **13.1, 13.2, 13.3** Axel Reis - Mitarbeiter, Oberderdingen; **14.1** Fotolia.com (ARochau), New York; **15.1, 15.2, 15.3, 15.4** February Films (Andrew Kemp), London; **17.1** Corel Corporation Deutschland, Unterschleissheim; **17.2** Klett-Archiv (Klaus-Peter Hackenberg, Drensteinfurt), Stuttgart; **17.3** Thinkstock (David Oxberry), München; **17.4** Fotolia.com (Sergey Nivens), New York; **17.5** shutterstock (Yuri Arcurs), New York, NY; **17.6** Fotolia.com (BlueOrange Studio), New York; **18.1, 18.2** February Films (Elke Bock), London; **18.3** February Films (Andrew Kemp), London; **19.1** shutterstock (Daria Filimonova), New York, NY; **19.2** February Films (Andrew Kemp), London; **19.3** February Films (Elke Bock), London; **21.1, 21.2** February Films (Andrew Kemp), London; **21.3** February Films (Andrew Kemp), London; **22.1** Fotolia.com (Pixelot), New York; **22.2** Thinkstock (~User4c1fb51d_286), München; **22.3** iStockphoto (Björn Kindler), Calgary, Alberta; **22.4** Thinkstock (~User4c1fb51d_286), München; **22.5** Fotolia.com (bbsferrari), New York; **23.1, 23.2, 23.3, 23.4** February Films, London; **23.5** Fotolia.com (alexlukin), New York; **23.6** shutterstock (Bork), New York, NY; **23.7** Thinkstock (Hemera), München; **23.8** Fotolia.com (Andrr), New York; **23.9** shutterstock (kotkot32), New York, NY; **23.10, 23.11, 23.12** February Films, London; **24.1, 24.2** Weccard, Thomas, Ludwigsburg; **26.1** Fotolia.com (Soloviova Liudmyla), New York; **28.1, 28.2, 28.3** February Films (Andrew Kemp), London; **29.1, 29.2, 29.3** February Films (Andrew Kemp), London; **42.1** iStockphoto (Spectral-Design), Calgary, Alberta; **42.2** Fotolia.com (Elías Gómez Muñoz), New York; **42.3** iStockphoto (Simon Krzic), Calgary, Alberta; **42.4** iStockphoto (Grigorev_Vladimir), Calgary, Alberta; **42.5** iStockphoto (Firmafotografen), Calgary, Alberta; **42.6** iStockphoto (Firmafotografen), Calgary, Alberta; **42.7** iStockphoto (RF/Mats Tooming), Calgary, Alberta; **43.1, 43.2, 43.3, 43.4** February Films, London; **44.1** Fotolia.com (erikdegraaf), New York; **47.1** Thinkstock (Mike_Colwill), München; **47.2** iStockphoto (Philartphace), Calgary, Alberta; **47.3** shutterstock (Lance Bellers), New York, NY; **47.4** Alamy stock photo (AKP Photos), Abingdon, Oxon; **48.1** February Films (Andrew Kemp), London; **48.2** Getty Images (Photographer's Choice), München; **49.1** Getty Images (Vetta), München; **49.2** laif (Polaris Images), Köln; **49.3** Thinkstock (iStock/Ratikova), München; **49.4** Thinkstock (iStock / Junghee Choi), München; **50.1** Corbis RF (Ramble), Berlin; **50.2** Fotolia.com (Milan Surkala), New York; **50.3** iStockphoto (ImageGap), Calgary, Alberta; **56.1, 56.2** February Films (Elke Bock), London; **56.3** February Films (Andrew Kemp), London; **56.4, 56.5** February Films (Elke Bock), London; **56.6, 56.7, 56.8, 56.9** Weccard, Thomas, Ludwigsburg; **62.1** Alamy stock photo (Justin Kase z11z), Abingdon, Oxon; **63.1, 63.2, 63.3, 63.4** February Films, London; **66.1** Thinkstock (Dusan Zidar), München; **66.2** Alamy stock photo (Brian Southam), Abingdon, Oxon; **67.1** Alamy stock photo (Pete Titmuss), Abingdon, Oxon; **67.2** Thinkstock (shalamov), München; **67.3** Alamy stock photo (veryan dale), Abingdon, Oxon; **68.1** February Films (Elke Bock), London; **68.2** Getty Images RF (Photo Disc), München; **68.3** Mauritius Images (Blend Images / Colin Anderson), Mittenwald; **69.1** ddp images GmbH (Jens Köhler), Hamburg; **69.2** Fotolia.com (Ivan Garcia Aguirre), New York; **70.1, 70.2** February Films (Andrew Kemp), London; **71.1** Thinkstock (Oli_Trolly), München; **71.2** shutterstock (Erika J Mitchell), New York, NY; **71.3** iStockphoto (RichLegg), Calgary, Alberta; **71.4** shutterstock (photoiva), New York, NY; **71.5** Fotolia.com (tinadefortunata), New York; **73.1** Klett-Archiv (Thomas Weccard), Stuttgart; **80.1** February Films (Elke Bock), London; **80.2** Adobe Stock (creativefamily), Dublin; **80.3** shutterstock (SpeedKingz), New York, NY; **80.4** Klett-Archiv (Weccard), Stuttgart; **81.1, 81.2, 81.3, 81.4** February Films, London; **83.1** Fotolia.com (Gelpi), New York; **86.1** iStockphoto (Image Source), Calgary, Alberta; **86.2** Getty Images (OJO+), München; **86.3** February Films, London; **87.1** Thinkstock (Jupiterimages), München; **87.2** shutterstock (Mikkel Bigandt), New York, NY; **87.3** Alamy stock photo (BRUCE COLEMAN INC.), Abingdon, Oxon; **88.1** Fotolia.com (Eléonore H), New York; **89.1** iStockphoto (Johnny Greig), Calgary, Alberta; **89.2** Thinkstock (Comstock Images), München; **89.3** Klett-Archiv (Weccard), Stuttgart; **89.4** iStockphoto (Linda Yolanda), Calgary, Alberta; **90.1** February Films (Elke Bock), London; **90.2, 90.3** February Films (Andrew Kemp), London; **91.1** February Films, London; **92.1** February Films (Andrew Kemp), London; **94.1** February Films (Andrew Kemp), London; **95.1, 95.2, 95.3, 95.4** February Films (Andrew Kemp), London; **96.1** Alamy stock photo (James Nesterwitz), Abingdon, Oxon; **96.2** shutterstock (Fer Gregory), New York, NY; **97.1** Picture-Alliance (dpa), Frankfurt; **97.2** iStockphoto (FatCamera), Calgary, Alberta; **98.1** Getty Images (Michael Nichols/National Geographic), München; **98.2** iStockphoto (zokov), Calgary, Alberta; **99.1, 99.2, 99.3, 99.4** February Films, London; **102.1** Thinkstock (iStockphoto), München; **102.2** Thinkstock (rufus young), München; **102.3** shutterstock (Kalim), New York, NY; **102.4** shutterstock (Zoran Ras), New York, NY; **102.5** Fotolia.com (mandritoiu), New York; **103.1** Alamy stock photo (Miroslav Liska), Abingdon, Oxon; **103.2** iStockphoto (groveb), Calgary, Alberta; **103.3** shutterstock (Goran Bogicevic), New York, NY; **103.4** Thinkstock (iStockphoto), München; **104.1** shutterstock (Nick Fox), New York, NY; **104.2** shutterstock (jessicakirsh), New York, NY; **104.3** shutterstock (Bill Florence), New York, NY; **104.4** shutterstock (Richard Cavalleri), New York, NY; **104.5** shutterstock (f11photo), New York, NY; **106.1** Thinkstock (Fuse), München; **106.2** Thinkstock (Photodisc), München; **106.3** Thinkstock (CPaulussen), München; **106.4** Thinkstock (ljubaphoto), München; **110.1** February Films, London; **112.1** February Films (Andrew Kemp), London; **113.1, 113.2, 113.3, 113.4** February Films (Andrew Kemp), London; **114.1** Fotolia.com (Denise Kappa), New York; **114.2** iStockphoto (Jacob Wackerhausen), Calgary, Alberta; **114.3** 123rf (Yanming Zhang), Nidderau; **115.1** Thinkstock (monkeybusinessimages), München; **116.1** Alamy stock photo (Mikael Utterström), Abingdon, Oxon; **116.2** Gordon Aeroball, Springville, Utah 84663; **117.1** Picture-Alliance (dpa - Report), Frankfurt; **117.2, 117.3, 117.4, 117.5** February Films, London; **118.1** Masterfile, Düsseldorf; **119.1** Thinkstock (DronG), München; **119.2** f1 online digitale Bildagentur, Frankfurt; **120.1, 120.2** Axel Reis - Mitarbeiter, Oberderdingen; **121.1, 121.2, 121.3** February Films (Andrew Kemp), London; **123.1** Corel Corporation Deutschland, Unterschleissheim; **123.2** Klett-Archiv (Klaus-Peter Hackenberg, Drensteinfurt), Stuttgart; **123.3** Thinkstock (David Oxberry), München; **123.4** Fotolia.com (Sergey Nivens), New York; **123.5** shutterstock (Yuri Arcurs), New York, NY; **123.6** Fotolia.com (BlueOrange Studio), New York; **123.7, 123.8** February Films (Elke Bock), London; **123.9** February Films (Andrew Kemp), London; **134.1** February Films (Andrew Kemp), London; **137.1** Weccard, Thomas, Ludwigsburg; **158.1** Thinkstock (iStock / vm), München; **158.2** Fotolia.com (Michael Rogner), New York; **161.1** Weccard, Thomas, Ludwigsburg; **166.1** shutterstock (Bikeworldtravel), New York, NY; **166.2** Fotolia.com (ang17a), New York; **166.3** shutterstock (JuliusKielaitis), New York, NY; **166.4** shutterstock (chrisdorney), New York, NY; **166.5** shutterstock (Renata Sedmakova), New York, NY; **166.6** shutterstock (nito), New York, NY; **166.7** Alamy stock photo (Justin Kase ztwoz), Abingdon, Oxon; **166.8** Corbis RF (Ramble), Berlin; **166.9** Fotolia.com (taxiberlin), New York; **166.10** Corbis RF (Dominic Burke RF), Berlin; **166.11** dreamstime.com (Galen Goyer), Brentwood, TN; **166.12** Corel Corporation Deutschland, Unterschleissheim; **166.13** dreamstime.com (Andreykr), Brentwood, TN; **170.1** Getty Images, München; **232.1** Pulse Creative Limited - Transport for London, Heaton Mersey, Stockport

Sollte es in einem Einzelfall nicht gelungen sein, den korrekten Rechteinhaber ausfindig zu machen, so werden berechtigte Ansprüche selbstverständlich im Rahmen der üblichen Regelungen abgegolten.

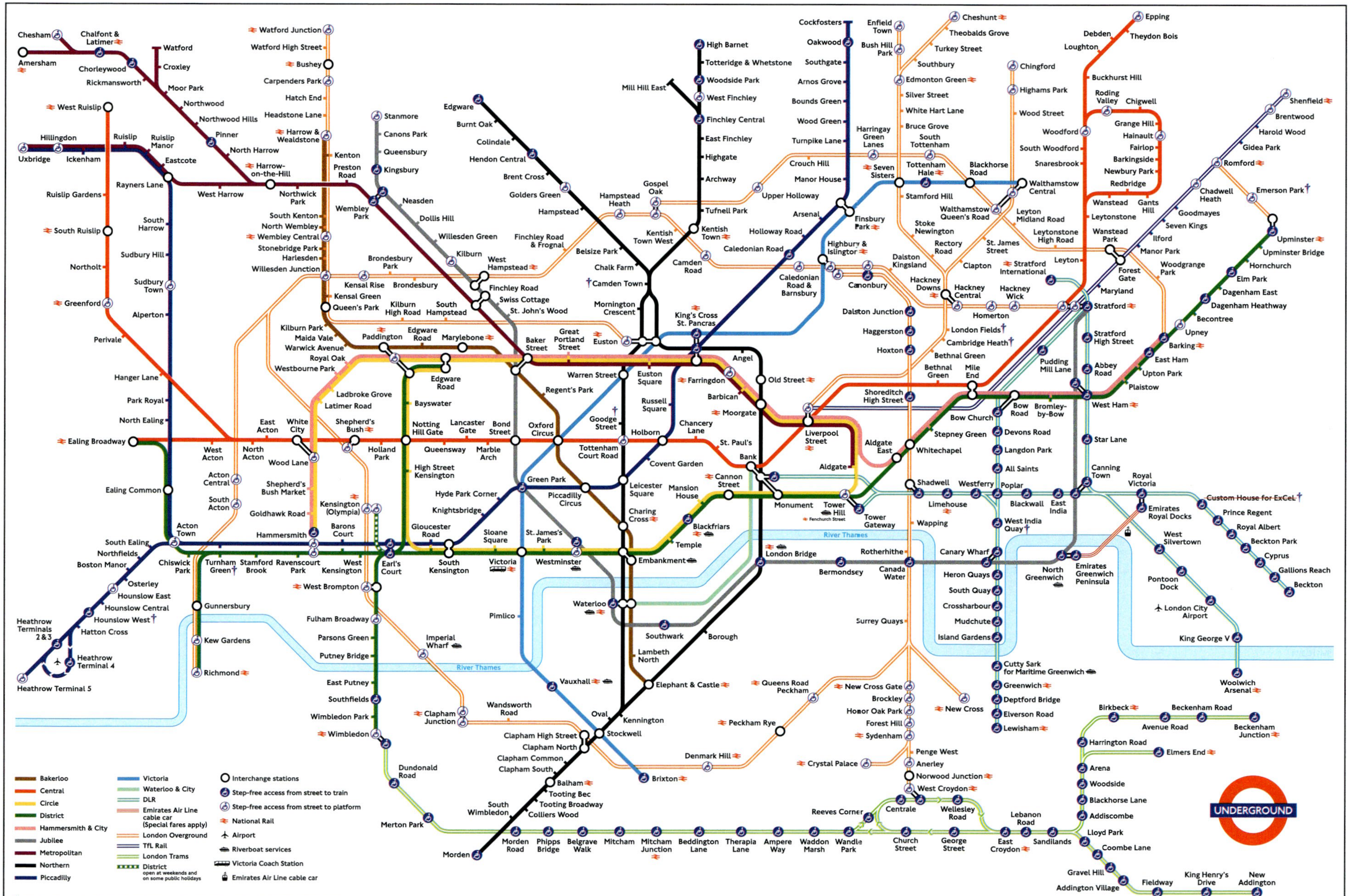

† Services or access at these stations are subject to variation. Please search 'TfL stations' for full details.

 Reg. user No. 17/E/3176/P **Improvement works may affect your journey, please check before you travel** Version A TfL 5.2017 Correct at time of going to print

THE UNITED STATES OF AMERICA

England
Scotland
Northern Ireland
"Union Flag" or "Union Jack"
Atlantic Ocean
Galway
REPU
OF IR
Cork